A NEW OUTLINE OF PEDAGOGY

Compiled by Li Haowu

Translated by Chi Dongyu, Zhuo Yaojun

Cosmos Publishing Group

Copyright © 2025 Cosmos Publishing Group.
All rights reserved.

No part of this book can be reproduced in any form or by written, electronic or mechanical, including photocopying, recording, or by any information retrieval system without written permission in writing by the author.

Compiled by Li Haowu

Translated by Chi Dongyu, Zhuo Yaojun

Published by Cosmos Publishing Group

Publication Date: Published December 2025

Although every precaution has been taken in the preparation of this book, the publisher and author assume no responsibility for errors or omissions. Neither is any liability assumed for damages resulting from the use of information contained herein.

Word Count 267,000 words

ISBN 979-8-90208-031-2

TABLE OF CONTENTS

Publisher's Note 1
Editorial Principles 3
Preface 6
Introduction 8
Chapter 1: The Essence of Education 14

    Section 1: What is Education 14
    Section 2: The Essence of Education and Its Transformation 24
    Section 3: Several Distortions of Education 63
    Section 4: The Efficacy of Education 94

Chapter 2: The Evolution of Education 110

    Section 5: Education in Primitive Communist Society 110
    Section 6: Education in Feudal Society 141
    Section 7: Education in Capitalist Society 162
    Section 8: Education in Socialist Society 200

Chapter 3: An Overview of Education 220

    Section 9: Education and the Economy 220
    Section 10: Education and Politics 234
    Section 11: The Teachers 254
    Section 12: Students 274
    Section 13: The Educational Movement of the Working Class 292
    Section 14: The International Organization of

Educational Workers 311
  Section 15: Education in the United States 340
  Section 16: Education in the Soviet Union 378

Bibliography **411**

PUBLISHER'S NOTE

In the twentieth century, the discipline of education in China grew from nothing to something—moving from translation to original authorship—and took shape as a system with its own distinctive style. Attuned to the pulse of the times, Chinese scholars of education drew broadly on China and the West, and fused antiquity with the present. Some independently compiled textbooks in education to meet the needs of normal (teacher-training) education in China; others authored scholarly monographs to lay a solid foundation for Chinese educational studies. Over a full century, many splendid works bloomed. To varying degrees they refracted the spirit of their age, reflected the visage of educational scholarship, and condensed the discerning insight of educational scholars.

Standing at the turn of the century, our press judged it necessary to bring anew to life the spiritual legacy of our predecessors. In the late spring and early summer of 2003, our deputy director and deputy editor-in-chief, Huang Xu, traveled to Shanghai to invite Mr. Qu Baokui and Professor Zheng Jinzhou of East China Normal University to serve as chief editors. We earnestly invited senior, mid-career, and early-career scholars to collate, annotate, and provide evaluations, and we solemnly launched the Twentieth Century Chinese Education Classics Series.

The works included in this Series have each stood the test of more than fifty years. They are of high quality, exert broad influence, and have led the field. Through these volumes we seek to present the scholarly wisdom of twentieth-century Chinese educators, to take stock of a century of educational science in China, and—learning from the past to guide the future—to lay a bridge for Chinese educational science across past, present, and future. This is an academic undertaking in education that inherits from those who came before and benefits those who come after.

We extend our sincere thanks to the chief editors and their working team, to the commissioned editors of the individual volumes for their great efforts, and to all rights holders for their full support.

We respectfully invite readers to criticize and correct any shortcomings or errors that may occur in the selection, editing, proofreading, or printing of this Series.

Fujian Education Press

August, 2006

EDITORIAL PRINCIPLES

1. Selection Scope. The Twentieth Century Chinese Education Classics Series (hereinafter referred to as the Series) selects educational works from the 20th century that have withstood the test of over 50 years, are of relatively high standard, significant influence, and led trends in the discipline. These works have played a role in carrying on academic traditions.

2. Edition Policy. The Series uses the first edition or revised edition as the base text. A copy of the original cover is printed before the title page of each volume.

3. Editorial Staff. The Series invites relevant senior, middle-aged, and young scholars to serve as "Special Editors" for each volume, responsible for collating the original text and writing the preface (mainly introducing the author's biography and the original work).

4. Editorial Principles. Respect the content and structure of the original work to preserve its original appearance; perform necessary formatting and technical processing to facilitate reading.

5. Layout Specifications. Original texts that were vertically set are uniformly converted to horizontal setting. After conversion, some expressions in the original text are adjusted accordingly, e.g., "the left column"is changed to "the following", etc.

6. Orthography. Replace traditional characters with simplified ones and regularize variant forms to the standard; retain the established adverbial usage of "的","得","地","底"

unchanged.

7. Punctuation Style. Where the original lacks punctuation, it is added; where original punctuation does not conform to modern usage, it is revised; where the original sentence breaks do not conform to modern Chinese grammar habits, they are adjusted. Special marks for proper names (e.g., personal names, place names) in the original are omitted. Book titles use the standard form 《 》 and 〈 〉; foreign book titles are set in italics.

8. Name-Translation Conventions. Foreign personal names, place names, etc., in the original text that differ from current common translations are generally changed to the current translation.

9. Number Style. Generally use Arabic numerals for representing Gregorian calendar years, eras, year, month, day, hour, minute, second, counting and measurement, and numerical values in statistical tables, edition numbers, volume numbers, page numbers, etc. Generally use Chinese numerals for representing Chinese cyclical calendar years and lunar calendar months/days, approximate numbers, grade levels, days of the week, or other fixed usages. Additionally, add Gregorian calendar year annotations after Chinese cyclical calendar years, etc.

10. Heading Numbering. Each level is assigned a distinct numbering style. If the source text already differentiates numbering by level, keep the source numbering. If a sublevel repeats the number of its parent level, the sublevel is, as a rule, to be renumbered.

11. Corrections and Emendations. Errors or omissions in the

original typesetting are corrected.

12. Notes Style. In-text notes in the original remain as in-text notes; endnotes in the original are changed to footnotes. Supplementary annotations by the Special Editor are (abbrev. SE notes) are likewise to be set as footnotes.

PREFACE

This is an introductory book on education, prepared for young readers with at least a junior-high education.

In writing it, I have this audience in mind and wish to address them about education. Therefore it cannot be a specialized monograph, nor a highly systematic textbook in pedagogy. As stated in the conclusion below, it is necessarily a selection of several key points to explain and analyze, so that readers may form a sound understanding of education.

At the same time, in my view, such young readers should also be those committed to social transformation and eager to acquire the basic knowledge of the "New Social Science"[1] so as to grasp a theoretical weapon they can bring to practice.

More specifically, this book is written for young fighters on the educational front: to set out the essence of education, clarify its functions, dispel superstitions about it, and correct common misunderstandings.

Accordingly, I hope all young people with at least a junior-high education will read this book—whether in school or out of school, employed or unemployed, and whether or not they intend to work in education—especially students in senior-secondary teacher-training programs, primary-school teachers, students in university departments of education, and secondary-school teachers.

---

1 [Special Editor's Note] After the May Fourth Movement, works introducing Marxist theory were referred to in China as "New Social Science", to distinguish them from "social science" in the traditional sense.

I venture to say: though this is a book for the general reader, it is by no means a collection of clichés. At the very least, it offers theories not previously articulated by Chinese writers and facts not previously brought to light. If you are already working, or intend to work, on the educational front, you will find here a new weapon; even if you do not plan to enter education, you will still gain many fresh insights. I am confident you will not be disappointed.

I also hope general students will read it, for it may awaken them to the true character of the education they are now receiving.

Let me reiterate and emphasize: most of this book is less academic research than exposé and plain talk. In our time, exposure is a necessary and powerful weapon. Let us use it to lay bare the tricks played in education!

Li Haowu
December 27, 1929, Shanghai

INTRODUCTION

Content of this book: 1. The Essence of Education; 2. The Evolution of Education; 3. An Overview of Education – A Critique of the Content of Current "Introductions to Education" – Education as "Propaganda", as a Tool – The Meaning of the "New" – Questions

Following the intent I stated in the "Preface", I begin writing this "Introduction" to A New Outline of Pedagogy.

What I aim to present here is an outline of this book's content and the reasons for selecting this content.

The term "education" encompasses a very wide range of content. The most obvious examples include educational principles, philosophy of education, educational psychology, history of education, educational administration, curriculum studies, and so forth. In terms of specialization, even dedicating a lifetime to a single field may not guarantee complete mastery. However, for a general overview, one book titled "Introduction to Education" is sufficient to cover it all.

Now, regarding the nature of this A New Outline of Pedagogy, it is neither a pedagogy text, nor a history of education, nor any other specialized educational treatise. It belongs to the category of so-called introductions to education.

Consequently, the content of this book is broadly divided into the following three parts: First, the essence of education, primarily explaining the origin of education, the function of education and its distortions, the efficacy of education, and correcting several misinterpretations of education. This enables readers to recognize the true face of education and avoid further deception by "pedantic scholars" and "scholars in the service of the ruling class". Second, the evolution of education, recounting the changes in the meaning of education and the facts and reasons behind the alterations in educational systems from primitive communist society to the socialist society now beginning to be realized. This allows readers to understand that education is governed by its fundamental determinants. Third, an overview of education, explaining the relationship between education and several related social phenomena—politics, economy, etc.; reassessing the nature of educators and educands who hold important positions in education; and describing the history and current situation of two major undertakings in education, namely the educational movement of the working class and the international organization of educational workers. Finally, taking American education as an example of education in capitalist society, and Soviet education as an example of education in socialist society, facts are cited to demonstrate the fundamental differences between the two types of education in the two types of societies.

Precisely because the content of education is complex and its categories numerous, and since we cannot cover everything, we naturally must select a few key aspects for dissection and clarification.

But why select precisely these aspects?

Here, I have sound reasons; it is not an arbitrary choice.

Let me first critique the books of the type "Introduction to Education" or "Gateway to Education" already published domestically.

Although their contents are not entirely identical, they can be said to be largely similar; and what differences exist are merely in chapters, sections, and phrasing, while the similarities lie in their fundamental standpoint.

They typically proceed as follows: first, they explain the meaning of the word "education", quoting definitions from Shuowen Jiezi[2], Latin[3], or various scholars[4]; next, they discuss some psychology and teaching, curriculum and teaching materials; then, they cover some school systems, some educational funding; and further, they present some educational theories and educational research. And with that, it's finished; this is considered a textbook, intended for general normal school students and educators to study and apply.

However, they do not address the reasons behind the changes in the meaning of education, the changes in its systems, or their

---

[2] Shuowen Jiezi: "To teach (教, jiao) is what superiors impart and inferiors emulate; to nurture (育, yu) is to rear children and make them do good." Duan's annotation: The character 育 (yu) uses not 子 (child) but an inverted 子, precisely meaning that those who are not good can be made to do good.

[3] Latin Educare, meaning "to lead out".

[4] From "Education cultivates moral habits to make one believe in Heaven...", "All things in the world live according to an eternal law... Education is to make one know this eternal law", "In illustrating illustrious virtue; in renovating the people; in resting in the highest excellence", "In making one learn to be a sage", down to "Education is the reconstruction of experience, which adds meaning to experience and enhances the ability to direct subsequent experience" – regardless of whether the former is extraordinarily vague and ambiguous, or the latter is relatively enlightened; such definitions, like the explanations of word meanings, entirely fail to capture the true meaning of education. Conversely, they only give readers a blurred conception and ultimately confuse them with the educational concepts of the ruling class. Therefore, the function of such explanations of "education" is akin to a (pretend) blindfold, masking the class bias and private interests of the ruling class. – See Chapter 1, Section 2, "The Essence of Education and Its Transformation"

functions. They do not address the reasons why many children receive no education, why many graduates become idle vagrants, or the solutions to these problems. They do not explain the relationship between education and politics, or with the economy. They are unaware that the machinery of education has been stolen by thieves and used like opium to poison people. Conversely, they speak of how sacred, how pure and lofty, how independent, how fair, how scientific, how populist education is, and even claim that education can save the nation, that education can solve the people's livelihood... a great heap of beautiful words and phrases eulogizing education.

Such are the educational books commonly used as textbooks or references; such are the educational books studied and applied by tens of thousands of normal school students and teachers; such are the educational books acknowledged by the general public!

Now, this A New Outline of Pedagogy of mine aims to be the direct opposite of such "hackneyed and stereotyped expressions". It seeks to loudly warn the reader: The machinery of education was long ago stolen by robbers; the robbers, for their own benefit, not for the benefit of the educands, possess and operate it; the robbers "carefully and deliberately... teach you not wisdom but foolishness, not justice but greed, not freedom but subservience, not love but hate." — quoting Upton Sinclair[5] from the preface to The Goose-step — Education is merely a tool, merely a form of "propaganda", merely a by-product, merely a batch of guards; education has been commercialized; education is magic, and it is also poison. In simple terms — using social science terminology — education is class-based, it is a weapon in the class struggle. Since the beginning of civilization, there has only been class

---

5 [Special Editor's Note] Upton Sinclair (1878–1968), American novelist, advocate for social reform experiments. The Goose-step is one of his social research works.

education, not human education; there has only been opposing education, not unified education.

Why do I dare to say this?

I have reasons.

Precisely to explain these reasons, I have selected the aspects mentioned above and completely omitted many other topics commonly found in general introductions to education or educational primers. This holds true whether in Part One discussing the essence of education, in Part Two discussing the evolution of education, or in Part Three presenting an overview of education.

Furthermore, because this book aims to dissect and elucidate these new perspectives and new facts, it is necessary to add the character "new" in the title. — Please note, readers: This is not a fashionable "new", but a "new" that signifies new meaning.

Questions

Try comparing the contents of introductions to education or educational primers published by several major bookstores. If you can access those books, ask yourself: "What exactly has it told me?"

What do I mean when I say "education is propaganda"? Please critique this statement.

Do you believe me when I say "the machinery of education has been stolen by robbers"? Who is the thief? How did he steal it?

Has your pedagogy teacher ever told you about the relationship between education and politics, and the economy?

If you are a normal school graduate and are now working as a teacher, haven't you felt that the "principles of education" you heard in school are utterly useless?

CHAPTER 1: THE ESSENCE OF EDUCATION

SECTION 1: WHAT IS EDUCATION

Education is one of the ideological domains of labor – Ideology and the real base – The origin of education – Science and utility – The practicality of education – The wondrous use of education scholars – The fact that education changes along with socio-economic changes – The relationship between education and other ideological forms – Questions

I will not explain the term by citing etymologies from Shuowen Jiezi or Latin, nor will I quote definitions from renowned educators. I shall state directly and plainly as follows: education is "one of the fields of ideological labour"[6], that is, one of the superstructures of society.

What is the superstructure or ideology? I believe this must be explained in detail in other volumes of this series[7]. Therefore, a brief explanation here will suffice.

According to the materialist conception of history, the economic structure of society is the real base, while the legal, political, religious, artistic, and philosophical spheres – in short, all various

---

6 [Special Editor's Note] It is equivalent to "ideology".

7 [Special Editor's Note] The "series" here refers to the New Social Science Series published by the Shanghai Nanqiang Book Company. Outline of the New Education is one volume in the series; others include A History of Socialism, On Ideological Forms (i.e., Ideology), and An Introduction to Dialectical Materialism.

conceptual forms (i.e., what is called ideology) – are the superstructure built upon this base. Education is precisely one such superstructure, one such form of ideology. The relationship of dependence of the superstructure on the substructure is this: The mode of production of the material means of life (i.e., the economic structure) determines the social, political, and intellectual processes of life (i.e., the superstructure); "With the change of the economic foundation the entire immense superstructure is more or less rapidly transformed."[8]

This is an established doctrine of the New Social Science, which we can use to explain the nature of education in this regard. It is indeed the fundamental concept we should bear in mind above all.

As for the explanation that education is "one of the fields of ideological labour", we can examine it by looking at its most concrete manifestation: the school. Ordinary schools, whether higher, secondary, or primary, are all fields of social labour, places that endow labour power with specific qualifications; that is, places where simple labour power is transformed into specialized labour power. Some people come here to become doctors, others to become lawyers, and still others to become philosophers, writers, scientists, etc. Thus, there is no essential difference between an industrial school training engineers and a religious school training clergy, because both are places that endow people with specialized labour power, fulfilling more or less specialized labour functions. Consequently, the structure of schools and their divisions into faculties (commerce, industry, teacher training,

---

8 [Special Editor's Note] The above quotation is from Karl Marx, the "Preface" to A Contribution to the Critique of Political Economy. It is rendered here as: "With the change of the economic foundation, the entire immense superstructure is more or less rapidly transformed." See Selected Works of Marx and Engels, vol. 2 (Beijing: People's Publishing House, 1995), p. 33.

medicine, etc.) are manifestations of the various skilled labour forces required by society.

This definition of education is based on the materialist conception of history. To provide readers with greater clarity, let us elaborate further.

We should start with the origin of education.

How did education originate? Was it based on human nature? On the consciousness of educators? Or on some divine mandate, as in the saying "appoint them as rulers, appoint them as teachers"? None of these. The origin of education does not lie in such mystical places. Education is merely a "daily necessity", closely connected to the process of social life and the relations of material production; moreover, it is based on this real socio-economic life. Whenever the real economic relations change, it inevitably changes along with them. There has never been an instance where education was determined solely by ponderings in someone's mind, unrelated to the real economic life.

Simply put, the emergence of education is limited to the actual life needs of the people in a given time and place; it is a means to help humans manage social life. This so-called life involves, on the one hand, the adequate acquisition of food, clothing, and shelter, and on the other hand, the free development of knowledge and ability. Furthermore, this life is collective and social, absolutely not that of an isolated individual. Therefore, the definition of education should be: one of the labours required by society, which endows social labour power with a special qualification. Wherever there is human life, there is education. Because wherever there is human life, there are needs of actual living. However, the needs of human life vary according to time and place; the content and methods of education also change along with these needs. The root of this change lies in the transformation of the social economic structure. Thus, in primitive society there was one mode of education, in feudal society another, and in capitalist society yet another. – For details, see Chapter 2, "The Evolution of Education".

Speaking of education originating from practical needs, some might view this as belittling education, even insulting it. But this is far from the truth. All sciences, whether natural or social, originated from practical use and progress alongside it. For instance, mathematics, known as the "science of pure thought", may seem on the surface quite distant from practical use, but initially it also originated from practical needs – namely, the very practical need to count things. Another example is astronomy, which originated from the necessity for early humans to determine direction on vast plains and deserts, and in agriculture, to know the climate and the years, months, days, and hours. Naturally, in the barbaric age of humanity, these fields of knowledge had not yet formed into sciences in the strict sense; initially, they were merely the sprouts of science. Their maturation and establishment as sciences occurred only after a certain degree of surplus existed in human life. That is, it was only possible when productivity gradually progressed, and humans had the leisure for sufficient observation and research of external things. Therefore, science, as such, initially emerged as a result of the progress of productive forces, and subsequently advanced directly or indirectly alongside the progress of productive forces. In other words, the content of science is based on the technological stage, i.e., the economic stage, of that society.

Thus, all sciences are entirely born from practical use and progress alongside it. The enterprise of education, whose duty is to transmit the content of various sciences, naturally cannot be separated from practical use.

But some might also say: In the development of learning, are there not times when it proceeds completely detached from practical use? That is, is there not such a thing as "learning for learning's sake" – knowledge pursued purely to satisfy the thirst for knowledge, or the pursuit of pure learning and pure knowledge without any regard for utility or application? This question can be answered on two levels.

First, not all scientific theories are necessarily directly practical; individual theories do not always have their applied aspects. However, no matter how pure a scientific theory may be, in an indirect sense, it certainly has full practical significance. All scientific knowledge, taken as a whole, is a socially useful thing. Although parts of it may not be directly useful, when viewed as a link in the entire chain of scientific knowledge, they are indirectly useful. There is not a single tool or machine in human society that is useless or unbeneficial; similarly, within human society, there is no knowledge that is useless or unbeneficial. But why is it indirectly useful rather than directly useful? This is because knowledge originating from practical use later becomes highly specialized into various branches due to gradual differentiation. Within these branches, they are further subdivided into numerous smaller sections. Consequently, a scholar engaged in one specialized branch may know nothing outside their own specialty. The entire scope of their own activity coincides with the scope of their research, while the practical application of their research is undertaken not by themselves but by other specialists. For example, the science of chemistry is divided into theoretical chemistry and applied chemistry. Thus, the specialist may come to imagine that their research is unrelated to practical use, unaware that in reality, the results of their research ultimately become products of practical necessity, either through utilization by other specialists or through broad social application via certain paths; moreover, their research itself, in practice, must take this practical necessity as its ultimate goal in order to be established.

Second, we must understand that by the time learning takes shape, those engaged in learning – such as law, religion, art, philosophy, and science – all belong to the upper strata of society, that is, the ruling class. Unless this were the case, they would not have the leisure to engage in such pursuits. Therefore, when they study and expound upon this learning, they inevitably reflect their standpoint within the social class structure. They acknowledge receiving an upbringing and possessing endowments completely different from those who actually engage in labour and maintain the socio-economic structure (slaves in ancient times, serfs in the Middle Ages, workers in modern society). Thus, they believe that the enterprise they are engaged in develops along a completely different track from the work of the labouring people. Here we can cite the views of Plato[9], a representative figure of philosophical idealism. In his view, only true philosophers can apprehend a certain sublime reality, while the children of artisans and workers cannot attain this level of spiritual training. Therefore, he explicitly advocated a philosopher-king polity, believing that only families possessing political, scientific, and aesthetic cultivation could produce geniuses who, after receiving careful training, could serve as the highest officials. Plato's views later expanded further with the development of class society. That is, the more class society developed, the more specialized these ideological pursuits became, falling into the hands of a segment of the upper social class. Consequently, the very essence of this learning came to be seen as a category increasingly distant and separate from the foundational structure of society and its actual needs.

---

9 [Special Editor's Note] Plato (427–347 BC), ancient Greek philosopher, founder of the Platonist school.

Education, as a means to help humans manage social life, is clearly practical. The successive progress of education has also suited the economic needs of society in each era (though not necessarily the needs of all humanity). But since the emergence of so-called education scholars who lecture on educational philosophy and propound educational principles, education, which was originally understandable by all and close to actual life, has been rendered incredibly profound and elevated, as if only philosophers could engage in it.

These educational theorists or philosophers of education, belonging to the upper class, consider themselves possessed of profound theories and understanding of abstruse philosophy. Therefore, in the educational doctrines they "compile", their concepts and terminology must seek profundity and mystery, avoiding all ordinary popular views and expressions. They first distinguish humans as the "paragon of animals" from other living beings; then they confine the facts of education within the school walls – and schools are "restricted areas, no entry for idlers". In fact, judging by the Latin origin of the word "school"[10], it was precisely a place where only idlers (the leisure class) could enter. Then, sitting comfortably within this "windless zone", they savor educational philosophy and deliberate educational theories. Even more admirable is their fervent desire to "transform" pedagogy into a science, striving to elevate the status of the pedagogy they "compile". Yet, they remain wholly unconcerned with, nay, wholly blind to, the ubiquitous facts that many children cannot enter the "school restricted area", that many poor people never get to taste the "wonder of education", and that many others,

---

10 [Special Editor's Note] "School", Greek schola, means leisure. Schola originally referred to places where the aristocratic class spent their leisure. The Latin ludus literarius also refers to a place for play/leisure.

although they have obtained graduation diplomas[11] and are sent to the labour market, cannot find employment.

The above explains the practicality of education as a social phenomenon and the origins of its perception as detached from practical use. Below, we will briefly cite facts to demonstrate the practicality of education and how it changes along with socio-economic transformations.

The feudal society of medieval Europe was one where religion was exceptionally developed. Consequently, medieval schools were imbued with a strong religious character. Religious schools are self-evident, but even other aspects of university life and curricula, etc., bore clerical colors and a theological spirit. Except for a few specialized universities like those for medicine and law, all other educational institutions, whether elementary schools or universities, primarily aimed at clerical instruction. However, by the end of the Middle Ages, with the development of cities and the concomitant rise of the commercial bourgeoisie, specialized schools aimed at training merchants were established. Later, with the development of industrial capitalism, industrial specialized schools emerged accordingly; and to meet the needs of large-scale industry for technicians, supervisors, and planners, the establishment of various advanced specialized schools and universities increased.

This demonstrates the nature of education through the changes in school content.

Looking further at those who have served as teachers throughout history: initially, perhaps mothers or chieftains (though certainly not in the formal, strict sense of teachers), later monks and

---

11 [Special Editor's Note] It means graduation certificate/diploma.

scholars, and still later, professional teachers and officials, etc. – this too followed actual needs. The reason modern states establish normal schools and implement specific preferential policies for normal school students is rooted in the needs of the state to monopolize education and maintain capitalist social order.

Having reached this point, we should now have a clear concept of what education is. Namely: Education is one of the social superstructures, one of the fields of ideological labour, and is based on the economic stage[12] of society.

However, it is worth noting here that although education, like law, religion, morality, art, philosophy, science, etc., is part of the social superstructure, it has a special characteristic: unlike other forms of mental production which each have their own specific content, education takes the content of other forms of mental production as its own content. For example, the curricula within schools, whether in science, philosophy, or art – the content of these various subjects is entirely consistent with the general content of science, philosophy, and art in contemporary society. In other words, the style, tendencies, etc., taught in school subjects are all based on the general styles and tendencies of the era. But note: this "general" refers precisely to what is dominant in a given era, for "the ideas of the ruling class are in every epoch the ruling ideas"[13].

Therefore, when the New Social Science explains various forms

---

12 [Special Editor's Note] "Economic stage" refers to the economic structure.

13 [Special Editor's Note] The above quotation is from Karl Marx and Friedrich Engels, The Communist Manifesto. It is rendered here as: "The ruling ideas of any given epoch are nothing other than the ideas of the ruling class." See Selected Works of Marx and Engels, vol. 1 (Beijing: People's Publishing House, 1995), p. 292.

of mental production, i.e., the superstructure, education is often not listed separately, precisely because education is merely an activity, a technique, whose task is to deliberate on how to implement "ruling ideas". Education's lack of independence is not only because its aims and implementation are conditioned by economics and politics, but also because its content and methods are conditioned by other forms of mental production.

Questions

What is ideology?

What concept of education did you originally hold?

What definitions of education did your pedagogy teacher provide?

Education has practicality, so why does current education often lack practical results?

The practicality of education is different from so-called pragmatist education or vocational education. Can you explain the difference?

SECTION 2: THE ESSENCE OF EDUCATION AND ITS TRANSFORMATION

The emergence of social classes and the evolution of the meaning of education – Education in the era of primitive communism – Private property and education – The state system and education – The class character of scholarship – Five major characteristics of class-based education: 1. Separation of learning and labour – The separation is a result of social division into classes – The division of labour theory of scholars in the service of the ruling class – Liberal education and vocational education are manifestations of separation in modern education – 2. Educational rights follow ownership – Education becomes the private possession of the propertied class – How many people in China lack educational rights? – "The poor shall not receive education" – Wealth/poverty and intellectual capacity – 3. Solely for the benefit of the ruling class – Education becomes a tool of the ruling class – The two functions of national education – The three functions of higher education – 4. The opposition between two types of education – Educational systems and educational practices – But the difference between primitive society and class society – The antagonism of dual educational rights in modern society – 5. Inequality in education between men and women – The beginning of the distinction – The view of women in civilized society – The prerequisite for solving the problem of women's education – Questions

The essence of education, as stated in the previous section, is one of the labours required by society, which endows labour power with a special qualification. In other words, education is a means to help humans manage social life. But such education, originating from the actual life needs of humanity, has not remained constant throughout the ages; its meaning and content have constantly changed.

In primitive society, education was accessible to all humanity, and all enjoyed it fairly. When society divided into classes, education also took on a class character. On the side of the ruling class, there were established educational systems, clear educational rules, and educational materials specifically for the use of their own class. As for the ruled classes, they were either completely excluded from this educational system or subjected to deceptive education.

Because of this, since the emergence of class antagonisms and struggle in society, there has been a continuous emergence of antagonisms and struggle in education as well. The historical changes in the meaning of education in the true history of education are the forms manifested during periods of historical change in social class relations, and thus become one sector, one front of the class struggle – quoting my friend Gongpu[14].

The turning point for this transformation lies in the division of society into classes. In societies without classes, i.e., in the era of primitive communist society, education was universal and unified; when society divided into classes, i.e., in the so-called era of civilization, education became class-based and antagonistic.

Class-based and antagonistic education has been the characteristic of education throughout the history of the civilized era. Yet, in terms of the essence of education, this constitutes a

---

14 [Special Editor's Note] Cited from Ye Gongpu, "The Features—Symptoms—of Modern New Education," The Education Magazine 20, no. 8 (August 1928). "Ye Gongpu" is the pen name of Yang Xianjiang.

transformation.

Let us examine the general outline of the changes in the meaning of education through history.

The greater part of humanity's past, perhaps nine-tenths, can be called the era of the clan system. Assuming the entire history of humanity is fifty thousand years, then perhaps forty-five thousand years belong to this era, the era of primitive communist life. In clan-based society, production aimed for the needs of society, and consumption followed the principle of satisfying everyone's needs. That is, production was not for the purpose of buying, selling, or making profit, and consumption ideally satisfied everyone. In other words, everyone laboured, and everyone consumed. The coexistence in the same era and society of two kinds of people – those who gain without working and those who starve despite labouring – would have been an absolutely incomprehensible riddle to people of this clan system era. That their descendants would suffer greatly because of this riddle, even finding themselves in desperate straits, was something they could not even dream of. How different the morality of this society of shared labour and shared enjoyment was from today's social morality is not difficult to imagine.

As for their education, it goes without saying that it was none other than for the biological purpose of so-called "preservation of the species" – that is, the purpose of adapting to the needs of actual life. In the clan system era, apart from transmitting the social heritage from one generation to the next, there was no other meaning to education. That is, beyond the purpose of "preservation of the species" (including "preservation of the individual"), there were no other educational objectives. People of the time, on the one hand, utilized the spiritual and material heritage passed down from previous generations, and on the other hand, added new experiences and inventions to transmit to future generations. Therefore, this was not an individual matter but a social one; it was also not a matter of domination but of equality.

However, once private property emerged and gradually developed within human society, a fundamental disparity appeared in the life of all humanity.

Because private property emerged and developed, inevitably a morality supporting this private property also emerged and developed. Education, which previously had no purpose beyond the simple biological one, now incorporated this new morality of upholding private property, aiming to transmit it to future generations and assign them this new task. Whether this new morality was consistent with the happiness or interests of all humanity was irrelevant to education. Consequently, the original task of education – "preservation of the species", i.e., the productive needs of the whole society – gradually lost its significance.

In clan-based society, although individuals differed in ability, their rights to subsistence were equal. After the emergence of private property, disparities in individual private property arose. Those with more private property and those with less no longer had equal rights to subsistence. On one side, "the wine and meat rot in the mansions of the rich"; on the other, "the bones of the frozen dead lie by the roadside"[15]. Thus, those with little or no property had to submit to those with more. The latter held the power of "life and death, reward and punishment" over the former. In such a society, a morality suitable for the propertied

---

15 [Special Editor's Note] The original line from Du Fu is "the bones of the frozen dead lie by the roadside". The author slightly modifies it for context.

class gradually developed, and education became a tool for transmitting this new morality to the next generation.

Disparities in private property ultimately destroyed the organization of the peaceful primitive society; the single, equal society thus split into the rich and the poor. This split led to the disruption of the existing "order", resulting in continuous turmoil. The ruling class, i.e., the class holding economic dominance, found it necessary to create a new "order" to superficially conceal this turmoil, mitigate the conflict between rich and poor, and thereby legally secure property. The state system was thus established.

To use a metaphor, the state is a revolving stage[16] built upon the ruins of primitive communist society.

This revolving stage was constructed only a little over four thousand years ago, yet it has already revolved several times to this day. But on any stage setting, the lead roles are always played by the "haves", while the "have-nots" and "have-littles" are always the extras. And the so-called "whip" of education is always held in the hands of the lead roles, used to drive and command the extras.

Look at Western history. Ancient times: The stage setting was the era of Greece and Rome; the lead roles were the nobles, the extras were the slaves. The education of this era aimed to confirm and praise the superiority of the noble lead roles and make the slave extras feel their own insignificance and despair. The nobles believed themselves to be particularly noble by birth, regarding

---

16 [Translator's Note] "Revolving stage" suggests a platform for changing scenes or performances, metaphorically indicating the state as a new structure facilitating the ongoing drama of class relations atop the old society's remains.

slaves as not quite human. They extracted the labour of slaves to build their own extravagant lives. And the task of education was to legitimize this fact.

Middle Ages: The stage revolved to the Middle Ages; the lead roles were feudal lords and clergy, the extras were serfs. The lords and clergy stood high above the serfs; the task of education was to keep the serfs unenlightened, living the life of groundhogs. Christianity, using the name of God, said that good groundhogs could ascend to heaven after death.

Modern era: The stage revolved further to the modern era; here, capitalists became the lead roles, while workers, peasants, and the poor became the extras. On this stage, naturally, all the scenery, costumes, and even dialogues are set up for the lead roles. So-called education is none other than making the performance of the lead roles more vivid and impressive.

Therefore, if we focus on the history of education in the course of human evolution, we can see that the original origin of education was truly to aid life; its function was merely a means to sustain life. But with historical progress, the meaning of education has greatly changed. The general outline of this change is as follows:

First, in the era of the clan system, education was for the maintenance and development of the race, transmitting the physical heritage[17] and spiritual social heritage from one generation to the next, purely for biological purposes.

Second, when the private property system began to rise, society split, and thus education, beyond its biological purpose, added

---

17 [Special Editor's Note] The original likely reads "物质" ("material").

the purpose of being a tool for domination.

Third, after the private property system was fully developed, the purpose of education consequently shifted to neglecting the first meaning and emphasizing the second.

The history of education beginning from Greece and Rome is already the history of transformed education. This kind of education has not yet ended even today. Hence, it is entirely in character for ordinary education scholars to disbelieve that the purpose of education lies in "preserving the race", in adapting to the needs of actual life, and instead feel compelled to dress it up with other high-sounding facades, making the general public superstitiously believe that the educational enterprise is sacred and noble – this is precisely the hallmark of "scholars in the service of the ruling class".

The class character of education is an obvious fact, but to provide readers with greater clarity, I will briefly explain the class character of learning in general.

As stated before, all learning arises from the actual demands of society. Once classes emerged in society, and one society split into several classes, then what could be called simple social demands ceased to exist, replaced by the demands of a particular class. From then on, learning, as such, emerged and developed precisely due to the demands of this class. Consequently, no matter what kind of learning, it inevitably carries a certain class nature, a class color. Although some might say that science seeks pure truth and thus can lack this class nature, one must understand that since science cannot be separated from practical use, in a class society, there can never be practical use completely detached from class. This is especially pronounced in the social sciences, as evidenced by the stark opposition between bourgeois economics and proletarian economics. Even in the natural sciences, class significance exists or lies latent, differing only in degree, whether great or small, direct or indirect.

Take astronomy as an example. When astronomy first emerged, it was indeed for the benefit of society as a whole. But later, as primitive productive society gradually changed, and private (or semi-private) class systems like the patriarchal system emerged, astronomy transformed from knowledge for the benefit of the whole society into knowledge for the benefit of a minority (i.e., the patriarchal class, the ruling class). That is, astronomical knowledge (and the same goes for other knowledge) became a secret monopolized by priests and shamans, primarily to protect the interests and power of the ruling class. For instance, the astronomy of Egypt and Babylon both possessed, to some extent, a religious (and ritual) ideological form for this reason. By the Greek era, although astronomy broke free from the hands of the priests and declared independence from religion, this time it became subordinate to philosophy. In Greece, all learning was philosophy, so astronomy also became a part of philosophy; the idealist philosophies of great philosophers like Plato and Aristotle[18] influenced astronomy. By the Roman era, Ptolemy[19] completed ancient astronomy. This was quite a valuable achievement, but behind his advocated geocentric theory lay, on one hand, the philosophies of Plato and Aristotle, and on the other, the Christian Bible. Therefore, Ptolemy's astronomy largely coincided with the structure of the universe described in the Bible and was based on the profound philosophies of the two

---

18 [Special Editor's Note] Aristotle (384–322 BC), ancient Greek philosopher and scientist.

19 [Special Editor's Note] Claudius Ptolemaeus (90–168 AD), Egyptian astronomer, proponent of the "Geocentric Theory". He believed the Earth was stationary at the center of the universe, with the sun, moon, and stars revolving around it. This theory remained authoritative in astronomy for over a thousand years before Copernicus. His works include Almagest, Geography, among others.

great philosophers. In the Middle Ages, his astronomy held absolute authority. Just as no one could doubt the Bible, no one could oppose Aristotelian philosophy, and no one could raise objections to Ptolemaic astronomy. Thus, astronomy after Rome, as the philosophical and religious geocentric theory, became knowledge that upheld ruling power and the ruling class. For a thousand years, astronomy showed not a trace of progress.

However, around the 15th century, the social darkness that had lasted over a thousand years began to show a glimmer of dawn. The so-called new era of the Renaissance, the new movement of the Reformation, new discoveries and inventions occurred successively, and new scientific research flourished. Where did this change originate? Naturally, it was none other than the result of the collapse of the economic foundation of the feudal system and the development of the new capitalist system. Among the villages dominated by lords and the church, commercial and industrial cities gradually emerged. The merchant-industrial class, i.e., the bourgeoisie, resisted the aristocratic class, using free thought and scientific thought as their weapons. Hitherto, so-called learning was completely monopolized by the clergy. Now the bourgeoisie demanded science and embraced it. Science became independent from its position as the handmaiden of the church; science rebelled against the church. And the bourgeoisie was the ally of science. Commercial and industrial cities became centers of new civilization, centers of new learning. To develop industry and facilitate transportation, the bourgeoisie found various sciences necessary. Simultaneously, to overthrow the old system and attack the old forces, they demanded science as an ideological weapon. The so-called Renaissance was the social phenomenon adapting to these demands. The so-called Reformation was merely about changing the Roman Church, which was allied with the feudal nobility, into a religion serving the bourgeoisie. Consequently, a new era emerged, new learning developed, and our astronomy also underwent great changes and made great progress. The heliocentric theory in astronomy at that time was the new learning of the new class. But in the modern era where capitalist society is established, although various academic fields have achieved rapid progress, learning, as such, still cannot avoid being the ruling class's serving knowledge. The so-called "academic freedom" is limited to the scope that does not hinder capitalist domination. As for history and the social sciences, they have clearly become bourgeois knowledge, displaying conservative, reactionary, oppressive, and dominating attitudes. What is more, even the natural sciences, often celebrated for their freedom and independence, are themselves faltering—whether through doubt or obsequiousness—and increasingly lapsing into reactionary and idealist philosophy. In our astronomy, it greatly serves the function of indirectly upholding ruling power. For example, it is said that studying astronomy can broaden the mind, explore the mysteries of the universe, thereby disseminating thoughts of "peace of mind and accepting one's fate" and "seeing through the vanity of the world" among the general public. When the class struggle intensifies and the ruling class feels incessantly uneasy, it has become a prevalent fashion worldwide to utilize things like popular astronomy lectures and film explanations in an attempt to divert the gaze of the masses. Its effect, precisely like that of religion and art, can be comforting, hypnotic, and narcotizing. Yet, general scholars, educators, and even journalists approve of and strive for such things. Unconsciously–though some are fully aware, or half-aware–they do their utmost to indirectly support the ruling class.

Since the class character of learning is thus, it is perfectly obvious that the educational enterprise, which takes various fields of learning as its content, cannot but have a class character.

From class-based education, we can discern five major characteristics of this education.

The first characteristic is the separation of education and labour. In primitive communist society, everyone laboured, and everyone learned the knowledge and skills required for labour as needed, wherever they were, or received guidance from elders. Thus, learning was also shared by all and connected to labour. But when class society emerged, with the appearance of the ruling and the ruled classes, the former became the so-called "mental labourers", the latter the so-called "manual labourers". Politically, "mental labourers" and "manual labourers" are in a relationship of domination and subordination; in education, this is the relationship between "learning" and "labour". The ruling class solely engages in "learning" (though many indeed do not engage in "learning" but only live in debauchery) and absolutely does not engage in "labour", while the ruled class solely engages in "labour" and absolutely does not engage in "learning". In other words, the brain and the hands split up, knowledge and industry/commerce divorced; the two form opposing camps, as if not allowing a single step across the line. The previously cited views of the Greek philosopher Plato serve as evidence.

The result of this kind of education, on an individual level, is that scholars become "too weak to truss a chicken", become "ignorant of physical labour and unable to distinguish the five grains"; workers become "illiterate", become "unknowing and unlearning, obedient to the emperor's rule". On a social level, scholars occupy the "head of the four classes"[1], viewing labour as lowly, while workers belong to the lower orders, viewing learning as useless. A person's status and occupation even become hereditary and irrational, such as a scholar's son always being a scholar, and a carpenter's son forever being a carpenter. A chasm seemed to lie between them, extremely difficult to bridge. However, while the direct cause of this situation must be attributed to the social division into classes, class education plays a role in fostering it. Thus, scholars inevitably become people alienated from productive activities, people who inevitably rely on the ruling class (or are themselves the ruling class) for their livelihood; while workers are doomed from birth to death, from morning till night, to engage in productive labour to support the general idle consumers. Hence, the two groups have different interests and must adopt hostile attitudes towards each other.

This phenomenon is actually an abnormality; it is never the case that one kind of person is born only fit to study and not work, and another kind is born only fit to work and not study. Unexpectedly, because this abnormal social phenomenon has been passed down for so long, some scientists actually arose to prove that such a division of labour in humanity is natural. What is their evidence? They cite the existence of division of labour in the biological world, such as among bees and ants. For example, the queen bee only reigns, the drone only mates, the worker bee only flits among flowers and makes honey, etc. Then our scientist infers that in human society, some people being capitalists and others workers is precisely "ordained by nature", perfectly reasonable. What a clever scientist in the service of the ruling class you are!—Dr. Kyū Asajirō, the famous Japanese scientist.

The separation of education and labour is not only a thing of the past; it remains so even in modern times.

Pre-1917 Russia was "mostly uneducated throughout the country," said Nadezhda Krupskaya[20] (Lenin's wife). Only the children of a small segment of the population, the special classes, could receive the benefits of education; other children of workers

---

20 [Special Editor's Note] Nadezhda Konstantinovna Krupskaya (1869–1939), Soviet educator.

and peasants who had sunk to the lower strata really had no opportunity or possibility of receiving an education. Even those nominally considered to be receiving education, after three years of primary school, found that church language[21], church singing, prayers, and other religious rituals occupied half of the class time, while Russian language, arithmetic, and penmanship were merely formal. The subject of history served only to inculcate a spirit of loyalty to the "Tsar", and nothing else. As for secondary schools, Alexander III's Minister of Education, Delyanov, once said, "There is no place in secondary schools for the sons of cooks."[22] Thus, those who could enter secondary schools were naturally only the children of landowners, nobles, and the wealthy. The curriculum of secondary schools focused on Latin, Greek, and the history of emperors, so the students produced were isolated from actual life, only fit to be minor bureaucrats under the then-existing system. This was indeed the purpose of secondary schools at that time. Another example is adult education; besides the four arithmetic operations (addition, subtraction, multiplication, division), teaching fractions was forbidden. If this ban was violated, the school would be closed.

This is one example of the separation of education and labour in the 20th century.

Let me give another example, which is the debate between

---

21 [Special Editor's Note] "Church language" was one of the subjects taught in Russian parish schools; it referred to the Slavic language used by the church.

22 [Special Editor's Note] In 1887, the Ministry of Education of the Tsarist government issued a secret circular known as the "Circular on Cooks' Children", which instructed secondary school principals to refuse admission to children of cooks, coachmen, and menial servants.

Liberal Education and Vocational Education[23], the opposition between the general track and the vocational track. But here, I do not wish to critique this issue extensively. I believe that regardless of whether one advocates separation or integration, the very existence of such opposing names and facts in education is sufficient proof that the separation of education and labour still persists even in this so-called developed and widespread era of capitalist education. That is, so-called education remains class-based, not universal.

Could it be that such a separation has no progressive role whatsoever in the course of social evolution? Perhaps someone will raise this question. Indeed, we do not deny that this separation has its progressive aspects. The brilliantly splendid civilization of Greece could be said to be entirely built by slaves. If there had not been 360,000 slaves at that time, using their physical labour to support 90,000 free citizens, and if a few wise men among the free citizens did not have ample leisure for contemplation, then the philosophies of Plato and Aristotle might never have been established. Plato argued that slaves were indispensable; Aristotle said philosophy presupposes necessary leisure. These are indeed heartfelt words, words "gained from experience".

However, there is a distinction here. It is a fact that ancient

---

23 [Special Editor's Note] "文雅教育" (Wényǎ jiàoyù), also translated as "liberal education", "general education", or "liberal arts education", refers to the traditional education model dating back to Ancient Greece. It aimed at the general cultural cultivation of the individual, prioritizing knowledge for knowledge's sake rather than practical utility. By the end of the Middle Ages, this form of education became incompatible with the demands of capitalist production. Consequently, bourgeois vocational education emerged, advocating that education should primarily serve societal needs and focus on various forms of vocational training.

civilization, and even modern civilization, was built by slaves. But because of the abundant and continuous input of slave labour, the Athenian people were able to devote themselves to politics, art, philosophy, physical education, and all other liberal pursuits. Consequently, acknowledging that the free citizens of Athens indeed sacrificed slaves for their own benefit and used them as tools for their own enjoyment, and furthermore advocating that there should indeed be slaves in human society, letting them forever live inhuman lives—or even if not explicitly advocating this, but accepting this division of labour as necessary and natural—is wrong.

The reactionary aspect of the philosophy of Plato and Aristotle (idealist philosophy) is revealed precisely in its relation to the slave system. Because this philosophy was the philosophy of a slave-owning society based on slave labour. The society of that time had already discovered many contradictions but found no way out. Thus, idealist philosophy emerged among the ruling class. The social purpose of this idealism was to idealize and perpetuate the existing social conditions, and to generalize the idea of rule by reason, i.e., the philosophy of the philosopher-king. According to this view, the masses are unreasonable; only a minority of the ruling class can be reasonable and possess rationality. This idealist philosophy of reason dominating all things, after thousands of years, became the most powerful argument for the general claims of the ruling class.

Without looking further, just considering the contradictions inherent in Greek society at that time, we can cite two examples to make it clear. In a society based on slave labour, a concept among free citizens despising occupational labour inevitably arose; they attached the stigma of baseness to labour, viewing it as solely the business of slaves. As a result, a great many propertyless free citizens had to rely on state funds to live. In other words, they became parasites of the state. Thus, the state had to engage in war to gather the means of subsistence for these propertyless free citizens, intensifying social unrest. Another point is an important contradiction arising in the economic sphere. Namely, slave labour obstructed technological progress and halted the development of productive forces. Because slaves only performed forced labour, only crude tools could be used in slave labour. Therefore, when the ancient slave economy reached its peak, we see technological stagnation and a stagnation of interest in the natural sciences (which were already flourishing in the Asian Minor colonies).

Therefore, nowadays, if anyone advocates a philosopher-king polity, or argues that education should emphasize liberal, broad, and "free" learning, it is definitely a reactionary view, definitely a view upholding ruling power, and should be vigorously attacked in our new education.

The second characteristic is that educational rights follow ownership.

The distribution of education is primarily determined by the amount of ownership; that is, the privilege of ownership is linked to the privilege of cultivation, so that the propertied class becomes the educated class, and the proletariat becomes the uneducated class. Such education is fundamentally the exclusive possession of a wealthy minority; the proletariat need not, and indeed are not permitted, to enjoy it. For example, Japanese imperialism, its education can certainly be said to be widespread, and the government's implementation of education can be said to be wholehearted. Yet, in the Elementary School Ordinance, it explicitly stipulates that if the guardian is poor, children may be allowed to delay schooling or be exempted from it. Is this not evidence that educational rights follow ownership?[24]

So, in a classless society, do you believe such unfairness would exist?

According to the preliminary plan for compulsory education implementation by the Ministry of Education published at the end of October 1929, the recent total number of school-age children in China was 43.6 million, with 6.41 million enrolled, leaving 37.19 million children not in school. These 37.19 million unschooled children exist precisely because they have little or no

---

[24] Examples of educational opportunities being greatly limited by the amount of ownership are right before our eyes, needing little explanation. But for reference, an actual case can be cited. The following is quoted from Gongpu's "The Characteristics–or Maladies–of Modern Education".

This instance was provided by Aoki Seishirō, assistant professor at Tokyo Imperial University, and another person, Okada Shinichi, based on their 1925 survey of the relationship between wealth and secondary education attendance in one area of Yamagata Prefecture, Japan.

Examining this table clearly shows how access to secondary education is profoundly influenced by financial capacity. In detail, children from the highest wealth bracket (over 12,000 yen) had an attendance rate of over 85 students per 100 households. As wealth decreases, this opportunity diminishes significantly: the middle bracket (1,000-3,000 yen) had 41.0 students per 100 households, the lower-middle bracket (500-1,000 yen) had 18.6, and finally, the lowest wealth bracket (under 500 yen), despite having the largest absolute number of households, could only send 2.7 students per 100 households to secondary school. We know that the number of children in lower wealth brackets is certainly not proportionally smaller. Therefore, it can be inferred that low financial capacity severely restricts the opportunity for children to receive secondary education. Moreover, the sequential decrease in the number of secondary education attendees as wealth diminishes further confirms the accuracy of this inference.

[Special Editor's Note] There appear to be calculation or typesetting errors in the original table. Necessary revisions have been made here. The Complete Works of Yang Xianjiang, Vol. 3, p. 284, published by Henan Education Press in 1995, also made corrections to the original table, though some points remain debatable.

wealth.

According to the draft preliminary plan for adult supplementary education implementation by the Ministry of Education, the number of those who should receive supplementary school education (i.e., the illiterate) reaches 195.15 million, nearly 200 million. These illiterates, constituting about half the national population, also exist due to having little or no wealth.

According to the statistics on school enrollment surveyed by the China Education Improvement Society[25] in 1923, the number of students in primary schools across various provinces was over 6.6 million, in secondary schools over 182,000, and in higher education over 34,800. Here, many who could not graduate from primary school or, after graduating, could not enter secondary school, and many who could not graduate from secondary school or, after graduating, could not enter higher education—aside from reasons of death or illness—are also due to having little wealth.

If you have ownership, you have educational rights.

Even if a child is mentally handicapped, as long as their father or elder brother is a landlord, wealthy man, comprador, bureaucrat, or warlord, there is no fear of lacking educational rights. They can not only enter any school but also study abroad.

But if it is the child of a poor person, then no matter how brilliant a genius they are, there is no opportunity for it to be discovered, because so-called scientific tools like intelligence tests cannot be applied to poor children. Nor can they dream of a day

---

25 [Special Editor's Note] The China Education Improvement Society was one of the Chinese educational organizations. It was established in 1921 in Beijing through the merger of the Practical Education Survey Society, the New Education Co-advancement Society, and the New Education Editorial Society.

when they become literate and read. Following Japan's example, they are "imperially ordered" exempt from the obligation to attend school (!); following Russia's example (in Tsarist times), "there is no place in secondary schools for the sons of cooks."

It is predestined: the poor shall not receive education!

Think: from the time they can talk and walk, many children of the poor must help their fathers and elder brothers earn a living. If you force them to study, you actually deprive them of the opportunity to make a living. Unless you can provide them with study grants, how can such compulsory education be implemented? A secondary school student costs about 200 yuan annually, a university student about 400 yuan. Among the national population, how many families can afford such expensive secondary and higher education fees?

Because the poor are originally not supposed to receive education, stories like "bore a hole in the wall to steal light [for reading]" and "hang books on ox horns [to read while herding]" are passed down as beautiful tales.

Because the poor are fundamentally not meant to receive an education, if one of them should suddenly gain a rich patron and actually succeed in their studies and career, they are expected to be "so overwhelmed with gratitude that they feel there is no place to hide themselves."[26]

---

26 On November 11, 1929, Shanghai newspapers carried a manifesto for raising the "Siyuan (Remembering the Source) Student Aid Fund" initiated by Wang Zhishen, a bank general manager, and Pan Xulun, an accountant. The full text is reproduced below to show readers how these two sons of poor families—now "wealthy men" themselves—"profuse tears of gratitude" towards the capitalists!

"Zhishen was born into a family of humble means and was orphaned in his early youth. Relying on his mother's laborious efforts, he barely managed to attend school. The hardships and difficulties of that time still move him to tears when he recalls them today. Xulun was also orphaned early, and his family's circumstances were below average, allowing him only to barely complete) his basic education.

Both of us were each on the verge of dropping out more than once. However, being young and ardent, determined to improve ourselves, we occasionally took on jobs to earn tuition money. Yet the road ahead was long, our hearts anxious but our steps lagging, leaving us at a loss. Heaven took pity on our isolation and poverty, and there was Mr. Li Zhaobei of Xiamen, whom we barely knew, who, believing Zhishen had promise, generously mailed 3,000 yuan to cover the costs of studying abroad. Receiving this unexpected aid from a 'helper', we prepared for the journey, feeling such gratitude that there was no place to hide ourselves. At the same time, Mr. Jian Zhaonan, general manager of the Nanyang Brothers Tobacco Company, an industrialist with a philanthropic heart, took pity on aspiring students in dire straits. He personally allocated a huge sum of money and set up a competitive selection process. Xulun, though undeserving, was accepted and sent to study in the United States for over three years, at a cost exceeding ten thousand yuan. Without Mr. Jian, given Xulun's limited capabilities, how could he have achieved this? Now, although Zhishen and Xulun have gained little substantial knowledge from their studies, we are fortunate to have society not discard us and have each come to hold a professional position, striving to fulfill our aspirations. Reflecting on this in the quiet of the night, we cannot help but shed tears and say to each other: Those who gave us life are our parents; those who taught us are our teachers; but those who provided the resources for our success, are they not these two gentlemen?

A guest once advised Lord Wuji of Wei: 'My Lord, if you have shown kindness to others, I hope you will forget it. But if others have shown kindness to you, you must not forget it.' Now, these two gentlemen have given and are able to forget their charity. How can we, the recipients, simply forget it?

But if we do not forget, what can we do? If we try to return the full amount to the two gentlemen, they will not accept it, nor would that be their intention. What, then, is their intention? It is simply their sincere love for young people who have ambition but lack resources, and their desire to help them achieve success. Why not uphold the intention of the two gentlemen and propagate their virtue? Though our own strength is inadequate, Zhishen and Xulun resolve to strive towards this goal. After discussion, we have decided: Zhishen will contribute 3,000 yuan, Xulun will contribute 10,000 yuan, and together we will establish a student aid fund named 'Siyuan' (Remembering the Source). Since we have drunk from the well, should we not remember its source? Since we remember the source, should we not let others also drink from it? Zhishen's contribution shall be named the 'Zhaobei Fund'. Xulun's contribution shall be named the 'Zhaonan Fund'. Each is to remember their benefactor, and also to make those who drink from it in turn remember them. All organizational details are outlined in the simplified regulations. In the future, if

Perhaps some may argue that the root cause of wealth and poverty lies fundamentally in differences in intellectual capacity. Therefore, it is only "inevitable under the circumstances and perfectly justified in principle" that the rich have the opportunity for education while the poor do not. But this view is clearly a

---

Zhishen and Xulun's financial capacity increases, we certainly dare not let these meager sums be our limit.

Alas! Who, knowing the desire to do good, is not like us? A beginning may be small, but the end can be great. Should others encounter circumstances similar to ours and be moved to reflection; should those who receive this money in the future strive diligently to complete their studies and be moved to reflection... Through wind and rain, the cock crows; why not rise up and join us? Zhishen and Xulun respectfully await your arrival.

The Republic of China, November 1929.

Initiators: Wang Zhishen, Pan Xulun."

Do you also wish to receive their funding to complete your studies? Then take a look at the qualifications they have set:

"Article 5: Young people receiving support from this fund must possess the following qualifications: A) Come from a poor family; B) Have excellent character and scholarship, and upright, proper aspirations; C) Be physically healthy."

So, first, if you lack nourishment and are physically weak, or if your health has suffered due to diligent study, forget about receiving support. Second, if in their view—for there are no objective criteria—your character and scholarship are not excellent, your aspirations not upright and proper; in other words, if you are a revolutionary youth, forget about receiving support. Finally, and most notably, those born without any opportunity to receive 'schooling' in the first place have no possibility whatsoever of receiving funding. This is just as effective as so-called scientific intelligence tests: for poor children, it is fundamentally a way to 'sever relations'.

"Alas!" Poor child! You receive neither sustenance from the state nor support from the capitalists. With such "double cold"—Heaven pities the isolated and poor (?), but does not pity the doubly destitute—where, pray tell, can you go?

grave error. As noted in the Education Reader by the Japanese author Nakasone Genwa: When the rich see the poor, they say they are poor because they lack ability; when the poor see the rich, they also think he is rich because he is great. In fact, in schools, the academic performance of the children of the poor often far surpasses that of the children of the rich. If children of the poor had the opportunity to be in the same environment as children of the rich, their intellectual abilities would be truly equal.

He also cites an interesting example: Suppose we take 9,000 useful members of society – 9,000 people whom anyone would consider capable – such as:

Schoolteachers with an annual income of $2,000: 1,500 people

Doctors with the same annual income: 1,500 people

Farmers with the same annual income: 1,500 people

Skilled workers with the same annual income: 1,500 people

Musicians with the same annual income: 1,500 people

Mining engineers with the same annual income: 1,500 people

These 9,000 people mostly spent long years acquiring their training and experience, and then performed useful work for society, yet their annual remuneration is only $2,000. Continuing for 40 years, the total money earned by these 9,000 people over this period would be $720 million. However, this sum is still $280 million less than the wealth of the single American magnate John D. Rockefeller in 1915 alone. If the distinction between rich and poor were due to intellectual capacity, then, collectively, are the brains of these 9,000 people really far inferior to that of a single Rockefeller?

Furthermore, the total salaries of 8,079 first-rank American politicians and educators amounted to $20,456,500. Yet, compared to Rockefeller's annual income, this was still over $10 million less.

Also, the average salary of the 100 highest-paid university presidents in the world was only $6,000 per year. But Rockefeller's income was at least 50 times greater than the combined salaries of all 100 of these university presidents. I ask you, was Rockefeller's brain really worth the combined intellectual value of these 100 university presidents?

Therefore, intellectual capacity cannot be measured by wealth. Consequently, we cannot say that the sons of the poor are not intelligent, nor can we say that they should not receive the same education as the sons of the rich.

Thus, in modern times, if anyone claims that promoting education is for the diffusion of culture among humanity, or that establishing schools is to cultivate talent for society, yet pays no attention to the vast majority of the poor who lack clothing and food, and ignores the multitude of impoverished children deprived of education and care – such talk is undoubtedly deceptive rhetoric meant to whitewash the facade.

The third characteristic is that it is solely for the benefit of the ruling class.

Class-based education, for the ruled class, is neither adapted to their own interests nor to the requirements of society as a whole. Its primary function is to implement an education convenient for the ruling class, designed to captivate the minds of the oppressed and make them into instruments serving the ruling class.

That education in ancient and medieval times was aristocratic education is an obvious fact needing no elaboration.

Although in modern times there are slogans of "equal opportunity" and "universal education", the substance of modern education is still governed by highly unreasonable standards. In the end, it cannot escape being rooted in the privilege of ownership, manifesting the privilege of cultivation at every turn.

Let us dissect modern education a bit.

National education can be considered the education generally available to all citizens. In terms of its scope, one might still say it is not entirely based on the ruling class. But if we proceed to examine the impoverished and minimal nature of what is provided to the proletarian masses, we can still discern the hue of the ruling class — and indeed, a more pronounced hue of the ruling class. Wherever national education exists under the control of the ruling class, it invariably performs two functions. These two functions are: first, as a means of political domination; second, as a means to maintain and promote economic exploitation. The education imparted in elementary schools naturally bears the marks of these functions.

First, let's discuss its function as a means of political domination. This involves teaching children in schools that the current capitalist social and state order is the best and most perfect among all possible natural and immutable social orders, and that the ruling class representing this social order are innate leaders possessing the greatest benevolence, justice, intelligence, and power. Consequently, the duty of the national masses is to regard the existing order as sacred, to respect and defend it, and to view the ruling class as good teachers and benevolent fathers, to revere and support them. Simultaneously, they are taught that any thought or doctrine opposing this is heresy and should be rejected.

Next, its function as a means to maintain and promote economic exploitation works as follows: After children receive four, six, or even more years of primary education, the labour capacity of the proletarian masses is enhanced, conditioning them to become obedient wage slaves. In subjects like Morality or Civics, moral lessons of diligence, effort, thrift, and frugality are vigorously instilled. Concurrently, on the societal level, systems like savings banks and postal savings are established, along with methods in factories that compel workers to save a portion of their wages. What the ruling class expects from the proletarian masses is to work as much as possible while consuming as little of the product of their labour as possible. In other words, to be content with the lowest possible wages, thereby leaving a larger surplus for the exploiting class to utilize. This is precisely why primary education places special emphasis on "diligence and hard work" in this specific sense. Furthermore, what the ruling class expects from the proletarian masses is loyalty to their masters and obedience to superiors. To this end, school education strives to cultivate habits of "honesty", "obedience", "rule-following", and "emphasis on cooperation". At the same time, Christianity fulfills its mission of social education by preaching the gospel, saying that suffering in this life leads to heaven in the next, and strongly advising against strikes!

Thus, the social task of primary schools is to tame the children of the proletariat, moulding them into an obedient and efficient industrial army and into loyal soldiers.

Can one still claim that national education is for the benefit of the general populace themselves? Only the lackeys of the ruling class would hold such a belief.

If this is true for primary education, what about higher-level schools?

The social tasks of higher-level schools can generally be summarized in the following three points:

To cultivate the intermediate classes that are subordinate to the ruling class. Various strata such as officials (serving in state and public organs), clerks and employees (serving in capitalist enterprises), and independent operators (owner-farmers, small merchants, upper-level artisans, and liberal professionals) – all possessing a fixed ideology and a certain level of specialized knowledge – are educated in higher schools. Whether as direct servants or indirect supporters, they are absolutely indispensable elements for the existence and maintenance of the capitalist society and state.

To nurture individuals from within the ruling class itself who are suited to hold their dominant position. To consolidate the position of the ruling class, they must, on the one hand, possess fundamental knowledge about domination and exploitation, and on the other hand, acquire the necessary conviction that the society they represent is natural and the best possible order. Hence, the higher schools of today, particularly universities, exist primarily to supply this necessary knowledge and conviction. Furthermore, these schools provide the ruling class with a humanistic cultivation (Bildung). The function of this cultivation is twofold: firstly, in principle, it secures the privilege – exclusive to the ruling class – of appreciating and enjoying the fruits of modern culture, such as music, literature, song and dance, painting, and even the utilization of electricity, power, etc. Secondly, as a side effect, when the ruling class, having tasted a bit of culture and acquired the polish of cultivation, is reflected in the eyes of the proletariat, they appear truly innately noble and elegant, while the proletariat see themselves as base and insignificant. This leads them to believe that serving the ruling class devotedly is perfectly "right and proper", absolutely justified.

To promote research in the academic disciplines and technical skills necessary for maintaining and developing the ruling class's order. Capitalism, in order to maintain its expanded productive forces and seek further development, finds it necessary to dominate nature and natural forces more extensively and reliably. Therefore, it vigorously encourages research in the natural sciences. The result of this encouragement is that capitalism can claim a great achievement in the discovery and application of new theories and technologies, preparing the potential for a uniquely human happiness on an unprecedented scale. However, this applies only to the natural sciences, not the social sciences. When the modern ruling class (the bourgeoisie) was itself a revolutionary class, it indeed encouraged the social sciences as well as the natural sciences, in order to smash feudal ideas and traditions, and to establish its own domination and strengthen its organizational structures. But once this necessity was fulfilled, and furthermore, when scholarly research began to target capitalism itself – the very system they had built – the ruling class became displeased with social scientific research that subjected the ruling class to thorough critique. Not only did they cease to encourage it, they actively began to suppress it. Thus, for example, in Japan today, academic research in higher schools concerning the social sciences is, in principle, permitted and encouraged only if it aligns with the standpoint of the ruling class, i.e., if it directly or indirectly contributes to maintaining and promoting the interests of the ruling class. As for student-initiated research movements in the New Social Science, these are banned, and participants face expulsion and arrest.

Can anyone still believe that such higher education involves the pure research of profound learning, unrelated to class? Only devotees of the ruling class harbor such superstitions.

The fourth characteristic is the opposition between dual

educational rights.

This so-called dual educational right refers to the two types of education that coexist and even contend with each other in class society. Namely, the organization of educational systems and the existence of educational practices are opposed rather than unified.

These two forms of education did exist among primitive peoples.

For instance, among the savage tribes of the South Seas, there were large communal houses—Western researchers call them Club houses — established for the training of youth, with prescribed circumcision and initiation rites. This setup can be said to constitute a somewhat organized educational system. Simultaneously, within this society, although such a system was not organized everywhere and at all times, various social life practices were informally transmitted and learned in daily life. This is called the substantive existence of education. Moreover, this substantive education was indeed the primary form of education in primitive societies.—See Section 5, "Education in Primitive Communist Society". However, we must pay close attention here: the two forms of education among primitive people do not constitute two separate educational rights, nor are they two opposing educational rights. Whether it is the educational system or educational practices, they are consistent in essence. They served the life needs of the entire society, not the interests of any particular special class. Their two forms of education are fundamentally different from the two forms of education in class society and must not be confused.

So, what exactly are the two forms of education in class society? In class society, the so-called civilized society, there is an educational system dedicated solely to the use of the ruling class. The ruled classes are excluded from this educational system; they rely only on a substantive practice that does not constitute a formal system.

Before the Middle Ages, education as substantive practice occupied a more important role than education as an organized system. The education for the vast majority outside the state class and the church class was accomplished entirely through substantive practice. The apprenticeship system was perhaps the only organized institution. But this organization did not actually change the substance of educational practice; it was merely like school rules, not affecting the content of the subjects. Therefore, within the apprenticeship system, the substance of education still belonged to practice and was not systematized, and it was precisely through this that the exquisite crafts of the Middle Ages were produced. Similarly, in the earlier Greek society, composed of free citizens and slaves who outnumbered the citizens several times over, the production of all means of social subsistence and all technical arts—indeed, all productive physical and mental labour—was borne by the slaves. Thus, in reality, besides the educational system recorded in general educational history, which served the military and civil dominative life or the leisure life of the citizen class of the Greek state, there was also an "unconscious" educational practice among the slaves, aimed at fulfilling the physical and mental labour life necessary for the "society's" production. The architecture and sculpture that concretely expressed the Greek aesthetic sense were entirely products of the "education" of the slaves. This education naturally aimed for substantive effects, demanded by the "societal" life of that time. It's just that those effects were no longer purely "biological" demands, and that society did not belong to the slaves themselves.

Those who typically write histories of education pay attention only to the educational systems of the ruling classes and completely disregard the educational practices of the ruled classes.

Therefore, the facts recorded as Greek education in Western histories of education are limited to the education of the citizen-state class. The reasons for this are partly, of course, perhaps due to a lack of documentary sources, but on the other hand, it is truly because the compilers, standing from the standpoint of the rulers, mistakenly or deliberately recognize only organized educational systems—specifically, education controlled by state apparatuses—as education, while forgetting or obscuring the education inherent in the human practices that sustained social life—not dominative life. Originally, since the beginning of history—the history of the so-called civilized era where society is divided into classes—the rulers have viewed their own class as the whole of society. What they call social life is actually the life of their own class; what they call social education or culture is actually the education or culture of their own class. The more civilization advances, the thicker this cloak becomes, to the extent that they claim oppression is for the happiness of the oppressed. And "scholars in the service of the ruling class" often adopt the rulers' perspective, so how could they not equate the education of the rulers with the education of all human society?

The above explains that in class society, the educational system of the ruling class and the educational practices of the ruled classes—the reason being their exclusion from the educational system—coexist simultaneously. However, the two are not necessarily mutually exclusive or antagonistic. For example, in medieval Europe, alongside the education of the ruling class, there was education for workers and peasants. Their educational conditions were certainly distinct, yet there was little interaction between them. In other words, the two forms of education coexisted but were not antagonistic.

But since the development of the modern class system—capitalists and proletarians—that is, since the modern revolution—the bourgeois revolution—class has become not merely a relation of natural opposition but also a relation of conscious opposition. This change in the relationship simultaneously gave rise to a relation of conscious opposition in the realm of cultivation. The vigorous modern cultivation arose consciously in opposition to the cultivation of the old state. Namely, the cultivation of the bourgeois class stood in antagonistic position to the cultivation of the militaristic state, ultimately achieving final victory.

Thus, as a modern phenomenon, cultivation (including education) is necessarily antagonistic. The cultivation of the modern state necessarily assumes an attacking stance towards the cultivation of the militaristic state. In other words, the characteristic of the modern era is this: class-based cultivation is definitely not "running parallel without mutual conflict," but is "mutually exclusive."

This early modern history of nations, progressing with the development of the bourgeois state, is continued by the history of modern class antagonisms. It is therefore natural that what is called education today cannot be universal or societal, but possesses a partisan character, aligned with either the bourgeois class or the working class in their opposition. Furthermore, these mutually opposing forms of education inherently possess a mutually antagonistic nature, aiming for the overthrow of the other.

Precisely because of this nature, from the standpoint of the modern state of the 18th and 19th centuries, it was inevitable to advocate free competition as the best method even in the "competition of cultivation." However, from the standpoint of a state where capitalism has advanced into the stage of monopoly, and the liberalist state has evolved into an imperialist state, it becomes equally inevitable to advocate "monopoly" and "imperialism" in the realm of cultivation as well.

Fundamentally, the modern state, having evolved to this stage, long ago lost its revolutionary practicality and its scientific progressiveness. The task of bearing the revolutionary mission in the historical process today, and inheriting the legacy of scientific development since the 18th century in culture, falls solely upon the proletariat. The social sciences, which had reached a dead end from the 19th century to the beginning of the 20th, were revived entirely from the proletarian perspective to explain the process of the capitalist system's collapse. This proletarian culture, both in its methodology and content, exhibits scientific growth. This is what makes the bourgeoisie tremble and fear, leading them to reject and suppress it. Yet, we must understand that it is just as impossible to exclude science from today's proletarian cultivation as it was a hundred years ago for the Church to interfere with the bourgeoisie's cultivation and exclude their science when the bourgeoisie were building their new order.

In this era of imperialism, it is precisely the time when the ruling class strives for a monopoly on education. But opposing this monopolistic education are not only the substantive, practical education of the ruled classes but also, furthermore, their organized, institutionalized education. This dual educational right exists right now and is actively struggling—see Section 13 below.

In such times, if anyone still claims that the universal education of the modern state is already the education of all humanity (or all the people), is unified education, and further advocates that no other educational practice or organization should be permitted besides state education or education sanctioned by the state, then this can only be the propaganda function of bourgeois[27] pedagogues.

Finally, the fifth characteristic is inequality in education between men and women.

As mentioned before, in the era of primitive communism, everyone laboured collectively, consumed collectively, and also received education collectively. In that era, of course, both men and women equally had access to societal education. Although in the savage era, gynocracy was particularly prominent, and in the barbaric era, women's status remained very high, this did not lead to differential treatment in education for men. Because clan society was truly a society of freedom, equality, and fraternity, without class divisions.

However, as animal husbandry and agriculture gradually developed, men's productive power gradually surpassed women's, eventually leading men to claim even the houses owned by their wives as their own. Furthermore, to obtain "their own sons" to inherit property, they began to demand absolute chastity from their wives. Thus, the patriarchal system replaced the matriarchal system. Under patriarchy, women's status became part of men's property, alongside livestock, farmland, and houses. This marks the civilized era of private property, where women fell into slavery even before male slaves existed.

Since the disappearance of matriarchal power, i.e., the collapse of the clan system, and humanity's entry into the civilized period, a great transformation occurred in the history of education. That is, women from then on not only could not "study together" with

---

27 [Special Editor's Note] It is a phonetic translation of the French word Bourgeois, meaning the capitalist class.

men and had to receive a differential education, but they were simply driven towards being "unlearned," severed from education.

"Obedience to the father at home, obedience to the husband after marriage, and obedience to the son after the husband's death" defined the social status of Chinese women. "For a woman, lack of talent is a virtue" was the educational policy for Chinese women.

Christianity regarded women as equivalent to maidservants and livestock, and also viewed them as unclean and impure.

God created Adam, the man, and the woman Eve was made from one of Adam's ribs. Throughout the ages, Christians not only scorned women, but a Christian council in the 6th century AD even raised the question: "Are women even human?"

The Reformation was a revolt of the emerging bourgeoisie against the feudal system in the Church, state, and society. But although the bourgeoisie gained the freedom to marry, the subordination of women to the privileges of men remained largely unchanged.

Superficially, it might seem that Western women receive more respect than men. "Ladies" are always placed before "gentlemen". On streetcars, women have the privilege of men offering them their seats. But we must ask about the reality. Taking education as an example, how many Western women actually receive a university education? (In the United States in 1924, the number of female students in universities and specialized schools was only about one-third of the total student population). What percentage of students in coeducational universities are women? Isn't it obvious that women cannot receive higher education on an equal footing with men?

The Japanese example is even clearer. Japan has seven national universities (Tokyo Imperial University, Kyoto Imperial University, Kyushu Imperial University, Tohoku Imperial University, Hokkaido Imperial University, Keijō Imperial University[28], Taihoku Imperial University[29]). By statute, none are stipulated to admit female students, nor have any national women's universities been established separately. Secondary schools that admit girls are called "Kōtō Jogakkō" (Higher Girls' Schools). While the name sounds more impressive, in substance, it reflects a disdain for women, using fancy words to pander to female vanity.

The situation in China is even more deplorable. According to the Statistical Overview of Education in China, from May 1922 to April 1923, excluding schools run by the Catholic Church, there were a total of 6,819,468 students in the country. How many of these were female students? Only 415,398 (excluding mission school students)! The total number of female university students was less than 500!

The first National Education Conference of the National Government passed a resolution to establish separate secondary schools for boys and girls. At the time, Zhejiang representative Liu Dabai declared that this would crush the educational opportunities for female students in Zhejiang and they could not comply (see Report of the National Education Conference, Part B, p. 64). Indeed, educational opportunities for Chinese women

---

28 [Translator's Note] Japan illegally occupied the Korean Peninsula from 1910 to 1945 and established this institution during that period; it has since been renamed Seoul National University.

29 [Special Editor's Note] Taipei was illegally occupied by Japan in 1895 and recovered after the victory of the War of Resistance against Japan in 1945. And then the uinersity has been renamed National Taiwan University.

are already pitifully small. If further eroded, won't they be completely blocked off?

But why can't women have educational opportunities equal to men's? "Valuing men over women" can certainly be cited as the direct cause. However, the emergence of this "social morality" of valuing men over women is not accidental. All social subordination and oppression arise from the economic dependence of the oppressed on the oppressor. The establishment of the patriarchal system represented the seizure of power by the propertied class over the propertyless class, and the overthrow of the matriarchal system was, in fact, the first social revolution in human history. Thereafter—to the extent that private property existed—all world history has been a history of various forms of class domination of the same type. Therefore, as long as women are not economically independent, they cannot escape the domination of men. Not only women, but the general labouring masses also cannot escape their subordinate status until the economic power held by a minority is overturned. This is where the women's issue and the labour issue connect. To solve the problem of women's education, it is imperative to first solve the problem of women's economic status. To be frank, women's suffrage and women's education are secondary issues.

I have now spoken at length about the essence of education and its transformation. Let me conclude with a few summary points.

The essence of education is the biological purpose of "preserving the species" (including the preservation of the individual), that is, a means to help humans manage social life. This education is societal and unified. However, since the emergence of the private property system, society has been divided into classes: the rulers and the ruled. The ruling class, in all matters, takes the maintenance and consolidation of its own interests as the starting point. The legal systems it creates, the morality it establishes, the philosophies it advocates, etc., are all aimed at upholding its ruling power. Even the education it provides is primarily for the convenience of the rulers. Therefore, this education is clearly class-based.

In class society, this class-based education manifests the five types of transformation described above: first, the separation of education and labour; second, educational rights following ownership; third, the benefits serving solely the interests of the ruling class; forth, the existence (and antagonism) of dual educational rights; and fifth, the inequality in education between men and women.

These phenomena could not exist in the primitive communist society, the classless society. Therefore, they all represent a transformation of education. This transformed education further differs according to changes in the economic base of class society. The detailed circumstances will be described in Chapter 2, "The Evolution of Education".

Although education is clearly thus transformed, clearly thus class-based, many education scholars still stubbornly claim that education is fair and independent. This can only be described as their "self-deception and deception of others".

Regarding the many misinterpretations and superstitions about education, we must correct and explain them. Now, let the reader please turn to the next section, "Several Distortions of Education".

Questions

What exactly is the essence of education?

How has the meaning of education changed?

Having read this section, you should now understand how the practicality of education has been transformed. Please explain this in your own words.

What is meant by "class-based practicality"? Can you give an example?

Based on what you know, where is the class character of education manifested? Please explain in detail.

Modern education speaks of life and adaptation; ultimately, to what kind of life is it supposed to adapt, and how does it adapt?

How did the separation of education and labour originate?

Do you feel it is glorious and fortunate to receive financial support from the rich? Do you have any desire to receive support from the rich? If so, why? If not, why?

In the area where you live, do you know how many children, youth, and adults are deprived of educational rights? Why are they deprived?

For whom do you think the education you are currently receiving is ultimately intended? Why?

If you are a primary or secondary school teacher, do you truly believe you are working for the children of the general impoverished labouring masses? How are you working for them?

If you are a female student or teacher, what are your thoughts on education for men and women?

Does China currently also have dual educational rights? If so, what form do these dual educational rights take?

Critique the division of labour theory of scholars in the service of the ruling class.

What method do you think could restore education's original function, that is, restore education for the life needs of all humanity?

SECTION 3: SEVERAL DISTORTIONS OF EDUCATION

The theory of the sanctity of education – The theory of the purity and loftiness of education – The theory of the neutrality of education – The theory of the independence of education – Questions

Education certainly plays an important role in the process of human life. But to attribute to it irrelevant fine words and add imposing false masks is not only far-fetched but also deceptive and fraudulent.

Of such misinterpretations, let us consider the most prevalent and superstitiously believed ones. There are four main types: the first is the theory of the sanctity of education, the second is the theory of the purity and loftiness of education, the third is the theory of the neutrality of education, and the fourth is the theory of the independence of education.

These four types all obscure the true face of education and have a deceptive and narcotizing effect. Therefore, we must expose them and explain their origins.

First, refuting the theory of the sanctity of education.

How do they regard education as sacred? They say education is the enterprise of enlightening the world and guiding the people, education is the enterprise of spiritual cultivation, education is the enterprise of austerity and integrity, education is the enterprise of nobility and transcendence, and there may be other reasons for elevating education to a sacred status.

But we know: "Enlightening the world and guiding the people" is not the nobility of education, nor is "spiritual cultivation" its capability. Political directives, literary and artistic policies, etc., all relate to "enlightening the world and guiding the people". Economic systems, social order, etc., all contribute to "spiritual cultivation". We have not heard of politics being sacred, literature and art being sacred, or the economy being sacred, society being sacred. So on what basis, for what reason, is education alone said to be sacred? Without solid basis or valid reason, to insist that education is sacred—is this not arbitrary and superstitious?

Furthermore, the claim that education is the enterprise of enlightening the world and guiding the people, while having "existed since ancient times" and seeming particularly earnest amidst current slogans of "universal education" and "mass education," proves upon practical examination to be "utterly erroneous." Let me explain:

Since Emperor Wu of Han revered Confucianism, Confucius – who has been revered by "everyone from the Son of Heaven to the common people" throughout history and even enjoys commemorative days today – did indeed utter the famous saying "in teaching, there should be no distinction of classes." But did he not also say, "The common people can be made to follow a path of action, but they cannot be made to understand it"? What kind of "enlightening the world" and "guiding the people" is this? Mencius, who carried on Confucius's orthodox tradition, wanted "to secure the most talented students in the world and educate them." I ask, where could the common people, who are not "talented students," find opportunities for education? This question of mine is by no means intended to slander these "ancient sages." On the contrary, I can explain the "theoretical background" for them.

Originally, in the feudal era, the ruling class did not provide education for the common people, and the so-called education of that time was also limited to moral education. The reasons were as follows:

First, the economic foundation of the feudal system was a closed, natural agricultural economy, an agricultural economy with very rudimentary production techniques. In such an agricultural economy, one only needed to follow elders into the fields; all production necessities like planting, fertilizing, weeding, and harvesting could be learned entirely through experience. The economy of the time was also self-sufficient and organized in small local units. Therefore, in the feudal era where agriculture was the main social industry, the common people actually had no need to study scholarly knowledge. Even if "completely illiterate," they could still fully engage in productive activities.

Second, the feudal system emphasized rituals and etiquette. "Three hundred rules of ceremony, three thousand rules of demeanor." So-called impropriety was considered "insubordination and rebellion." Furthermore, free competition was absolutely forbidden within the feudal system. "To yield while contending" was a quality of a gentleman. Thus, education in the feudal era almost entirely consisted of "moral" education. Its main purpose was to make everyone "know their place and abide by their duties." From this, it is clear that education in the feudal era only "kept the people ignorant," it did not "guide them"; it only "confined the world," it did not "enlighten it."

Then, what about the capitalist era? In this era, things naturally changed dramatically: Education was to be provided to the entire nation, and it was compulsory. The content of education also expanded in scope, aiming to transmit the knowledge and skills of daily life. Beyond this, there were actions like "international peace education" and "World Education Conferences" encompassing the entire world and "all humanity." It truly seemed as if "enlightening the world and guiding the people" had become a reality. But don't be too hasty; allow me to explain the reasons why capitalist society alone possesses an education so vastly different from feudal society.

The reason is also extremely simple: it is because the economic base of the capitalist era is large-scale factory production and international trade. In this era, small-scale local self-sufficiency was no longer possible; its ideal lay in massive commodity production and gaining international markets. Let's look at the relationship with education from these two aspects. In factory production, the capabilities of an unlearned and unskilled person versus someone who can read and write are vastly different. Simply remembering the name of a machine, for an illiterate person, is an indescribably difficult and arduous task. Therefore, in today's world, the ability to read and write is a requirement of the work itself. Furthermore, in the era of self-sufficiency, transporting goods required only hands, carts, etc. But in the capitalist era, besides needing cars, trains, and ships for transport, the written word is also essential. If you want to be a chauffeur or a waiter, don't even think about it if you're illiterate. This shows that the capitalist socio-economy itself demands literacy. The reason capitalist states implement compulsory education is definitely not for the well-being of the citizens themselves, but to prepare the national labour force to function within its economic structure, with the compulsory education term representing its minimum requirement. Some humanitarians, without investigating the details, even claim that "universal education" is a gospel for humanity; even if this is not deliberate propaganda, it is ultimately foolish and ridiculous. If "universal education" were truly a humanitarian measure as they claim, then why can't the children of the poor advance in their studies like the children of the rich? Why are there dual-track school systems that limit educational opportunities? And why does the state exercise multifaceted supervision and approval over educational endeavors? In a word, compulsory national education itself ultimately serves only the masters of the capitalist system (the capitalist class).

In this society, all pleasant-sounding and impressive new facilities and plans are likewise for the benefit of the capitalist class. Take workers' education, for example: "The establishment of educational (or training) institutions by factory and mine operators initially was mostly a policy action to win over the hearts of workers... Mr. Fukagawa Masao, the head of miners at the Miike Mining Station, was one very enthusiastic about miner education, diligently guiding them through various educational facilities. Three or four years ago, a dispute arose at the Miike Coal Mine, but at that time, among more than ten groups of miners, only one group did not participate in the dispute – the group guided by Mr. Fukagawa. This was undoubtedly because his usual guidance methods were effective, so they did not act rashly. Because he was seen as having this ability, he was appointed as the guide for all the miners." This was written by Mr. Obi Noriji, head of the Social Education Section of the Japanese Ministry of Education (published in the Education Weekly on February 23, 1929; I did not fabricate it). This frankly tells us why capitalists promote workers' education. Some have theorized that schooling under the capitalist system has the following three major tasks: First, to instill reliance upon and respect for the capitalist system in the laborers of the future; Second, to cultivate 'educated' individuals from among the youth of the ruling class to manage the labouring masses; Third, through the technical application of science, to aid capitalist production and increase capitalists' profits (see Section 7, "Education in Capitalist Society"). Judging from the reasons I have explained and the examples I have cited, we absolutely cannot say this "theory of the three tasks of schooling" is "baseless nonsense." So then, even in capitalist society, where is there so-called education for "enlightening the world and guiding the people"?

As for "spiritual cultivation," that is also not factual. As explained in the previous paragraph, education is merely a means to create tools for the use of the ruling class; there is absolutely no "spiritual cultivation" to speak of. Oh, it does exist — such as "rectifying the heart and making the thoughts sincere," "loyalty, filial piety, chastity, and righteousness," and even "cherishing the fatherland," "obeying the laws," etc. — there are plenty. But isn't it obvious that these aim at narcotization and deception, serving a class function? Even conceding that "spiritual cultivation" is opposed to the "material" and the "physical," carrying a philosophical, spiritual meaning, this still remains highly unscientific. Look at education today — what aspect of it is separable from material things? Without school buildings, desks and chairs, books, laboratories, sports grounds... would there be education? In the "Republic of Dollars," where higher education is most developed, isn't the value of education determined by the amount of money? We naturally do not admire the "omnipotence of gold," but we believe education deals with human life; it is not about engaging in mystification. It concerns practical problems; it is not about preaching "morality and righteousness" emptily. The human world is just the human world, not the "Kingdom of Heaven." To say education is "sacred" because of "spiritual cultivation" — is that not self-deception and deception of others? Yes, spiritual cultivation could also refer to the liberation of thought and the transformation of consciousness. If that were truly the case, we would certainly express approval. But in past history, we have only seen the shackling of thought, or the indoctrination of fixed ideas; the obscuring of the consciousness of the oppressed classes, or the forced instillation of the oppressors' consciousness. How so? According to the history of thought, intellectual production changes along with material production; the ideas dominating any given era are invariably the ideas of the ruling class of that era. To genuinely hope for cultural prosperity and the free human spirit, the following prerequisites are necessary: the abolition of all cultural monopolies, making culture the property of all people, replacing class consciousness with a scientific materialist worldview; furthermore, it is necessary to foster the development of world social productive forces, shortening the time required for material production to allow leisure for thought and creation. Humanity must not only achieve legal freedom but must also achieve complete material freedom before it can attain complete spiritual freedom, liberating itself from religious thought and idol worship. Yet, how could this be realized in the past feudal society or even the present capitalist society?

Regarding the opinions that education is an enterprise of integrity and nobility, I will provide further critique later. But here, I can state my conclusion in advance: The enterprise of education is by no means one of integrity, nor is it noble. To call it "sacred" is mere superstition. On the contrary, we have witnessed with our own eyes how within the "sacred" educational circles, there have emerged model instructors who turned robbers, "thought guides" who embezzled lecture fees (both incidents occurred in Japan in 1929), and various individuals who monopolized positions and ran "Confucius shops" for profit. Have these not already torn off the false mask of "sacredness"?

However, regarding education as sacred is not entirely without basis or reason from another perspective. It is originally a product of fantasy, but all fantasies, all fabrications, also have their own definite basis in experience.

What is this definite basis in experience?

Originally, the concept of "sacred" is most easily associated with religion, as if religion were the very base of "sacredness." I will start with religion, as this explanation can be applied by analogy.

The meaning of "sacred" encompasses solemnity, mystery, even inviolability. The reason religion is considered sacred lies in this secrecy. Let us attempt to unveil this mystery.

To clarify the essence of religion, I can give an example. This example contrasts religion with science. Let's consider the natural phenomenon of rain. Rain is a very important phenomenon for human material life. For agricultural peoples, the fate of their inhabitants is greatly influenced by the frequency of rainfall, its amount, and its geographical distribution. Yet, rain is a phenomenon beyond human power; one cannot make it rain or stop it at will. Now, how does religion deal with this? How did primitive villagers deal with it? They imagined it this way: the phenomenon of rain is produced by an imaginary, personified rain god. Humans can influence the god's will through rituals like sacrifices, prayers, or threats, thereby achieving their desires. But science's attitude towards rain is completely different. Science has a specific discipline called meteorology; it observes the phenomenon of rain, discovering its causes and effects. Thus, the natures of religion and science are vastly different: religion is based on faith, science on knowledge; religion adorns its experiential basis with fantasy, while science organizes its experiential basis through experiment and reasoning.

The main origins of religion are twofold: one stems from humanity's relationship with nature, the other from various social relationships. Early humans, because they were so greatly dominated by nature, tended to view all natural phenomena through the lens of religious fantasy. This is the first origin of religious views. Secondly, in primitive times, the entire society exerted an immense influence on the individual. Morality, law, customs, practices, general social norms, etc., all had a compelling, commanding effect on the individual. Primitive society itself was also a kind of natural entity, so the impact of social norms and customs on the individual was as powerful as natural forces. Individuals could not fully perceive or understand the meaning and purpose of all these things, and thus believed that spirits or demons issued these commands and established these rules to compel people to obey. Therefore, from this nature of social relationships, religious views naturally arose to provide reasons and sanction. For example, ancestor worship arose from the clan system[30]. In other words, social order relied on religion for its security. Furthermore, another root strengthening religious views emerged when class antagonisms developed within society. At that time, religious concepts became a means for the ruling class to keep the oppressed class in a subordinate position. Moreover, as a result of class antagonism and social division of labor, a special class dedicated to religious affairs, the priesthood, emerged. Religious concepts, for the priests, also became a means to build and maintain their own socially superior position (i.e., divorced from direct productive labor and living off the surplus product of others' labor).

From this perspective, religion possesses a "sacred" significance because people, failing to understand their relationships with nature and society (both impacting their own lives), sought to express awe and expectation through religion. Furthermore, because the ruling class and the priestly class each utilized religion for their own benefit, religion came to seem truly powerful.

The reasons for viewing education as sacred are similar. Just as

---

30 [Special Editor's Note] Clan system refers to the family system constituted by blood ties from a common ancestor, also known as a kinship society.

people regarded religious ceremonies as capable of influencing deities, seeing them as marvelously effective, people viewed education's ability to enlighten intelligence and "open the people's minds" as containing an incomprehensible power. Additionally, the ruling class's use of education to keep the people ignorant, and the "scholars'" emphasis on education to enhance their own status, also parallel the situation with religion. Furthermore, the earliest teachers were originally priests, and early education was closely linked to religion in many aspects (e.g., teaching materials and applications). Therefore, the perception of education as "sacred" indeed has its unsubstantiated basis and improper reasons – from a scientific viewpoint.

Everyone knows that religious views are products of faith and fantasy, but they do not realize that the view of education as sacred is also a product of faith and fantasy. Some recognize the irrationality of religious superstition and seek to break it, yet the superstition of education's sacredness seems not to have been exposed by anyone; on the contrary, it is still earnestly and happily propagated. Is this not a grave error?

The ruling class is not "omniscient and omnipotent"; without the scheming and calculations of scholars in their service, it is not easy for them to maintain their ruling power. Therefore, since ancient times, the ruling class had to use official positions, wealth, and fame to entice talented individuals, making them serve and achieve merits for themselves, thereby preventing subjects from "insubordination and rebellion." Simultaneously, out of gratitude and a desire to repay, these scholars in service fabricated various sayings, such as "Heaven sets up the ruler and the teacher"; "The Son of Heaven values heroes, literature teaches you all; All other pursuits are low, only studying is high." On one hand, they created theoretical justifications for the ruler's power; on the other hand, they also built the factual basis for their own position as the "head of the four classes." Therefore, the perception of education as "sacred" actually contains this clever function of class domination.

Now we can say: Those who regard education as sacred, who eulogize its sacredness, not only demonstrate their own ignorance and superstition but also prove that their "scholarly conscience" has been utilized and narcotized by class domination.

Without breaking the superstition of "education as sacred," education will forever remain, like religion, a tool for the ruling class to "keep the people ignorant," never becoming the education needed for human life.

Just as eliminating religious concepts and their roots was not achieved by the 18th-century French philosophers using rationalism (i.e., adopting an intellectual stance to struggle against religion and the church; this stance was ahistorical because they only saw religion as irrational, a delusion that could be swept away by enlightenment), nor was it accomplished a few years ago merely by propaganda (e.g., anti-Christianity) or recently by brute force alone (e.g., smashing temple idols) – such enlightenment work certainly has its function in the stage of preparing for revolution, but to truly eradicate religion, it is necessary to completely overthrow the social roots and foundation that produce religious concepts, i.e., fundamentally change the existing social organization. Similarly, to eliminate the concept of education as sacred, it can only be achieved when the social basis that produces this concept is overthrown.

Second, refuting the theory of the purity and loftiness of education.

The meaning of purity and loftiness implies, on one hand, austerity and hardship, and on the other hand, nobility and elevated status.

Why do they say the educational enterprise is one of austerity? They say, first, because it is not like business, constantly seeking profit, or like being an official who "scrapes the land" and takes bribes; it is very honest and clean. Second, because it requires "sitting on a cold bench," and being a "teaching craftsman" is very hard work.

As for its nobility, of course, it's because it is the great enterprise of "it takes a hundred years to nurture people," the vital task of "cultivating talent for the nation," and the sole "superior class," venerating the Supreme Sage and Teacher Confucius as its model, whom even the "dignity of the Son of Heaven" dare not look down upon. Another point is its transcendent stance, uninvolved in politics, not for money, truly "aloof and peerless in the world," truly "of renowned nobility, a model for all."

These are the reasons why the general public believes the educational enterprise is pure and lofty. Now let us examine these reasons.

The "hardship" of the educational enterprise is indeed a fact, but its "purity" is not necessarily so. Many teachers, barely managing to hold on, just manage to keep a rice bowl to support their families. We can hardly bring ourselves to praise this kind of passive honesty. And as for educational administrators, principals, or senior school teachers, their monopolizing positions, excluding those of different views, and taking on multiple jobs and teaching assignments – how is this any different from the generally acknowledged filthy, corrupt political world or the despicable, cunning business world? Frankly, its "purity" is not necessarily superior to that of a "street sweeper," and its "hardship" falls far short of that of a "coolie." It's only because society restricts a certain group of people in such a way that, for a time, they have no other shortcut to make a living or rise in status; thus, they use the school as a lodging place, wielding the teacher's pointer to get by, seemingly forced into contentment, even willing to dedicate their lives to it. In reality, if an opportunity for "making a fortune properly" arises, they can go to the stock exchange, the army, or, even more readily, a government office – how then can they maintain so-called honesty? Thus, when they can succeed, they turn away without a second thought, and when unsuccessful, they can use it as a refuge. On one hand, they live a life of unavoidable austerity; on the other, they unexpectedly gain the fine reputation of being "honest." The life of a primary school teacher, acknowledged by most as the most austere, is precisely this kind of affair.

As for its being noble, in my opinion, it is nothing more than a case of "beauty is in the eye of the beholder." As stated in the previous paragraph, the reason education has seemingly become noble is none other than the manipulation by the ruling class and the self-aggrandizement of scholars in their service. We fail to see any difference in rank or value between education and other enterprises (such as military, transportation, public health, etc.). In terms of the hierarchy of government ministries, education ranks below foreign affairs, internal affairs, and military administration. I ask, what privilege does the educational enterprise possess that it dares to arrogate to itself the title of "noble"?

If education, because it deals with nurturing people and is thus of great importance, should be particularly valued and therefore naturally become "noble," unfortunately, this view treats education as omnipotent or expects miracles from it; it is ultimately an excessive, superstitious extravagant hope. The responsibility of "nurturing people" cannot be borne by education alone; at the very least, the public health department shares part of it, and the regulation of production and distribution is even more fundamental. Look at current society: although the minds of the poor may be ten thousand times smarter than those of the rich, as stated in the previous section of this book, because their wallets are too small or they are simply penniless, they ultimately cannot enter the "school restricted area." This sufficiently shows that the nurturing power of education is very limited. Here, we can say that only property is truly "omnipotent" compared to education. Moreover, only private property possesses the sacred and inviolable nature. Education only gets its turn before property; it itself can never stand independently or hold its head high. How can it be worthy of being called "noble"? Therefore, in the modern era where finance capital reigns supreme, education is truly a lowly enterprise. Except for those with full stomachs and nothing to do who use it to embellish their facade, or those without food who use it like gnawing bones to barely survive, who is happy to pay it any attention? When military funds are insufficient, they can print bonds or levy special taxes anytime, anywhere to make up the shortfall. Sometimes they even unabashedly misappropriate educational funds. When educational funds are insufficient or even misappropriated, no matter how much teachers shout their grievances or "petition" tearfully, which dignitary will pity you? At such times, is it still acceptable to emptily chant about education being sacred and noble?

Previously, because successive emperors respected Confucius, venerating him as the Supreme Sage and Teacher; before children read the Great Learning and the Analects, they first had to pay respects to Confucius; the spring and autumn sacrifices were major state ceremonies. This was at least a key reason why education could claim to be noble and sacred. But recently, the fervor for worshipping the Sage and honoring Confucius seems far less intense than before. Taking the example of 1928: except for Generals Lu Diping[31] and He Jian[32] in Hunan, who strongly advocated for restoring Confucian ceremonies and personally performed the ancient rites of three kneelings and nine prostrations on Confucius's birthday (according to reports from the Shanghai Times), the National Government merely ordered that "the proposal to designate Confucius's birthday as a memorial day is feasible; there is no need to stipulate rituals." Later, the Ministry of Education, after "deliberation," merely stated that "henceforth, on Confucius's birthday, all schools nationwide should suspend classes for two hours to lecture on Confucius's deeds as a memorial." Thus, the National Government's ceremonial honors for Confucius seemed almost abolished, and the act of "venerating the Sage" henceforth seemed to become a "thing of the past." Doesn't this mean the concepts of education's sacredness and nobility derived from venerating the Sage and worshipping Confucius have lost their basis? And might tearing off the "noble" mask of education not even be considered a loss of face?

"The Master seldom spoke of profit." Mencius advised King Hui of Liang, "Why must Your Majesty speak of profit?" That education should not concern itself with profit seems to have a long-standing tradition. But today, the situation has clearly

---

31 [Special Editor's Note] Lu Diping (1887–1935), courtesy name Yong'an. Native of Ningxiang, Hunan. Participated in the Northern Expedition early on, served as commander of the National Revolutionary Army's Second Army. In 1928, became Chairman of the Hunan Provincial Government, strongly advocated honoring Confucius and studying the classics.

32 [Special Editor's Note] He Jian (1887–1956), courtesy name Yunqiao. Native of Liling, Hunan. Graduated from the Baoding Military Academy early on, served successively as regiment commander, brigade commander, division commander, and corps commander. In 1929, served as Acting Chairman of Hunan Province and Commander-in-Chief of the 4th Route Army against rebels, advocated restoring antiquity and honoring Confucius.

changed dramatically. Not only is profit no longer taboo, but there is even loud advocacy for vocational education and vigorous efforts to open up productive avenues. Educators sell their eloquence for profit, and students also study knowledge and skills for profit. The value of education is now determined by how much income it can generate. So then, will the view of education as 'noble' because it supposedly did not concern itself with profit not also be stripped away, now that it is being so greatly exploited?

As for the nobility of not involving itself in politics and adopting a transcendent stance, these are merely words of concealment and deception. The reasons for this will be explained in the next section; for now, let us just look at the facts. Have you not seen the quite prominent and influential 'academic warlords' of the militarist era? They were considered leading figures in the national education circle, yet they were the most adept at flattering the militarists and colluding with the financial magnates! And have you not noticed the gentlemen of the nationalist[33] clique who advocate the theory of saving the nation through education? They operate under the cover of the militarist banner. If political activity is considered filthy, then from what aspect can we perceive the nobility of this kind of education?

The above has already examined the reasons for considering education as pure and lofty. Below, we will further study the possible impacts of this view and its historical origins.

The impacts of viewing the educational enterprise as pure and

---

33 [Special Editor's Note] The Nationalist Faction was one of the political factions in modern China. It was primarily composed of members of the China Youth Party, with representatives such as Zeng Qi, Li Huang, and Zuo Shunsheng. They advocated nationalism and opposed communism. They published the journal "The Awakened Lion Weekly" and were also known as the "Awakened Lion Faction."

lofty can be summarized as at least the following items.

First, it isolates itself from politics. In their view, the political sphere is a path for seeking fame and rank, a place where filth and corruption are gathered; those in the pure and lofty educational world should not approach politics. Consequently, whether politics is clean or not does not become an issue in education. The more corrupt politics becomes, the more education distances itself from it. Even Confucius said, "The scholar who has completed his learning should enter public service," which does not prevent educators from participating in politics. Yet, on the other hand, he also said, "He who is not in any particular office has nothing to do with plans for the administration of its duties," and "The superior man does not think beyond his position," and even more, "The common people may be made to follow a path of action, but they may not be made to understand it." Consequently, educators not only themselves wish to have nothing to do with political affairs but also teach students not to concern themselves with political matters. The so-called "being wise and safeguarding one's person" is essentially an attitude towards politics of "respecting ghosts and spirits while keeping aloof from them." Initially, the ruling class did not want the people to concern themselves with political affairs. With the emergence of this kind of "educational philosophy," it seemingly provided a theoretical basis for education to keep its distance from politics. Later, due to the actual corruption in the political world, educators who prized their own worth increasingly sought to isolate themselves from politics. Since education did not concern itself with politics, those engaged in politics could act more recklessly and without restraint, "harming the country and bringing calamity to the people."

Second, it isolates itself from labour. Since not engaging in production is considered noble, the educational enterprise naturally becomes an empty-talk, sit-and-eat undertaking. Although ancient times also emphasized "sweeping and sprinkling," that was merely a form of etiquette, not productive labour. Moreover, the 'scholars', who ranked at the head of the 'four classes', considered themselves naturally born to "rule others" and "be fed by others." If they had to use physical strength to obtain food, not only would it affect their dignity, but fundamentally, why would they need to study? Physical labour is lowly, using the mind is noble; producing profit is base, studying is superior. Consequently, "too weak to truss a chicken" and the "too delicate to stand the wind" consumptive-type woman were both praised, and society added a large batch of people who only consume but do not produce. The higher the class of idler, the more they belonged to the so-called 'scholars' of the upper class. This is the pernicious effect generated by the nobility of education.

Third, it provides politicians who have failed on the political stage with a temporary refuge. Because, on the surface, education does not involve politics, politicians can transform into 'academic guests' overnight. Under the name of managing education, they extensively build connections and cultivate their factions. To outsiders, they appear to be fervently dedicated to educational affairs, deserving of praise. Have we not frequently encountered such people?

However, the reason why education possesses these noble attributes is also historical. Since human society divided into classes, and the ruling class possessed the state apparatus of power, it most feared resistance from the masses and had to devise various methods to prevent it. It used either forcible coercion by military means, or the intimidation of law, or the constraints of ritual and morality, or the "softening" approach of education, to achieve the thorough implementation of the policy of keeping the people ignorant: "The common people may be made to follow a path of action, but they may not be made to understand it." On the one hand, the state used fame, profit, official salaries, and rank to capture the hearts of scholars, making them serve the rulers loyally; on the other hand, it taught them to "aspire to be sages and worthies" and to "rectify the heart and make the thoughts sincere," making every educated person a superman—a high-class idler—who "cannot distinguish millet from wheat" and "does not inquire into order or chaos." Therefore, the more one received this pure and lofty education, the more one would "preserve one's purity and self-respect," and the more carefree the ruling class could be.

Another reason for education possessing nobility, as mentioned earlier in this book, is that class-based education separated education from labour. In other words, since human society entered the period of civilization, there has never been education universal for everyone; education has always been exclusively possessed and enjoyed by a portion of people. Like a luxury item, education was something for the aristocracy and the propertied class to play with, adorn themselves with, and use for pastime. The common people and the propertyless were only fit to contribute their labour power as the price for survival; a luxury like education absolutely allowed no room for the poor and lowly to have a share. Thus, education came to wear a golden crown.

In reality, the "purity and loftiness" of today's educational enterprise has already been self-evidently broken: it must fight for funding, demand payment of arrears, promote vocational education—all the characteristics once considered marks of purity and loftiness have been swept away completely. Only one aspect of "hardship" remains, which at least a portion of the teachers cannot avoid; and because they lack the kind of united strength that laborers have, they can only admire the latter's bravery while lamenting their own backwardness, or perhaps regret having been poisoned too deeply by the concept of purity and loftiness!

Third, refuting the theory of the neutrality of education.

This superstition is as follows: Education stands on a fair and impartial footing, adopting a moderate and neutral attitude, without partiality or extremism. For instance, regarding doctrines and factions, it is considered part of education's inherent duty not to adhere to any particular one; regarding political issues, it is considered impermissible to hold any stance; similarly, research into various scholarly theories must also be free of "personal views"; and most characteristically, theory and practice are "divorced." For example, one reason for the forced resignation of Professor Kawakami Hajime[34] of Kyoto Imperial University (in 1928) was that during the general election, he went to campaign for candidate Mr. Oyama Ikuo. This implied that scholarship is neutral, and for a university professor to engage in practical movements damages the dignity of scholarship. Therefore, Kawakami Hajime had to resign. Many so-called scholars recently are followers of this "religion of neutrality." For instance, when a certain economist expressed his views on some factory legislation, he first declared that he neither supported the capital side nor favored the labor side, but was merely speaking impartially from the standpoint of economic principles. Another example: when the May Thirtieth Incident occurred in Shanghai, some students

---

34 [Special Editor's Note] Kawakami Hajime (1879-1946) was a Japanese Marxist political economist and member of the Japanese Communist Party. He served as a professor at Kyoto Imperial University, was forced to resign in 1928, and was imprisoned in 1933. His works include History of Modern Economic Thought and Studies in Historical Materialism.

had already been shot dead by the running dogs of British imperialism, others had gone on strike and were running about actively engaged in anti-imperialist work. What about the educators? They also held meetings, wanting to discuss remedial measures and to "take responsibility" towards the students' families. But their capability ended there. As for high-class Chinese scholars like Ding Wenjiang[35], they actually advocated a "fair investigation"—this can be considered the thorough implementation of the "religion of neutrality."

Furthermore, another basis for the claim that "education is neutral" is Confucius's saying, "In education, there should be no class distinctions." Indeed, in a single school, there may be children from wealthy families and children from poor families; there may be bright students and dull ones. Graduates from lower-level schools can advance to higher levels just the same. Providing equal educational opportunities to all people—what could be more impartial than this?

But what is the reality? First, let's examine the actual situation of the doctrine of equal educational opportunity. Those who have studied the introduction to education know that there is something called the "dual-track system" in educational structure, meaning that from the very first day of receiving an education, children from wealthy families and those from poor families must go their separate ways. No matter how excellent the academic achievements of Zhang San's son might be, because Zhang San is a carpenter, his son can only receive a national education. Yet Zhang San's son is still somewhat fortunate; consider Li Si's son,

---

35 [Special Editor's Note] Ding Wenjiang (1887-1936), a native of Taixing, Jiangsu Province, courtesy name Zaijun, was a modern natural scientist specializing in geology. At the time, he served as the Director of the Geological Survey of China and authored over twenty reports, including The Geology of the Lower Reaches of the Yangtze River below Wuhu.

who has had to earn his own food since learning to walk—pitifully, he cannot even afford a school bag. In contrast, the youngest son of the Zhao family, though not as stupid as a wooden ox, failed his exams twice in three years but has now managed to study abroad. Furthermore, primary school teachers, following textbook instructions, encourage students to be diligent and thrifty. Yet they can turn a blind eye to the local gentry next door who scrape the land clean, or even to the school trustee who smokes opium. Schools teach that humanity should be peaceful and loving, yet they can ignore the warlords carving out territories and the imperialist nations expanding their armaments. Class struggle is too brutal, so education must preach labor-capital harmony; student involvement in political and social movements is too radical, so education must encourage them to focus on academic research. Speaking of academic research, it seems any field of study is permissible—except Marxism. Assembly and speech are, of course, free, but they must first be approved and must not "defy central resolutions." Educators say: "We must adopt a scholarly attitude to conduct detailed research and arrive at impartial conclusions, but only within the limits of not violating the Three Principles of the People."

Behold the impartial face of such unbiased, non-extremist education.

To what degree, then, is this impartial education truly impartial? I can use the judicial independence touted by modern civilized nations as an example. All are equal before the law, so surely no injustice goes unredressed in court. Yet, on one side, there are lawyers who mutually guarantee human rights, able to cite the law in defense whether representing plaintiff or defendant. On the other side, there are extralegal torture and prison abuse, while those in power can enact any criminal law at any time and order judicial officials to enforce it. For instance, in 1928, Japan's

Tanaka Cabinet felt the Peace Preservation Law was insufficient to suppress the labor-farmer movement, so it could issue an emergency imperial decree amending the Peace Preservation Law, and the so-called independent judiciary had to comply immediately. See how such "class justice" is considered a progressive system in civilized nations! Perhaps you think our impartial education might not deceive people to this extent? Then consider this: the educational systems of various civilized nations that claim to implement impartial education are formulated by those who control state power; educational funding is determined by them; textbooks require approval; teachers require certification; curricula require authorization. As long as you understand the nature of the modern state and grasp the purpose of these procedures, you should not doubt the designation "class education." Yet shameless scholars still dare to proclaim that "education is impartial" and "education ought to be impartial." As long as "whoever feeds you is your master," isn't it utterly ridiculous! Moreover, some liberals believe that government interference with academic freedom undermines the dignity of university autonomy. This is like prisoners criticizing the use of handcuffs and shackles—no different from the ravings of a madman.

This superstition about education can lead to three flaws: First, refusing to take a stance. Because they champion "impartiality," they can only push everything aside and remain uninvolved, at most dealing in vague, insubstantial generalities. Second, having no sense of right and wrong. Because they take no stance, they naturally need not concern themselves with right and wrong, or even if they clearly know the difference, constrained by the banner of "impartiality," they simply keep silent. But sometimes they do take stances and distinguish right from wrong—however, the motivation comes not from themselves but from those in power. Thus, those who strenuously opposed "party-based education" during the warlord era, upon the arrival of the Kuomintang era, surprisingly began loudly advocating Three Principles of the People education, either taking office or publishing theories, acting like "loyal believers." Yet I believe even at such times, they likely still cling to the view that "education is impartial." Due to the influence of the above two outcomes, a third result emerges: impartiality in name, bias in reality. In other words, it is an impartial education that benefits the ruling class, an impartial education that forbids resistance against the ruling class. No matter what, it refuses to openly declare itself class-based, always seeking to conceal its class nature.

Without dispelling this superstition, education will remain unable to escape the "social relations of human exploitation" and will only serve as a tool for the minority ruling class. But to truly and thoroughly break this superstition, we must first abolish the "social relations of human exploitation." Otherwise, the golden signboard of "impartiality" will always hang on people's lips (see the discussion on commercialization in Section 7).

Fourth, refuting the theory of educational independence.

The notion of "educational independence" has several aspects. One argument is that education should stay aloof from political tides and not fall into the vortex of politics. This is a factual and essentially passive stance. Another argument, based on so-called educational principles, is that education should be child-centered, aiming for the full development of the individual, and should not restrict individuality with the doctrines of any single party or faction. Both of these argue that education should be independent, transcending political relations. Additionally, some argue for the independence of educational administration, others for the independence of educational funding, and still others for independence from religious influence.

The most important concept here is the independence of education from politics. Let us examine this point.

Throughout history, wherever the power of a ruling class has been established, one could say that no affair remains free from political control. Education has always been a tool for keeping the people ignorant; to consolidate their power, the ruling class absolutely cannot allow the people to understand the truth. It either restricts the people's opportunities for knowledge or entices them to believe in "theories" beneficial to the ruling class. Because Confucian teachings emphasized loyalty, filial piety, and deference—morals most advantageous to the emperor in feudal society—they were favored by emperors throughout the ages after Emperor Wu of Han "elevated it to exclusive honor," remaining "valued" even by warlords into the 1920s (for instance, the former Beiyang warlord and "dog-meat general" Zhang Zongchang performed the three kneelings and nine prostrations at Shandong University, and Chu Yupu ordered all schools to study the classics). In the West, Christianity, teaching submission and love, has been adopted by ruling classes whether in the medieval Roman Empire or in the modern imperialist era, who spare no force or expense to achieve missionary goals. Religious doctrines have even become the main content of education overall. This is politics actively controlling education. Other examples, like China's "burning of books and burying of scholars" and "literary inquisition," the medieval Roman Empire's closing of the University of Athens, the recent banning of the teaching of evolution in a certain U.S. state, and the Japanese government's dismissal of "left-leaning professors," represent politics negatively controlling education. Yuan Shikai's mandate for primary students to read the Analects and Mencius, and secondary students to read the Great Learning and Doctrine of the Mean, the aforementioned warlords Zhang and Chu ordering schools to study the classics, and Japanese primary students worshipping the emperor—all are instances of education's inability to transcend political influence.

As described above, education cannot escape political influence, whether in ancient times, foreign countries, or modern capitalist civilized nations. Even in socialist Soviet Russia, its education is also political, and moreover class-based—for them, naturally, it is the proletariat. The difference is that Soviet education openly declares itself political and class-based (though this class education differs from that described earlier in Section 2; see Section 16 for details). In other civilized countries, it is called independent, universal education—on the one hand, making every effort to ensure that universities concern themselves only with advanced scholarship while lower schools impart only common knowledge; on the other, making every effort to conceal the political role of education and to forbid educators from engaging in practical movements—even as "patriotic" or "loyalty-to-the-sovereign" training, military drill, and field exercises are all heavily emphasized.

In terms of the essence of education (referring to class society) and its administrative system, the reason it cannot be independent is simply that education is merely one tool among many for maintaining political power. Especially in the modern era dominated by finance capital, all cultural and educational undertakings—from school education, news and magazines, religion, science, art, radio, telephones, to films, sports, etc.—are monopolized by the bourgeois class (see Section 7 for details). The political power of modern civilized nations is bourgeois political power; the education of modern civilized nations is also bourgeois education.

This education finds its most concrete and stark expression in American education. I will dedicate a separate section later for detailed discussion (see Section 15); here, I will offer only a brief glimpse.

Upton Sinclair, in his work The Goose-step, published his observations and conclusions on American higher education institutions. According to him, in North American universities, 600,000 young people receive an education that systematically trains them to be the vanguard of big capital. All higher education, without exception, receives funds from trusts[36] or banks; corporate managers or other agents of big capital occupy positions on the boards of trustees of higher schools. Every large trust or major financial club has its "own" university. Generally, the substantial assets of higher education institutions are invested as stocks in those companies, seeking to form a solid "co-development" with the capitalist oligarchy.

The special funds of Rockefeller, Morgan, and others also hold significant importance for American national education and science. The Rockefeller Foundation, whose charter aims "to promote the well-being of mankind," has vast sums invested in stocks (in 1920, $185 million), earning millions in profits, and is exempt from taxes due to its "charitable" work. A portion of this money is used for scientific research institutes, medical undertakings (the Peking Union Medical College Hospital and Rockefeller Hospital in Beijing indirectly serve the imperialist aims of Standard Oil), missionary teams (opening paths for investment in distant colonies), etc. Another portion is used for secret "military purposes." A considerable amount is also invested in organizing the suppression and breaking of strikes.

---

36 [Special Editor's Note] It represents an advanced form of monopoly organization.

Furthermore, the Rockefeller Foundation's "General Education Board," worth hundreds of millions, is specifically designated for national education. According to its stated purpose, it is "to educate the masses to be satisfied with their condition... to educate them to follow the example of their parents." In many places, this fund exerts great influence even on lower-level schools, systematically teaching children to adhere to the Rockefeller religion and the general religion of capital. The scientific Carnegie Foundation is entirely of the same nature. Superficially, it funds thousands of meaningless, pedantic studies and the training of hypocritical clergy, but in essence, it solely pursues the interests of the steel company that supplies the funds.

The churches, completely like all educational and charitable organizations, also serve capital. The churches defend the interests of capitalists in certain spheres, and the capitalists pay the churches in return. One need only look at the Y.M.C.A. to understand. It establishes branches worldwide, receives funding from large capital, acts as the vanguard of American imperialist policy, and serves the function of economic espionage. The famous "ARA" (American Relief Administration) also performs similar functions.

In European countries, the school system is regulated by the state, and the relationships described above are somewhat whitewashed. Unfortunately, we cannot detail here the means of indirect influence on education through state organs (which are assistants of modern centralized capital). We can only cite, as an example, the direct material assistance scientific facilities received from trusts during Germany's period of precipitous decline.

Modern science increasingly requires research institutes, laboratories, and specialized facilities for research that demand enormous funding. Today, most discoveries are the products of collective, collaborative work. Technical accomplishments are made in factory research institutes or special facilities maintained by trusts.

Fundamentally, science proceeds in the direction of pursuing capitalists' interests, even if scholars themselves are unaware of it. But this fact holds great significance for humanity. One need not elaborate much; simply consider the vast amount of energy, money, and knowledge expended on countless military discoveries, and it should be startling enough.

The influence of centralized capital is fully exposed in the officially sanctioned "science" within the field of social sciences. In Germany, every lecturer and professor of economics must begin their career with a "refutation" of Marxist doctrine.

Among such facilities, the Kiel Institute for the World Economy, one of the largest and most influential in Europe, is sustained by big industry and tasked with conducting specialized research on export markets and capitalist expansion.

The above simply illustrates how modern education is subordinate to politics—the ruling methods of finance capitalists—through the influence of centralized capital on schools and science. This implies two things: first, this education relies on capitalists for support; second, this education exists solely to meet the needs of the capitalists who fund it (refer to the discussion in Section 2).

If we also consider the influence of capital on news, films, sports competitions, and wireless telephony, it becomes even clearer how today's human spiritual culture is being exploited. If those who believe in the "independence," "sanctity," "purity and loftiness," and "impartiality" of education were to hear this, they would likely be utterly ashamed and furious enough to die—if they are true believers.

The above materials all elaborate on education's inability to be independent and detached from politics. As for the independence of educational administration, at most it differs in form, while its spirit remains "subordinate." Arguing for independence from religion as an educational principle is certainly possible. However, one must understand that in a society ruled by class domination, which still uses religion for "ideological control," it is impossible to expel religious influence. Taking China as an example, as long as missionary schools continue to exist, who can believe that education is independent?

These four superstitions are interconnected. Viewing it as "sacred" leads to viewing it as "pure and lofty," "impartial," and "independent"; because it is "pure and lofty," it becomes "sacred"; because it is "impartial," it must be "independent," and only through "independence" can "impartiality" and "sanctity" be preserved. Judging by the current situation, what the general public superstitiously believes is "sacred" is somewhat "base"; what they believe is "pure and lofty" is somewhat "filthy"; what they believe is "impartial" is merely deceptive talk masking "bias"; and what they believe is "independent" is like servants putting on airs and boasting in front of the crowd, ashamed of their own disgrace.

We dare to reiterate: Since humanity's internal division into classes within society, education has only been a tool for class domination. It serves only the interests of the rulers, and only a minority privileged class can enjoy it. By the capitalist era, "universal education" also serves the needs of capitalists, creating efficient machines for them in peacetime and patriotic soldiers in wartime. Due to the concentration of capital, a monopoly of so-called "spiritual production" accompanied it, and schools are merely factories for "manufacturing ideas."

Therefore, regarding this entity called education, in contrast to "sacred," I shall call it "secular"; in contrast to "pure and lofty," I shall call it "commonplace"; in contrast to "impartial," I shall call it "class-based"; and in contrast to "independent," I shall call it "subordinate."

Questions

What is the basis for claiming that education is sacred?

How many kinds of detrimental effects have arisen under the theory of education's purity and loftiness?

Under class-based education, can impartial education truly be realized? Why or why not?

Based on your knowledge, approximately how many schools of thought are there in China advocating the independence of education? What are their reasons?

Besides the four types discussed in this section, can you identify other misinterpretations of education? Please explain in detail and provide critique.

SECTION 4: THE EFFICACY OF EDUCATION

The Possibility of Education – A Critique of Three Erroneous Views on Educational Efficacy – 1. The Theory of Educational Omnipotence – 2. The Theory of Saving the Nation Through Education – 3. The Theory of Education Before Revolution – Questions

Regarding the essence of education, I feel it would be somewhat incomplete if I did not also discuss the efficacy of education. Therefore, I will now specifically explain the efficacy of education.

The motivation for my need to specifically address the efficacy of education is that people both within and outside the educational field have often held an inappropriately excessive estimation of it, leading to many errors – both in education itself and in the process of revolution.

These erroneous views on educational efficacy can be broadly categorized into three types: The first is the theory of educational omnipotence; the second is the theory of saving (or building) the nation through education; and the third is the theory of education before revolution – the latter two can also be seen as derivatives of the first.

Before critiquing these erroneous views on educational efficacy, I should have the reader first recall what has been discussed above.

Initially, we explained that education is one of the superstructures, one of the fields of ideological labour that endows people with a specific kind of labour power. In other words, it is a means to help humans manage social life. At the same time, we know that education does not grow out of nothing or exist independently; it is conditioned by economic relations (and simultaneously by the political system, which will be discussed in more detail in Sections 9 and 10 below) and is a by-product of a certain economic and social order, a reflection of a certain economic and social formation. It is true, we might add, that education also has a function of taking the lead or promoting. For example, before the 1911 Revolution, schools in many places were already propagating revolutionary ideas, and the heroic actions of the Seventy-two Martyrs of Huanghuagang can largely be considered a product of such propaganda. From this, we can see that education indeed has an effect; it is definitely not merely a 'tail'. However, here we must ask: Why did such revolutionary ideas emerge before the 1911 Revolution? Were they born from the 'innate conscience' of educators? Or from the 'foresight' of revolutionaries? Neither. They were born from an objective stimulus. To be more specific, they were born from the imperialist powers gradually intensifying their aggression against China, and the Qing government's inability to resist, which caused the living conditions of the masses to become increasingly difficult, forcing everyone to seek a way out; only then did such revolutionary ideas emerge. Therefore, in terms of the various facilities in education as well as the content of teaching, all correspond to the economic and political conditions of the time. Whether reactionary or revolutionary. Education absolutely cannot, and never could, transcend the era and environment to possess particularly novel and pleasing content and methods, as if it descended from heaven.

In essence, humans absolutely cannot create anything beyond the realm of objective possibility; humans can only advance and guide within the limits of what is objectively possible.

The possibility of education naturally also has this limit.

To say that education has extraordinary capabilities, that it possesses an existence independent and transcendent above all else, is either delusional or surely megalomaniacal.

Now let us proceed to critique the aforementioned three views on educational efficacy.

The first is the so-called theory of educational omnipotence.

Allow me first to recount my own past experience, for which I now feel somewhat ashamed.

About fifteen or sixteen years ago, just after I graduated from primary school, due to my family's poverty, it seemed obvious that I would be disappointed in my hopes of advancing to further studies, so I had no choice but to take the path of making a living. It is embarrassing to say, but I became a primary school teacher immediately after graduating from primary school myself. However, over half a year, the school principal paid me only a little over ten dollars in total salary. But my ambition to continue my studies still stubbornly remained. At that time, I had several fantasies: to enter an industrial school, to take the exam for telegraphy students, to enter the preparatory class for studying in America (the predecessor of Tsinghua University), and I even discussed it with my father. But my father scolded me severely, saying, "Are you still dreaming?!" My father was an artisan, and due to poverty, naturally believed that a poor child was fated (in reality, it was the inability to pay) not to receive much education.

Dreaming after all! My dream actually came true – I was admitted to a teachers college. I chose teacher training, partly because it waived tuition and even board fees (this is no longer the case now); but on the other hand, it was also because I was a believer in the "religion of educational omnipotence."

Perhaps this is a method of self-consolation. Because I wanted to enter teachers college, because I was admitted, I placed the highest hopes upon it. Regardless, at that time, I truly believed education was omnipotent, thinking that education could provide people with knowledge and skills. Even more fantastically, it could make the mute speak and the blind read. Furthermore, the enterprise of education was so noble, so pure. In the educational circles of that time, teacher trainees indeed appeared more disciplined and frugal than regular secondary school students.

After five years of teacher training, I became even more convinced that education was truly the foundation of all national endeavors. During my studies, I recall when Yuan Shikai was about to become emperor and specially issued an educational directive; we students all read it and considered it the "gospel of education." After graduation, although I never "took up the teaching pointer," I still held education in high regard, believing that if education was not properly managed, certainly nothing else could be managed well.

However, in the last five or six years, I have come to congratulate myself for finally awakening from this dream. I discovered that my past was indeed "mere dreaming," indeed superstition.

This is not only because "common people like me have no food to eat," causing the "religion of educational omnipotence" to collapse on its own; but truly because both facts and theory have proven the "religion of educational omnipotence" to be unreliable.

The theoretical explanation can be understood from the beginning of this section.

Now, I will provide proof solely based on facts.

Those who believe in the theory of educational omnipotence, aside from childish and ridiculous nonsense like "Zhao Pu[37] governed the empire with half the Analects" — which no one with the slightest common sense would believe — surprisingly, many still believe that the so-called modern education, the new education, is nearly omnipotent. Their reasoning is: new education is scientific education, is education for the masses. This kind of education cannot be compared to the aristocratic education that kept people ignorant in the past. The sky has airplanes, the seabed has submarines, heat relief has electric fans, warmth has electric heaters. These many tools of civilization have made the world more progressive than before, and this can be said to be the product of education. So, although education is not omnipotent, it is close to it.

But is this really true?

Using so-called "scientific education" to test children's intelligence, examine their schoolwork, and conduct other surveys and statistics, etc., seems like very fair and accurate tools are being applied in education.

Using so-called "education for all the people" to establish public schools, promote continuing education, and publish books and newspapers for the common people to read, also seems as if education is breaking down barriers and being immensely inclusive.

---

37 [Special Editor's Note] Zhao Pu (922–992) was one of the founding statesmen of the Song Dynasty, holding official positions including Privy Councilor and Grand Preceptor, and was enfeoffed as the Duke of Wei. According to legend, he once said to Emperor Taizong of Song, Zhao Guangyi: "I possess one copy of the Analects. With half, I assisted Emperor Taizu in pacifying the empire; with the other half, I assist Your Majesty in achieving peace and prosperity."

But examining the reality, does every child enjoy the bounty of "scientific education"? Does every commoner receive the lessons of "education for the common people"?

In education, just as in politics, economics, law, and society, there exists much inequality, much falsehood.

There are truly many scientific tools, aren't there? In transportation, construction, nutrition, entertainment, the modern era is certainly more advanced, novel, and interesting than pre-modern times. But how many people actually get to enjoy their benefits? Let's take a simple example: those who have electric fans to avoid summer heat and warm stoves to ward off winter cold – what fraction of the total population in this modern age are they? Similarly, no matter how many tools are invented in education, their maximum utility is limited to those who can attend school. So, how many people are actually excluded from the gates of education? These people will never get to see the face of "scientific education"!

Now consider "education for all the people." Speaking of "all the people," "all the people" is originally a wonderfully excellent term. But where in the world is this "all the people"? Is the United States, a democracy "of the people, by the people, for the people", has it perhaps reached the state of "all the people"? We know there is no so-called politics of "all the people" in the world yet, because the state apparatus that holds political power is not in the hands of "all the people," but in the hands of a "section of the people." Let's leave that aside for now. Looking solely at the modern so-called "education for the common people," firstly, it is not universal in quantity, and secondly, it has even more deficiencies in content. For instance, take the educational admonitions of modern wealthy and powerful nations, such as "serve the public and abide by the law," "diligence and thrift can lead to wealth and establish a family," etc., words aimed at cultivating law-abiding citizens. Actually, from the standpoint of opposing capitalism, these are slogans used by the ruling class of capitalist countries to deceive and soften the common people, to make the common people tractable. Because the general common people do not hold political power; those who hold political power are all from a special class; in other words, their state does not belong to the common people, but only to a special class. Therefore, such educational preaching merely constitutes education for the special class; it has no relation to the interests of the common people themselves. So, where does "education for all the people" come from then? – Gongpu's "The Characteristics – or Maladies – of Modern New Education".

This quoted passage can prove that many propositions in education, no matter how pleasing they sound, are extremely limited in their efficacy, speaking from education itself. A "cure-all" type of education exists only on the lips of educationists, never in reality.

Let me cite another practical example to prove that good methods in education do not necessarily produce efficacy.

Education for the blind and mute is education that the blind and mute should receive; everyone knows it should be actively promoted. But according to an article in Shen Bao in October of the 18th year [1929], by Zhu Weitao and Zhang Weixin, submitted to the Ministry of Education regarding the need to include blind and mute education in the education plan, it stated:

"Investigating the number of blind and mute in our country... should be over one million... Also investigating the history of blind and mute education in our country, it has been over twenty years. But currently, according to recent surveys, there are only five schools for the mute nationwide: in Nantong, Beiping,

Yantai, Shanghai, and Nanjing (among these, three are private, one is public, one is mission-established), with the total number of mute students less than three hundred; there are about thirty schools for the blind, mostly established by missions, with the total number of students only around one thousand several hundred..."

Originally, general ordinary education has not yet been universalized, so naturally this kind of special education is even less universal. But from this, can we not understand that education itself has very little power?

With over a million blind and mute people, yet only around one thousand several hundred receiving blind and mute education – this simply declares the impotence of education.

Why is education so impotent? It is because education is conditioned by the economy and by politics. Relying solely on ideas within the educational enterprise, operating within the educational sphere, no matter how clever the educational methods, they are futile.

What can believers in the theory of educational omnipotence say to this now?

Frankly speaking, the crux of modern new education lies precisely in what Gongpu stated: "It lies in the peculiar 'wealth' of the modern era. We know modern society is a society of 'wealth,' a society where wealth is concentrated in the hands of a minority, a society where those who hold the economically dominant position are simultaneously those who hold the politically dominant position. Just as the wealthy enjoy privileges in politics, economics, law, and society, so too do they enjoy privileges in education. In other words, those who hold property rights enjoy education rights. Consequently, the so-called 'scientific education' fundamentally cannot impact those without property; the so-called 'education for all the people' simply never existed."[38]

Therefore, without seeking solutions focused on the problem of "wealth," not only will education lack efficacy for things it fundamentally cannot do, but even for things it potentially could do (like intelligence tests, blind and mute education), it will also prove ineffective.

Second is the so-called theory of saving the nation through education.

This theory can be seen as derived from the first theory. Since education is considered omnipotent, it is naturally considered capable of saving or even building the nation.

Four or five years ago, the Nationalist Faction advocated the theory of building the nation through education. But those who esteem education as the sole method for national salvation certainly did not begin with them; and the types of education considered as national salvation are not limited to Nationalist education alone.

For example, some venerable old scholars vigorously promoted moral education, believing that people's hearts are no longer ancient, public morality is declining daily, and nothing but moral education can provide relief. With moral education, even the conscience of traitors like Cao, Lu, and Zhang[39] could be awakened. They utterly fail to realize that when the people are

---

38 [Special Editor's Note] Quoted from Gongpu's "The Characteristics - or Maladies - of Modern New Education".

39 [Special Editor's Note] "Cao, Lu, Zhang" refers to the three individuals: Cao Rulin, Lu Zongyu, and Zhang Zongxiang. They were pro-Japanese traitors.

impoverished and wealth exhausted, when everyone has no food to eat and is facing starvation, what morality is left to speak of? Furthermore, we already understand that something called morality, just like the legal system, is a tool used by the ruling class to protect itself; there simply is no such thing as social morality or human morality.

Then there are those who promote patriotic education, believing that China's weakness stems from the people's lack of national consciousness. If education vigorously propagates patriotic thought, making everyone know that the country should be loved, how could China not become wealthy and strong? This is precisely the logical deduction of the Nationalists who regard the nation as the highest form of social evolution. Patriotic thought is a product of the rise of capitalism, and thus a tool of the bourgeoisie. During the First World War, imperialists, even the Second International and the Social Democratic parties under it, unanimously shouted "Defend the Fatherland," resulting in tens of millions of lives being buried alive under this slogan. This counts as the ultimate achievement of patriotic education, and presumably something the Nationalists supremely admire? Such education can certainly serve the state owned by the capitalists, but it has nothing to do with the exploited and oppressed workers and peasants. Furthermore, something like "love" can only be maintained when "clothing and food are without worry." What parents do not love their children? Yet currently, in areas like Shaanxi and Henan, selling children has become an opportunity disaster victims seek but cannot obtain. Can you reprimand such parents for lacking love? The heart of love originally existed, but it has starved to death. Who starved them to death?

There are also more practical people who advocate vocational education, believing that the country is currently too poor, people's livelihoods too bitter; enabling people to have the ability to make a living independently, developing various industries and commerce to resist foreign goods, the country can then become wealthy and strong. They do not understand why China's industry and commerce are underdeveloped, why so many people are unemployed. Saying this is the result of imperialist economic aggression – perhaps they can acknowledge this now – but going a step further, saying that imperialist economic aggression is an inevitable result of capitalist development – I'm afraid they do not understand, nor dare to think in this way. Without overthrowing imperialist rule in China – economic, political, cultural, etc. – without eliminating feudal forces, and without defeating the bourgeoisie that surrenders to imperialism and compromises with feudal forces, China cannot escape its current semi-colonial status. The Chinese people cannot improve their current impoverished lives. Relying on vocational education to save the nation is simply a joke!

As for anecdotes like the Prussian General Moltke attributing victory in the Franco-Prussian War to elementary school teachers, or Japan's Itō Hirobumi saying victory in the Russo-Japanese War was due to the strength of elementary school teachers, these are merely the hypnotic effects orchestrated by the ruling class.

While education certainly cannot save the nation, education is also not absolutely exempt from the need to "save the nation." The deceptive and misleading saying "education for education's sake," we long ago recognized as a smokescreen used by the ruling class to avoid mentioning class education, a fabrication created by hired scholars to deceive themselves and others. But similarly, advocating saving the nation through education while despising the people's revolution is also a conspiracy to divert the sight of the revolutionary masses and lead them down the wrong path. Therefore, we must proceed to critique the third theory.

The third theory is the theory of education before revolution.

This theory has common ground with the second theory, namely, it asserts that education has an independent, contributory efficacy. However, while the second theory believes that relying solely on education can save the nation, this theory at least does not forget revolution. Yet the errors of this theory are also considerable, especially recently when the Chinese revolution has become an immediate issue. It deserves serious attention from those engaged in educational work.

Their idea is that to carry out revolution, one must first educate the people. If the people do not understand revolution and lack the ability to revolution, the revolution cannot succeed.

According to their logic, the 1911 Revolution was certainly meddlesome, and even the Chinese revolution of two or three years ago was premature. Because the majority of China's four hundred million people, largely as the Nationalist Party said, are "Ah Dou"[40] type characters, certainly they cannot understand revolution and lack revolutionary ability.

Let's not dwell on that for now. Simply criticizing this theory in one sentence: it is "waiting for the river to clear," who knows which year or month it will be achieved. Frankly, it is ultimately impossible.

As we have described above, education undergoes transformation; that is, in class society, education belongs only to the ruling class, it serves the interests of the ruling class. Attempting to overthrow

---

40 [Translator's Note] "Ah Dou" refers to Liu Shan, the incompetent and weak later ruler of the Shu Han kingdom during the Three Kingdoms period. His name is often used metaphorically to refer to a foolish, incompetent person who cannot be helped.

ruling class education from within this class education to implement revolutionary education and universally cultivate revolutionary talent — nothing is easier to understand than the impossibility of this. So, may I ask those who advocate education before revolution, what magic do you have to administer education that cultivates revolutionary talent?

Admittedly, the bourgeois revolution against the feudal system did indeed involve the maturation of its own culture within feudal society, superior to the culture of the ruling class. But simultaneously, we must not forget that within the feudal societal framework, it [the bourgeoisie] was already the economically dominant class in economic life, thus it substantially existed as this new class; and moreover, it certainly did not forget revolutionary action. Before the French Revolution of 1789, hadn't there already been the new era of the Renaissance and the new movement of the Reformation? While such a new era and new movement cannot be called the seizure of power by the bourgeoisie, they cannot but be called the struggle of the newly rising bourgeoisie against the collapsing feudal system, and indeed a successful struggle.

However, by the time capitalism developed into its final stage, the imperialist era, the situation became vastly different. As stated earlier, in the imperialist era, culture and education also inevitably tend towards "monopoly" and "imperialism." Ancient and medieval cultures and education were dualistic but "coexisted without conflict," whereas modern culture and education are dualistically antagonistic, dualistically engaged in "mortal combat." Therefore, in modern capitalist society, the position of the working class is one of economic exploitation, political oppression, and also cultural suffocation. It absolutely cannot be like the bourgeoisie within feudal society, which held a dominant position economically and also possessed its own matured culture.

For this class (the proletariat) to achieve the maturation of its own culture is only possible during the transition period, only after it has seized state power, only by destroying the bourgeois monopoly of education and gaining command over all learning, and only through the experience of great constructive endeavors, transforming its own nature to become the organizers of the new human society.

Therefore, in modern times, advocating education before revolution is again deceptive talk. The ruling class absolutely will not permit the emergence of education detrimental to it under its rule. Since you do not advocate immediate revolution, you naturally have to conform to its mold. Such an argument calls for everyone to take the path of legalist movements, the path of liquidationism. This is not merely "revolution later," it is simply "no revolution," "abandoning revolution."

So what is the correct approach?

We acknowledge that education has its own place within the revolutionary process, that is, it can serve as one of the weapons of revolution. This statement does not mean that education alone can accomplish revolution, nor does it mean that education is irrelevant to revolution; rather, it means that education must play its role within the overall revolutionary program and tasks.

Generally, the relationship between education and revolution can be stated as follows:

Before the revolution, that is, before the revolutionary masses seize political power, education is a weapon used for destruction, agitation, and propaganda, exposing the crimes of the ruling class to the fullest, disseminating the revolutionary platform as widely as possible. While this has a similar function to military offensives, its additional function, beyond destruction, is to arouse the revolutionary fervor of the oppressed masses and cultivate new elements dedicated to revolutionary work. In essence, before the revolution, education is used for struggle, aiming to be one of the weapons for seizing political power. After the revolution, that is, after the revolutionary masses have seized political power, the responsibility of education lies in educating the masses, training the masses, to support this political power, consolidate this political power, and maintain the close relationship between the masses and the government, ensuring their consistent trust in its policies. Because the government then is one elected by the masses to exercise political power; it stands together with the masses, no longer opposed to them. In essence, after the revolution, education is a function for defending and promoting political power. (Gongpu's "The Political Mission of Educators")

This indicates that education, in relation to revolution, cannot exist independently without relation to it; only when carrying out revolutionary work can there be (and is there a need for) revolutionary education. Moreover, even regarding this kind of education, we should not overestimate it; its effectiveness is ultimately limited. May revolutionary educators not unconsciously surrender again to the "theory of educational omnipotence" or the "theory of saving the nation through education"!

We know the meaning of the term revolutionary education: it is using education as a weapon of revolution, as a weapon of struggle. It can also be seen as a response to the unrealistic arguments of "education for education's sake" or the "religion of education." During the revolutionary period, everything must adapt to the overall revolutionary strategy, advancing in coordination; only then can revolution succeed. Since the Chinese revolution is not yet considered successful, educational workers should communicate with general revolutionary fighters and the revolutionary masses, march in step, and work together to realize the overall revolutionary program. In other words, education should be regarded as one front army of the revolutionary forces, moving towards revolutionary victory under the tasks of overthrowing imperialist rule and eliminating feudal forces.

This is our view on the relationship between education and revolution, and also our view on the efficacy of education.

Questions

How did old educational texts speak about the efficacy of education? (If you have received or are receiving teacher training.)

Try to explain the relationship between education and revolution.

On one hand advocating the theory of saving the nation through education, on the other hand insisting that students should not participate in political and social struggles – can you discern the purpose behind this?

Why is education not omnipotent?

We oppose the theory of education before revolution. Does that mean we can abandon educational work? If not, how should we proceed?

CHAPTER 2: THE EVOLUTION OF EDUCATION

SECTION 5: EDUCATION IN PRIMITIVE COMMUNIST SOCIETY

Overview of Primitive Communist Society – "Practical Education" and "Religious Education" – "Learning" without "Teaching" – Three Forms of Education – Imitation and Suggestion – Training – Initiation Rites – Characteristics of Education in Primitive Society – Slave Society and Education – Questions

After reading the sections of Chapter 1 above, the reader should already understand that education originally aimed at preserving the race (including the preservation of the individual) and served as a means to help humans manage social life. But later, due to the development of private property and the emergence of the family, education ceased to have the preservation of the race as its goal, instead taking the defense of private property and the consolidation of ruling power as its main purpose. This caused education to change in nature, becoming a tool of class domination – but also a weapon in the class struggle.

In this chapter, I will describe the various traces of educational change from the primitive communist society, through various slave societies (i.e., civilized societies), to the recently budding socialist society, thereby enabling the reader to understand the reasons for the changes in the meaning of education and educational systems, that is, to understand the patterns of education's transformation.

Now let us begin with education in primitive communist society.

We have already touched upon the situation of primitive communist society (clan system society) in Section 2 above, but to clarify education within this society, a more detailed account is still necessary.

Primitive society is the society of the pre-historic era (i.e., before recorded history). The author of Ancient Society, Morgan[41], divided the pre-historic era into three major periods: Savagery, Barbarism, and Civilization, with the first two being transitional to the third. Furthermore, based on the level of development of the productive forces – the means of obtaining the necessities of life – he subdivided the first two periods into Lower, Middle, and Upper stages. The Lower stage of Savagery is the infancy of humanity, the transition period from animal to human, where distinct speech was formed. Its Middle stage begins with the use of fire, and the Upper stage begins with the invention of the bow and arrow. The Lower stage of Barbarism begins with the application of pottery-making, the Middle stage begins with the domestication of animals and the cultivation of edible plants, and the Upper stage begins with the smelting of iron, field agriculture, the invention of writing, and its use for keeping records. It is from this point that humanity enters the period of Civilization.

In essence, the technology of production determines the degree of human conquest over nature. Savagery was the era of appropriating natural products, Barbarism the era of pastoralism and agriculture, and Civilization the era of more advanced industry and technology. With the invention of animal husbandry

---

41 [Special Editor's Note] Lewis Henry Morgan (1818-1881), an American anthropologist, who, from an evolutionary perspective, divided the development process of humanity from Savagery through Barbarism to Civilization.

and plant cultivation, and the discovery of iron, human labour power gradually increased, sufficient to produce more than what was necessary for their own sustenance, and accumulated wealth no longer belonged to the community but to individuals, thus giving rise to private property. Therefore, these two achievements accomplished an unprecedented great revolution in human history: from common property to private property. The transformation of our education also hinges on this.

Clan system society is the society that existed before the emergence of civilized class society, hence it is primitive communist society.

Although the organization of this society was extremely primitive and simple, it was truly a most astonishing organization. There were no armies or police, no state or nobility, no courts or prisons. Yet everything proceeded in an orderly fashion. In this communist society, there were no poor people, nor were there slaves; all people exhibited personalities of great justice, authority, dignity, and courage.

The most notable feature of this period was the superiority of women's rights. The era of Savagery practiced promiscuous marriage. Generally speaking, paternal relationships were unclear, so society necessarily became a matriarchal system, and the clan system, as a kinship group, was a matriarchal system. The era of Barbarism practiced pairing marriage, i.e., temporary monogamy – again, generally speaking – although paternal relationships became clearer, children still belonged to the mother, so in the clan system of the Barbaric era, women's status remained very high.

The living conditions of this clan-based society, as observed by Morgan among the Iroquois (Seneca tribe), were highly admirable. It was like this: This tribe consisted of eight clans named after animals like wolf, bear, and turtle. (1) Each clan elected a peacetime chief and a wartime military leader through the vote of all men and women. The chief's power was merely the moral authority of a patriarch; the military leader only had some command authority during war. (2) The clan could freely depose the chief and military leader; once deposed, they were merely private individuals, soldiers. (3) No one was allowed to marry within the clan; this was a fundamental principle. (4) When a man died, his belongings were distributed among his brothers, sisters, and mother's brothers; when a woman died, they were inherited by her children and sisters. Husband and wife did not inherit from each other, nor did children inherit from the father. (5) The clan had the obligation of mutual support, assistance, protection, and aiding in revenge for injuries by other tribes. (6) The clan had a common burial ground. (7) The clan could adopt people from other tribes. (8) The clan had a council, which was the supreme authority of the clan, a democratic assembly of all adult men and women. In essence, their clan system was a fraternal relationship of freedom, equality, and friendship. When Native Americans were first encountered, all of North America still practiced the matrilineal clan system; only two or three tribes had abolished it and adopted the patrilineal system.

In societies practicing matrilineality, all children belonged to the mother's clan, and things like land, houses, and food were all commonly owned by the entire clan. Therefore, although matriarchal power was said to be superior then, it was absolutely unlike the patriarchal power of civilized society, where the father monopolizes everything and holds privileged power over subordinates. Although clan society practiced matrilineality, property belonged to the clan, not to individual women. This is a major difference from the private property system of civilized society. In terms of the rights of men and women, they were equal in this society; everyone engaged in productive labour, and everyone shared the fruits of labour. Since the clan was such a closely-knit whole, its members, lacking a concept of private property, also lacked the concept of an individual independent of the clan. Originally, their group and the individual were so unified. Consequently, being expelled from the clan was, in their view, no different from a death sentence.

Fishing and hunting were the two major productive labours in primitive society. Additionally, gathering fruits, skins, and roots from wild plants was naturally known since ancient times. But animal husbandry and agriculture, as mentioned above, were discovered later. Morgan, who studied such primitive communist customs, also wrote the following in his book:

"Tribes on the plains subsisting almost solely on animal flesh show, in their hunting customs, tendencies similar to communism. For instance, the Blackfeet people form large groups comprising the entire tribe, including men, women, and children, hunting buffalo on horseback.

When beginning the chase, hunters leave the animals killed along the way for those following to pick up. Their method of distribution ensures that everyone gets a share of the game. Also, during the fishing season on the Columbia River, the entire tribe camps by the river, storing the caught fish collectively. Every day, fish are distributed equally to each person according to the number of men and women. They also gut the fish, dry them in the sun, and after they are dry, place them in baskets to be transported to the village."

In primitive society, all productive labour was carried out collectively in this manner, and the results were also collectively distributed. At that time, every individual was a labourer; among them, no one was lazy, nor did anyone monopolize the spoils. For example, the African Bushmen even distributed the majority of their catch to their companions, keeping only a very small portion for themselves. Similarly, the Fuegians, upon spotting a whale on the coast, would quickly gather their companions to hunt it, and then the eldest among them would perform a fair distribution on the spot. There is also a beautiful story told about the Eskimos:

All neighbours were entertained with games, choruses, feasts, and dances, continuing for several days. On the final night, the villagers were utterly exhausted. Then, the lavishly dressed host and hostess brought out their favourite gifts and gave them to all their friends, distributing in this way 10 guns, 10 pieces of clothing, 200 beads, as well as the pelts of 10 wolves, 50 does, 100 seals, 200 beavers, 500 antelopes, and much woolen cloth. Finally, they even took off all their own clothes and gave them to their friends. Standing naked, the host and hostess then gave the following speech to conclude the feast: "Friends, our hearts can now be at ease. Now we are poorer than any one of you. But we have no regrets whatsoever. Although we now possess nothing, we have gained your friendship because of this."

Among the Eskimos, even today, a custom remains quite prevalent: those possessing property above a certain level must hold a feast and distribute all their property among the entire tribe.

The examples of the Iroquois and Eskimos cited above are both examples from existing savage tribes. The customs practiced among them might not fully correspond to reality. But the spirit and even the fact of collective labour and shared property still exist.

Let us now examine their education within a society having such a material environment as its background.

Generally speaking, the content of education in primitive society falls into two main aspects: "Practical Education" for obtaining the necessities of life, and "Religious Education" for spiritual consolation. The former includes skills for fishing, hunting, warfare, and tool-making; the latter involves the transmission of customs and rituals.

At this time, education can clearly be divided into two types: The first type is not really education at all, but merely learning. It is the acquisition of various know-how and skills regarding the environment, livestock, beliefs, customs, and even language, dance, and singing through children's spontaneous imitation. This can be called having "learning" without "teaching". The second type constitutes the forms of education in primitive society, which can be further distinguished into the following three kinds: The first is the most primitive, taking the form of parental nurturing, focusing on the physical aspect and limited to passive protection. The second is a more advanced form, becoming parental coaching, aiming to actively assist the child's development, making them learn parental habits, containing conscious action and spiritual instruction. The third is general social training, centered on religious education for internal unity and military education for defense against external enemies. This social training can again be divided into four items: (1) Ordeal: For youths joining the adult group, physically arduous tests are administered, such as fasting or solitary isolation, to verify their will to endure hardship and pain. (2) Drill: In the practice of hunting and warfare, the focus is on practical skills, but it also has the task of cultivating obedience and habits of cooperation. (3) Initiation rites: These are religious, conducted in solemn secrecy, where elders teach about divine matters and the obligations of members, etc. After undergoing this ceremony, a youth becomes a member of society, signifying the completion of educational experiences in all aspects. (4) The teaching of legends, beliefs, "laws," and customs, formed by combining the above three forms. Later, with the increase of these traditions and the development of writing, specialized educators like priests gradually emerged, and "schools" thus began to develop.

In essence, the characteristics of education in the primitive era were its practical and social nature, and the consistency of education with labour, with women and men "studying together." So-called cultivated, liberal, or individual education naturally could not arise in a primitive communist society aimed at the interests of the entire clan; "teaching materials" that upheld ruling power and respected private property were naturally also nonexistent.

The above only outlines the general picture of education in primitive society, to give the reader a concept. Below, we will describe the methods and content of education in primitive society in more detail – based on Chapters 8 to 10 of the American Nathan Miller's The Child in Primitive Society.

First, education through imitation and suggestion. To be more precise, it is not "teaching" but "learning."

Children in primitive society, on one hand, needed to adapt to the material environment to obtain the necessities of life; on the other hand, they also needed to adapt to the experiences accumulated through countless efforts of their ancestors, passed down as heritage, in order to preserve the "culture" of the entire group. And the learning of these various life-activities could almost always be achieved through imitation. Simply by seeing, hearing, and touching, they could, unconsciously, react with appropriate behavior. It is said that among Australian Aborigines, Malays, Polynesians[42], and Melanesians[43], there was virtually no

---

42 [Special Editor's Note] Polynesians are the indigenous peoples of the islands east of a line stretching

formal education to speak of; almost everything was learned from nature. Among the Ainu of Hokkaido, Japan, "their children are never troubled by school or teacher. Mountains, rivers, are their classrooms; necessity is their teacher; inclination and climate are the only forces driving them to work." Among California Indian children, "once they reach the age of self-sufficiency – that is, catching mice and killing snakes – education ceases immediately. Once California youths have acquired sufficient skill and strength for these tasks, the presence or absence of parents is irrelevant. In terms of instruction or teaching, their parents accomplish nothing." Similarly, in the Arinoco[44] region of South America, parents do not educate their children because they have nothing to teach. Adults act, and children imitate, just like young goats leaping about in the mountains, growing up entirely naturally.

Even when children occasionally asked their parents about natural phenomena, they gained nothing. For example, Kaffir[45] children, "when they see the moon during the day and are greatly surprised, run to their parents and ask why. The parents' only reply is that the moon is in the sky because that is its place. This explanation is final and actually satisfies them." Because they all say: "What's the use of doubting these things? I haven't studied how trees grow, yet trees grow naturally." Or again, "Children ask

---

from New Zealand northeast through Fiji to the Hawaiian Islands, including Hawaiians, Tongans, Tahitians, and the Maori of New Zealand, among others.

43 [Special Editor's Note] Melanesians are the indigenous inhabitants of the Melanesian islands in the southwestern Pacific, including New Caledonians and Fijians, with some populations distributed on the island of New Guinea.

44 [Special Editor's Note] The Orinoco region of South America refers to the Orinoco River basin.

45 [Special Editor's Note] The Kaffir are a branch of the Bantu people of Southern Africa.

their parents: 'How do ghosts eat meat, as you say? We clearly see that after the ghosts have eaten, the meat remains just as much as before, yet you say ghosts eat meat.' Then the old people forbid them to speak, and they say, laughing, 'Ah, ghosts drink blood, or smell the essence; that's all they care about.' Or they might say: 'The ghosts have tasted the meat.'"

In essence, children's education was entirely left to nature, without guidance. Children acquired experience entirely on their own, just like chicks learning to peck without help. For instance, in Central Africa, all the knowledge children possess seems to be gained instinctively – because no one has ever seen them being taught. On the Gold Coast[46], once a child's senses come into contact with practical life, he participates in all practical actions.

Children not only learn about the natural environment very quickly; they also learn the details of tribal life very quickly. Through constant contact with the environment, family, and companions, by the age a child in civilized society just begins schooling, they are already thoroughly familiar with everything in nature and about their people.

For example, in Madagascar, a child's observations in nature provide him with extremely rich knowledge of natural history. He can know the names and habits of various animals and plants growing nearby. African youths "study every animal in the herd, its appearance, habits, and tracks..." "Most children of fourteen or fifteen know the names, habits, and even methods of catching the fish in rivers and streams. They also know the names and dwellings of animals in the forest; the names of birds, insects, trees, flowers, etc., are also well known to them and easily identified."

---

46 [Special Editor's Note] The Gold Coast is present-day Ghana.

Children also learn everything about fields, forests, and rivers through this method of natural observation. This knowledge is extremely necessary for them, as without it they cannot adapt. Methods of sustaining life – fishing, hunting, herding, farming, etc. – were not developed on a large scale and were acquired merely by imitating the behavior of elders. For instance, on the Loango[47] coast, children learn from a very young age how to fish and make palm wine. Among the Cheyenne[48] Indians, "children know about horses and their behavior from infancy; by two or three years old, they often ride with their mothers. Thus, they learn the methods of riding just as they learn to walk." Maya[49] girls, by observing their mothers, learn from childhood how to cook and grind grain.

Legends and customs are also learned largely in the same way. That is, by listening to the elders' discussions, they gradually learn the content of tribal history. No one teaches children worship; they simply watch the adults do it and imitate them when they grow up. From the stories of the elders, they learn who the tribe's enemies are and thus harbor feelings of animosity. By mixing in tribal and family councils, children "precociously" become familiar with public affairs and tribal law. Even language acquisition occurs without formal instruction. Dance and song are also learned solely through observation.

---

47 [Special Editor's Note] Loango is a place name in the Congo region of Africa.

48 [Special Editor's Note] Cheyenne, the capital city of Wyoming, USA, located in the southeastern part of the state near the border with Colorado.

49 [Special Editor's Note] The Maya are a group of Indigenous peoples of Central America, inhabiting areas such as Mexico's Yucatán Peninsula, who developed a high-level culture and constructed monumental architecture as early as the beginning of the Common Era.

The many beliefs and attitudes already formed within the tribe gradually influence the children, who consequently develop behaviors that last a lifetime. They "instinctively" obey the words of adults.

When children come into contact with this culture, they are also free from preconceived notions. Therefore, they imitate anything and everything without selection. Let's take examples from their play life. African children imitate the full set of weapons possessed by adults. For instance, spears are made from sharpened plant stems, and short guns from sharp wooden pieces, all made very appropriately. In North Queensland[50], adults often use wedges, so children also make wedges by combining several pieces of bark, applying the same decorations. By four or five years old, children carry small spears, using them to fight other children and to threaten their mothers and dogs. Among the Veddas[51] of Ceylon, children have bows and arrows, and five-year-olds have many skillfully made bows. On Borneo and the Gilbert[52] Islands, children build their own houses and toy canoes. Among the Chukchee[53] of Siberia, children have various toys, mostly imitations of everyday objects, such as small boats, sleds, wooden dogs and reindeer, snowshoes, bows and arrows, etc.

---

50 [Special Editor's Note] North Queensland is a state of the Commonwealth of Australia, located in the northeastern part of the Australian mainland.

51 [Special Editor's Note] The Veddas of Ceylon; Ceylon is present-day Sri Lanka. The Veddas, formerly translated as "Vedda people," now often Veddah, preserve remnants of matrilineal clan systems and animistic beliefs.

52 [Special Editor's Note] The Gilbert Islands are an archipelago in the central-western Pacific.

53 [Special Editor's Note] The Chukchi, also translated as Chukchee, reside between the Kolyma River and the Bering Strait, and in the northern part of the Kamchatka Peninsula.

Brazilian Indian children, besides small bows and arrows, have their own model musical instruments.

What is noteworthy here is that such play is difficult to distinguish from actual work. For example, those small wooden spears are used by Australian youths to dig up roots; similarly, in Brazil, children's toys are hardly different from the real objects.

The labour and activities of adults all become material for children's play. This kind of play contains the highest educational value. The school of primitive children is in their playground, and their playground exists everywhere. Their play also encompasses all the habits, attitudes, and institutions of their people. Before they formally participate in actual life, they live within this play life. Consequently, their play serves a fully preparatory and training function.

Religious rituals are also imitated by children and manifested in their play. For example, among the Pangwe[54] people, children imitate ancestor worship, dancing and praying just like adults. Filipino Igorot[55] children also have a game called fug-fug-to[56], which imitates the ceremony held by adults after the annual harvest.

However, later on, the things to be learned became complex, diverse, and remote. Consequently, relying solely on imitation

---

54 [Special Editor's Note] The Pangwe people, also known as the "Fang" or "Pahutu," are an ethnic group on the eastern coast of the Gulf of Guinea in Africa, who practice primitive beliefs and ancestor worship.

55 [Special Editor's Note] The Igorot people, also translated as Yigeluo or Yigelü people, are distributed in the highland regions of northern Philippines.

56 [Special Editor's Note] "Fug-fug-to" is a children's game of the Igorot people, which imitates the ceremony held by adults after the annual harvest.

could not fully adapt to social inheritance. Children's innate interests could not necessarily comprehend more abstract, evolved cultural artifacts, such as religious beliefs, folk songs, language, and legends. Thus, certain training methods had to be gradually created to guide children. Furthermore, because the "curriculum" did not much suit children's tastes, a compulsory or disciplinary system became necessary to instill the later-developed, more significant, artificial tribal customs into children. Now let us remember that the application of pure imitation ability is the foundation of children's education in primitive society, and from this, proceed to examine the elements of more formal education in primitive society.

Second, let's discuss education through training.

The education of children in primitive society was originally said to be entirely imitative. However, the elders in the tribe consciously paid attention to children to prepare them for participation in tribal life. But because primitive social life was simple, children could achieve independent status very early. Therefore, even such conscious training did not constitute a systematic or regular form of instruction. It merely used suppression and authority to make children reliably adapt to tribal life. Initially, the free permeation and adaptation of social culture to the child provided economic maturity; now, the social superiority of the elders was allowed to influence the child. Through this, children could develop appropriate emotional tendencies to match their economic maturity.

The necessity for training children also arose because culture gradually developed, becoming more refined and remote, beyond the reach of children's natural interests. This kind of social heritage could only be transmitted through the instruction of the elders. This society lacked reliable written records. All the cultural achievements of the entire society could only exist in the minds and behaviors of the younger generation. Therefore, without special training, the culture would risk being lost.

The motivation for imparting the results of social life to the young was also stimulated when one tribe came into contact with another. During contact, the distinctive characteristics of their own tribal culture became apparent. The reason elders told the younger generation about tribal customs and admonitions was not only to preserve these tribal characteristics but also, beyond preservation, to enable them to resist the encroachment and destruction by other tribes.

This primitive "curriculum" generally included two types of content: vocational and moral. Originally, skills like fishing and hunting, as mentioned above, were almost entirely learned by children on their own, without anyone providing special training. However, these methods of making a living later became complex quite rapidly. Without practical instruction, it was feared they might not be able to use those weapons and tools properly. To enable children to achieve economic independence early and acquire the ability to use tools promptly, the implementation of some training became necessary. This shows that the emergence of such training stemmed from social exigencies – a result of cultural evolution.

In Australia, when a father took his son out with him, he always used the opportunity to give his son some instruction. "For example, when they reached a place associated with some legend, if the son was old enough to understand, he would tell him the legend. Or the father would tell him the simplest method to obtain this or that animal, or other food." They also prepared small weapons for their sons. The father would demonstrate their use. One point worth noting here is that this kind of training is clearly based on the imitative play function described above and is interwoven with it.

When the means of livelihood became difficult, this also became a reason forcing fathers to instruct their children, rather than waiting for the children to imitate on their own. Australian children were often guided by adults to track animals and could recognize the presence of birds and reptiles based on the subtlest traces. Girls were taught methods of knotting ropes and making baskets. The Ainu of Japan had to teach their children to catch fish, hunt game, make bows and arrows, capture deer, and predict the weather based on the sky. A Bushman father would tell his son about the sources of food and methods of obtaining them from a very young age.

When life skills moved beyond the most primitive stage and progressed, preliminary training became truly necessary. Activities like trade, tanning hides, and pottery-making required considerable instruction. On the children's part, they needed to quickly learn these more refined methods of obtaining food and making a living. On the adults' part, they were no longer satisfied with leaving children to natural imitation alone. A Congolese child learning to paddle a canoe used a toy canoe given by his father to practice. Simultaneously, his father taught him how to paddle backwards, how to steer, and how to use the paddle. Besides this, there were over 50 different terms related to canoeing that he also had to learn from the elders' instruction. Another part of the children's "curriculum" included training in "not only the movement of beetles but also the crowing of chickens, the call of a certain bird, and the movement of the sun."

In the Tonga Islands[57], girls learning adornment had to be taught by women. Apache[58] girls were taught by their grandmothers to make baskets from yucca[59] leaves, starting from the age of six. Blackfoot mothers worked very hard to teach their daughters the skills of tanning hides and turning them into clothing; additionally, they taught them to recognize pasture grasses and wild plants used for food and medicine.

When the tribe had military exercises, it was an even more compulsory training opportunity. Here, organization and discipline were essential to achieve the required physical and mental control. Among the Mandan Indians[60], simulated warfare and simulated scalping were important parts of a boy's education. At that time, experienced warriors would lead a group of children aged 7 to 15 to the grassland early in the morning. They were naked, carrying only bows and harmless grass arrows, wooden knives, and fake heads made of grass. They would drill all the actions of Indian combat – feints, retreats, advances, and then melees. Apache children were taught by their fathers and grandmothers methods such as counting, running, jumping into cold water, and racing, all to prepare them to become brave and strong warriors.

Matters concerning sexual intercourse between men and women,

---

57 [Special Editor's Note] The Tonga Islands, located east of the Fiji Islands in the South Pacific, now constitute the Kingdom of Tonga.

58 [Special Editor's Note] The Apache are a branch of Native Americans.

59 [Special Editor's Note] Yucca, a plant name. Also known as Spanish dagger or Adam's needle, its leaves can be used for weaving baskets.

60 [Special Editor's Note] The Mandan Indians were distributed across the plains region of North America.

especially those that had become incomprehensible rituals and dogmas, were also instructed to children. For instance, on the D'Entre Casteaux Islands[61], elders guided children from an early age to participate in the "deeper mysteries of sex. The adults would go out for a few days to fish, buy areca nuts, or simply visit friends. The youths went with them. In the evening by the fire, they told the children which roots and leaves to rub together with tobacco or betel nuts, and taught them magical songs, so that when they had relations with their lovers, they could forever win their 'favor'." Things like this could not be learned except through practical teaching.

Life in primitive society was extremely harsh and severe. Without a robust physique, survival was difficult. Therefore, certain physical characteristics had to be developed first to gain an independent position in society. The custom among the Siseelis of British Columbia was to force children to bathe in the river every morning and evening. Initially, they also whipped their naked bodies with small whips (which were kept in the household fire). "They are whipped daily, and with this apparatus, he will become a lively and energetic person, capable of attaining much happiness." Later, the child's body was pricked with spears and cut with knives, "to let the bad blood out." At night, they slept naked in the open air so as not to fear the cold. Among neighboring tribes, youths had to lie all night by a river or lake with their hands immersed in the water.

Those who could not endure such harsh training were deemed unfit and could not attain full independent status within the tribe; they had to remain in a state of lifelong servitude and shame. The methods for implementing this severe policy were often dictated

---

61 [Special Editor's Note] The D'Entre Casteaux Islands are a dependency of Papua New Guinea, located in the southwestern Solomon Sea.

by the nature of the environment. Among the Kaffir people, children were forced to sleep on the ground without mats. The aim was to toughen their bodies. Many children died under this rule. Yet such deaths were of no concern to them. Girls also underwent training to endure hardship and pain.

It was not only the body; the emotions of the children also had to conform to the tribal mold, and their interests to tribal conventions. The cultivation of such mental attitudes and sentiments required conscious training; it could not be left to nature. This is because various attitudes, habits, and even minor points of etiquette were the results of social evolution from a process of trial and error by previous generations, being relatively complex and subtle. Children in the Andaman[62] Islands were often reprimanded for negligence and rashness; conversely, they were taught to be generous, self-controlled, mutually supportive, and to share food with others. The Ainu taught children to respect their elders, serve them, give way when elders passed, and remove their hats in front of elders. Among the American Indians, young people were trained in etiquette from childhood. Direct address was strictly prohibited. "Kinship terms, or certain honorifics, were commonly used instead of personal names... We were taught to care for the poor and suffering and to revere the heavens."

Where there was no writing, the preservation of past culture relied entirely on oral transmission. Primitive science and philosophy, like primitive tribal history, were preserved through storytelling. Often, rhythm was added, turning speech into poetry, making it easier for children to memorize. For example, the Boloki of the Congo region had no written historical records

---

62 [Special Editor's Note] Andaman, referring to the Indian Andaman Islands.

because no one in the tribe could write. However, through oral tradition, they could pass down the tribe's origins, migrations, etc., from father to son.

The content of these talks was didactic and moral. Each talk contained a point from local law, custom, or ritual. Many talks were, of course, the crystallization of cultural products of unknown origin, passed down through social force and convention. Among the Hova people of Madagascar, this body of traditional knowledge was called the "heritage of the ear." Additionally, there were fables, proverbs, etc., constituting the children's "textbooks." For example, in Ainu stories, we can find the purpose was to encourage diligence, respect for the aged, and to prohibit laziness and greed. Children enjoyed listening to these moral narratives and were able to put them into practice. As a result, "he learns to sing the love songs and affection songs of former generations; there is no new path for him to tread, he only follows the old road."

From the above, children's education was initially based on "self-learning," later receiving some training from parents and elders to develop the physical and mental tendencies necessary for social life. When physical development was complete, they underwent a special ceremony, which represented the culmination of all experience. Thereby, the child became a mature individual in society, an independent tribesman. This ceremony was the Initiation Ceremony.

Third, let us discuss education through the initiation ceremony.

The initiation ceremony signified that the child had become an adult, had been socialized, and thus was given a name, admitted into the group, and guided to approach the spirits of the ancestors and protective deities. In essence, through this, they gained public recognition. The various "technical" aspects of culture, such as methods for obtaining food, making tools, and building houses, were gradually absorbed through the child's innate impulses. However, the "moral" culture or customs, the principles or patterns of thought and emotion in tribal life, absorbed in this state, were naturally not complete. Therefore, these had to be more consciously instilled by the community. The initiation ceremony now to be discussed, by opening the door of tribal life to the child, served to thoroughly accomplish this purpose: creating a social psychology or personality.

During puberty, certain physiological and emotional changes in the child were sufficient to attract everyone's attention. This sexual maturity also implied a crisis in the youth's social status. Because during and after adolescence, he had acquired the potential to create new social relationships, enough to shake the existing social order. Therefore, in many places, the fundamental function of the initiation ceremony was to publicly acknowledge the existence of this physiological change in the individual, preparing him to participate in adult status, to enjoy recognized rights to sexual intercourse, and to fulfill tribal obligations. But in other places, the initiation ceremony did not correspond to the child's puberty. This is because the ceremony, which initially served to mark the individual's physiological change, soon became a symbol of introduction into the social life of the tribe, thus no longer based entirely on physiological maturity.

Depending on the nature of the culture, the age for the initiation ceremony could be specified. Among the Masai[63], children underwent circumcision and initiation ceremonies when they reached the age for military service. In Borneo, a child gained social status when he struck an enemy's head for the second time

---

63 [Special Editor's Note] The Masai are a famous pastoral area in East Africa, located in northern Tanzania.

in war. In terms of age, it was generally between 8 and 15 years old. So in practice, many older boys, having failed to take an enemy's head for years, were still considered children. In some places, such as Fiji[64], the initiation ceremony could be postponed as a punishment for misbehavior. Then he had to remain in the status of a child and suffer contempt.

The shift of the initiation ceremony from being based on physiological relations to emphasizing social relations is proof of the effort of custom surpassing personal matters. Thus, among the Kaonde women, the initiation ceremony was held not at puberty but before it. The reason was the belief that waiting until menstruation began was very dangerous. Among the Ila people of Nanzela, it was also believed that if women did not undergo the initiation ceremony early, they might never menstruate.

Most closely related to the initiation ceremony is circumcision (removal of the foreskin in males; or the inner labia in females). This clearly indicates suitability for sexual life. It is thus related to the child's physiological development. However, later, as culture evolved, derived meanings became attached to this practice, and it was incorporated into the general initiation ceremony. Thus, it became a symbol of the youth's entry into social maturity, not necessarily corresponding to physiological maturity.

A Kaffir man who has not been circumcised will be considered a child for life. Women will mock and despise him; in social terms, he is regarded as dead because he cannot participate in the council. Such a man cannot have property rights nor become a soldier. No woman would ever consider marrying such a wretch.

The age for circumcision is not fixed: "Once circumcised, even if

---

64 [Special Editor's Note] Fiji is a Pacific island nation.

he is only an eight-year-old child, he is considered an adult; he is a warrior with the obligation to fight." Among the Masai, children are circumcised when they are able to hold a spear and shield. However, although this ritual has lost its original biological significance, among peoples practicing circumcision, a belief still prevails that circumcision aids reproduction. Without it, the population would inevitably dwindle. Naturally, as mentioned above, tribes completely lacking this motivation also exist. Like the Jews and Arabs of today, they regard this custom solely as a standard for adult qualification.

Thus, the initiation ceremony signifies the youth's transition from social infancy to social maturity. This process of socialization is originally gradual and cumulative. But to primitive people, all these major changes were seen as sudden and abrupt. The purpose of the ceremony was to sever the youth's past relations, to consider him as having died in the past, and now reborn, entering a completely new world as an adult. Therefore, an extraordinary environment was specially created to make the youth aware of this significant change. During the ceremony, he felt cut off from his old life, placed in a state of solitary isolation to experience a new life.

For example, among the Nandi of East Africa, boys and girls took purgatives and had their heads shaved. This signified the severance of childhood ties and the acquisition of a completely new personality. In Dutch New Guinea, when men received instruction in the men's house, their eyes were covered, and they saw nothing. Only later could they see the various objects placed there, representing the new environment. Using Lafitau's[65] words: "These poor children have drunk so much of the water of Leth[66]

---

65 [Special Editor's Note] Lafitau, a Western scholar who studied the peoples of Western Irian.

66 [Special Editor's Note] Lethe, the River of Forgetfulness in Greek mythology (a river in the

that they have forgotten everything: parents, friends, their own past, even their own speech." Discarding old clothes was also used to symbolize separation. For instance, in Rhodesia[67], girls undergoing the initiation ceremony threw their old clothes onto the roof of their parents' hut, thus severing their childhood ties.

During the ceremony, to signify the new and major transformation, initiates were granted various privileges. For example, stealing grain, killing livestock, and even sexual promiscuity went unpunished. Also, the names of things were taught anew by the elders. All this signified that the old was gone and the new was coming.

During the ceremony, separation from women was also required. This signified that in the past, he belonged to his mother, but now he began to belong to men and male society. Most adult men of the tribe attended, signifying the transmission of the habits and customs of social life to the younger generation through this ceremony. From then on, the child gained a position in social life and shouldered responsibility for obligations to the community. That is, he could no longer act as he pleased but had to meet the demands of custom: to be the head of a family, a capable provider of food, a participant in rituals, a worshipper of ancestral spirits. It was through the ceremony that the youth acquired the sense of responsibility befitting an adult, the sentiment of obeying the elders and tribal customs, and the qualification not only to support his family but also to contribute to the entire society.

Particularly important in the nature of the ceremony were the

---

underworld). Legend says that the dead who drink its water forget everything about their previous life.

67 [Special Editor's Note] Rhodesia, located in southern Africa, is today's Zimbabwe.

many rights and obligations imposed on the youth. The so-called rights included becoming a warrior, hunter, voter, dancer, smoker, and other privileges that an independent adult man or woman should enjoy. But the acquisition of these rights was premised on solemn obligations. Most relevant here were naturally the obligations regarding food. Hence, there were practices of fasting and dietary restrictions. The intention was "to make each new member of society conscious of the social value of food... In short, to make him realize that food belongs to society, for which the individual should be grateful to society, not only for the right to obtain food but also for the right to use it without danger; the granting of this right also signifies that the individual must accept corresponding obligations." Therefore, to indicate this relationship of dependence, the child's food had to be given by a friend or relative who had already passed the initiation ceremony, according to ritual. The elders thus granted the initiate the "right to eat."

Secondly, the conferral of clothing was also one of the external characteristics of social maturity. Certain pleasurable activities, such as drinking and smoking, were only permitted at this stage. And shedding the blood of an enemy was a solemn obligation for formal admission into the tribe.

Because the initiation ceremony was the most serious single rite of passage in primitive society, severe warnings were given to the initiates against disclosing secrets; violation would incur the most terrifying punishments. Outsiders were naturally even less able to participate. Therefore, we know very little about the proceedings of the ceremony for this reason.

During the ceremony, children were not allowed to live comfortably. They had to be secluded, even forbidden to speak, laugh, or bathe. Sometimes the whipping and suffering endured were almost unbelievable. For example, Bechuana[68] boys lined up naked every morning. "The men of the town, carrying tough, long, thin rods... performed a dance called the 'Khoa', while asking the children: 'Will you do your utmost to protect the chief?' 'Will you do your utmost to guard the livestock?' When the children gave affirmative replies, the men rushed forward and struck each child's back with all their might... then brandished the flexible rods on their backs, letting the blood roll down. When the dance ended, the boys' backs were covered with wounds and welts, and these scars would remain for life." The ordeal endured by Nandi boys was: "Each boy held the waist of the one in front of him and had to bend down, placing his head under the buttocks of the person in front... At the entrance and exit of the enclosure stood warriors armed with thorns and hornets. They continuously stabbed the boys' faces and private parts with the thorns and dropped hornets on their backs."

There were various other pains and ordeals. If a boy showed the slightest sign of fear or difficulty, he was immediately scorned and bullied, often resulting in suicide. The Basuto[69] people would kill boys who attempted to escape; in the Euahlayi tribe of Australia, timid boys were sent back to their mothers, deemed unworthy of the initiation ceremony. "Soon after, a poisoned stick or bone would put him to death."

The most crucial activity that every boy had to contribute was obtaining food. To reinforce this impression, for example, Australian boys, when participating in the initiation ceremony, had to fast for a considerable period to encourage the sentiment

---

68 [Special Editor's Note] Bechuanaland was originally a British protectorate in southern Africa. It declared independence in 1966 and changed its name to Botswana.

69 [Special Editor's Note] The Basuto people are an indigenous people of Africa.

of self-control. Among the Papuan people[70], boys were taught to eat sparingly. Omaha[71] youths had to fast for four days and nights and were not allowed to use the bow and arrows given by their fathers during the period of solitary trial.

Under such ascetic practices, naturally, many boys lost their lives, unable to withstand the torment. When they died, they were secretly buried nearby, without any funeral rites or lamentations! Because such individuals were not considered to possess independent personhood.

Furthermore, terrifying methods were used to make the initiates feel the power of supernatural spirits. The elders attributed mysterious explanations to various powerful forces, terrors, and threats, interpreting strange sounds and vague omens as the workings of ancestral spirits. All these were used to overwhelm the will of the young people and eliminate their doubts about the ceremony's proceedings. After experiencing such pain and terror, he or she naturally had no choice but to turn to the elders for help and submit to custom.

The knowledge imparted often seemed to include lessons on hygiene, morality, and daily occupations. Take the natives of the Torres Straits as an example. Their instructions to children were as follows: "If two boys are friends, they must not marry each other's sisters, otherwise it is shameful. If someone needs food, water, or anything else, you should give it to them. If you have only a little, you may not give, but if you have plenty, you should give half. Share half of all the fish you have with your parents; never be stingy. Never speak ill of your mother. Father and

---

70 [Special Editor's Note] Papuans, the indigenous people of Western Irian, Papuans.

71 [Special Editor's Note] Omaha is the largest industrial and commercial city in Nebraska, USA.

mother are like food in the stomach; when they die, you will feel hungry. Also pay attention to your parents' brothers and their children. If your brother goes out to fight, you should help him, go together, do not let him go first." This shows the advice aimed to make the youth shoulder responsibilities towards parents and kin. Personal desires had to be sacrificed here.

The ceremonies girls underwent were often similar to those for boys and frequently imitated them. At the first menstruation, a girl had to leave the group. During this period, according to tribal custom, she was taught the attitudes and behaviors expected of an adult woman. During the ceremony, she also underwent ordeals. For instance, in the Amazon River region, when a girl menstruated for the first time, all her relatives and friends gathered, "each bringing elastic cane rods. Then the girl was placed naked in their midst, and each person present struck her back and waist heavily five or six times with the cane until she fainted; sometimes she was even beaten to death." Other practices included prohibitions on eating fresh fish, compulsory ditch digging to practice hard labor, and making daily utensils like baskets, mats, and ropes.

In essence, the combined force of these ordeals, ascetic practices, teachings, and admonitions had an immense impact on the character of the young. The duration of this process could extend for several months in some places. Upon returning from the completed ceremony, he was truly a new person. He felt everything was new, recognized no one, not even his parents. In fact, this new person was treated with the utmost kindness and favor until he had become familiar with his environment. He put on new clothes, shaved his head anew, bathed anew, and everyone came to celebrate the birth of a new life. He was now regarded as an adult; his spirit would exist eternally. When he died, his name would be bestowed upon another family member, signifying that his personhood had gained eternal recognition in tribal life. Therefore, the initiation ceremony was a very important opportunity for the individual in primitive society – a critical juncture determining whether one became an adult or not. We can say that the only formal educational system in primitive society was this general training of society (the initiation ceremony).

The above uses the primitive state of education among existing uncivilized tribes to aid our study of education in Clan System society. Although not exhaustive, it is sufficient to prove that education in primitive society lacked the several abnormalities described in Section 2. This education truly had only a biological purpose, namely, "the preservation of the race," containing no element of domination. Although there were teachings about respecting elders, it was not class-based; the elders deserved respect for representing the interests of the whole society. Respecting the elders was tantamount to respecting the whole society; there was no other function.

We have said that the transformation of education began with the division of society into classes, i.e., with the rise of the private property system and the state system. Therefore, the characteristics of education in Primitive Communist Society were its classless nature, the absence of content respecting private property or upholding ruling power, the integration of education and labor, and the fact that everyone, regardless of gender, had both the right and the obligation to receive education.

In such communist tribes, it was very difficult to eradicate the concept of common property fundamentally. For example, the thefts by Southern US Negroes were said to stem entirely from an inability to comprehend the concept of private ownership. In educational history, bourgeois scholars recorded that Spartan education taught children to steal, valuing the ability to steal daily necessities without detection, considering it an educational method encouraging bravery and resourcefulness. In fact, from a sociological viewpoint, this was the instinctive resistance of the surviving habits of the primitive communist system against the emerging private property system.

But since the collapse of the Clan System and the entry into the civilized period in human history, a great transformation occurred in education. The first class society was the slave-owners' society. In this society, the Ruling Class had leisure to receive liberal education, while slaves were only permitted to labor, thereby completely separating labor from education, i.e., beginning the separation of practice and theory. Originally, all who had the right to survive could enjoy education; now, the owners monopolized the privilege of education, while the non-owners had neither the right to livelihood nor the right to education. The education monopolized by the owners took on an aristocratic character, becoming an ornament rather than a necessity. Even the education provided for commoners did not correspond to their actual life needs. Therefore, in terms of educational purpose, it was no longer purely biological but aimed at upholding private property. Originally, after the Clan System was destroyed by the private property system, the owning Ruling Class necessarily required a new political form adapted to the new economic organization. Thus, the state system of class rule, connected by territory and property, emerged, and it had to use coercion and power to unify society. Education also inevitably had to undergo corresponding changes. Thus, about four to five thousand years ago, when the dawn of human history first appeared, we already had class-based states and hence class-based education.

Greek and Roman education was the education of the slave-owners' society, whose characteristics have already been discussed in Section 2. For convenience, we will not elaborate specifically here but proceed directly to discuss education in feudal society. After all, the serfs in feudal society differed little in status from slaves, only possessing slightly more human rights.

Questions

1. What are the characteristics of Clan System society?

2. In this society, what is the relationship between the individual and society?

3. What is the relationship between what children learned in primitive society and the social life of that time?

4. What are the essential differences between educational activities and educational systems in primitive society?

5. By whom was this education implemented, and for whom was it implemented?

6. When did class education arise, and what were its root causes?

SECTION 6: EDUCATION IN FEUDAL SOCIETY

An Overview of Feudal Society – Education in European Feudal Society – Education under Christian Dominance – Chivalric Education – University Education – Civic Education – Characteristics – Education in Chinese Feudal Society – Education Exclusive to the Nobility – Education Emphasizing Ritual Propriety – Education for Training Ruling Personnel – The Struggle between Feudal Ideology in Education and Anti-Feudal Forces – Questions

What kind of society is feudal society? This, we must first explain – naturally, briefly.

Feudal society is a society centered on land ownership. In Europe, it was a social system prevalent from the 9th century to the end of the Middle Ages, i.e., the 15th century, in Northern and Western Europe. The characteristic of the feudal system was that land belonged to the great lords (commonly called kings). He granted the land beyond his direct domain as fiefs or territories to lesser lords – commonly called princes; the princes further distributed land to their vassals; the vassals subdivided it to allocate to serfs. The relationship between great lords, lesser lords, and vassals was an absolute command relationship of sovereign and subordinate, with military service as the primary obligation. The serfs were the sole producers at that time; they engaged in agriculture, and from the total production, except for the minimum means of subsistence for themselves, everything was expropriated by the lords; they did not even have the freedom to relocate. Industry at that time was still rudimentary, being the era of handicrafts. These artisans employed apprentices, residing in cities. Although they were also exploited by the lords, they managed independent cities, seemingly opposing the lords. The social order established by these various strata of landowners is called the feudal system. In other words, the feudal system was a social system built upon an Economic Base where land was the most important means of production[72]. The serfs were the sole productive class of this era; all upper classes were parasitic upon them, relying on them for support.

When the feudal system flourished in Western Europe, the power of Western Christianity was already immense. Since allying with Emperor Constantine[73] and becoming the state religion of the Roman Empire, Christianity, with the support of political power, managed to spread widely in Europe. The Roman Church had become the protector of Roman culture. After the invasion of the Germanic barbarians from the south, the Church also educated and guided them in methods of cultivation and manufacturing. Therefore, although the Western Roman Empire fell, the Holy Roman Church remarkably maintained a dominant power like an emperor.

As the Germanic barbarians gradually settled, the Christian Church also served the function of rural organizer. Originally, the Church was the sole repository of past culture; the clergy could read and write, provide medical treatment, and knew the times for sowing and harvesting. Consequently, the Church's influence penetrated deep into the internal life of the people, eventually becoming a political organizer.

---

72 [Special Editor's Note] Means of production, referring to the materials used in production, not the organizations managing production.

73 [Special Editor's Note] Emperor Constantine (Flavius Valerius Constantinus, approx. 280–337), Emperor of ancient Rome (306–337).

The leader of the Roman Church was the Roman Pope. He allied with the most powerful princes and their military forces, aiming to restore the Roman Empire. By the end of the 12th century and the beginning of the 13th century, the Church's power even surpassed that of kings and princes, making them vassals of the Church. Thus, the Church secured its own position even more firmly within the political structure of feudalism. In other words, the Church possessed the authority to rule over the material and spiritual life of all Europe, casting a religious hue over all thought in the feudal era.

As for China's feudal system, it peaked during the Zhou Dynasty and disintegrated during the Spring and Autumn and Warring States periods. But since the Qin Dynasty, although the feudal system no longer existed, feudal forces were not eliminated. The reason lies in the fact that the agricultural economy, which is the essence of the feudal system, did not undergo transformation. Thus, despite dynastic changes, the ingrained habits of feudal society persisted. Consider the current exploitation methods of feudal landlords in the countryside: the smaller the landlord, the more severe and vicious his exploitation methods, the harsher his tenancy conditions. Although there are progressive (bourgeois-style) forms of land ownership, they collude with backward semi-feudal methods of exploiting peasants. Consequently, the general agricultural economy stagnates and declines, and the masses of peasant producers face starvation. So-called public land rent, ostensibly income for public institutions, is actually income for local gentry, who economically are landlords. Moreover, warlords' levies are equivalent to rent collection, and warlords even implement a form of feudal-style military corvée. Therefore, it is erroneous to claim that there are no feudal remnants or feudal exploitation in rural China now, and thus to advocate that the current stage of the Chinese revolution has grown into a socialist revolution.

The foundation of the feudal system was vast feudal estates, and these vast estates were maintained by exploiting the peasants. Corvée labor and taxes took up most of the peasants' time and resources. The hardships of peasants during the Warring States period can be evidenced by the words of Mencius. Mencius said:

"Now, the property allocated to the people is insufficient, above, to serve their parents, and below, to support their wives and children. In good years they live in constant hardship; in bad years they cannot escape death. Thus, they are solely occupied with saving themselves from death and fear they will not succeed; how then can they have leisure to study ritual and righteousness?"[74]

From this, the severity of exploitation suffered by peasants in the feudal era is evident. Even now, remnants of the feudal system still exist everywhere, as landlords, local tyrants, and warlords are everywhere. International imperialism also attempts to collude with feudal forces, thus the exploitation suffered by peasants is even more severe. The current Chinese revolution still must include the task of eliminating feudal forces, precisely for this reason.

The above roughly outlines the general situation of feudal society in Europe and China. Now we continue to discuss education in feudal society, examining how it underwent **Transformation** and how it adapted to the social stage of that time.

First, let's discuss education in medieval Europe.

The Ruling Classes in medieval Europe were, on the one hand, the feudal nobility, and on the other, the Roman Church. The

---

74 [Special Editor's Note] This passage is from the "King Hui of Liang II" chapter of Mencius.

former consisted of secular kings, princes, and knights; the latter was a religious empire, nominally non-secular but in fact also owning land (monastic and church lands accounted for at least one-third of all land) and having princes (bishops, archbishops) little different from ordinary secular princes. These two forces colluded and worked together for their mutual benefit. By the end of the 8th century, the Roman Pope, exploiting Charlemagne's naive vanity, crowned him emperor, restoring the Western Roman Empire. From then on, the secular authority of the Christian Church was sufficient to dominate the kings of the European nations during the peak of feudalism. Although there were conflicts between the Pope and feudal monarchs, these were internal conflicts within the Ruling Class; the general serfs and urban commoners were the oppressed.

The education provided in this social environment included, firstly, Christian education, aimed at training clergy or spreading Christian faith. Although the peasant masses were not entirely without education, illiteracy was still very common, and the education they received focused mainly on preparation for the afterlife, unrelated to real life. Secondly, there was chivalric education, exclusively for the sons of nobles, an institution for training the guards of the feudal class. However, this was education opposed to Christian ecclesiastical power. Although these two types were not entirely consistent, they were the same in being education provided by the Ruling Class and for the benefit of the Ruling Class. The educational aims were, for the former, to uphold church doctrine, and for the latter, to foster loyalty to the king; in short, both remained within the scope of religious morality.

There were two other types of education: university education and civic education. Their origins contained elements of opposition to the Church and even the feudal class. However, by the end of the Middle Ages, they still had not completely shaken off the Church's dominance.

Below, we will provide a more detailed explanation in order.

As mentioned before, schools in medieval Europe bore an extremely heavy religious character. Thus, not only were monastic and cathedral schools clearly ecclesiastical and theological, but other school life and curricula were also imbued with the same ecclesiastical and theological spirit. This Christian education initially used the catechism method, originating before the beginning of the Middle Ages, focusing on moral cultivation; later it became the education of the Church Fathers, vigorously rejecting Greek thought and refusing pagan knowledge; scholars like Augustine[75] even declared that "those who build the kingdom of heaven are the unlearned." Thus, thick clouds of superstition and ignorance, layer upon layer, enveloped Europe under the rule of the Roman Church. By the 8th century, darkness reached its peak, and the word "learning" had almost vanished from the entire European continent.

After Charlemagne was crowned Western Roman Emperor by the Pope, although he established so-called universal education associations, ordering monasteries to set up schools teaching singing, arithmetic, and grammar, and although the most famous scholar of the time, Alcuin[76], notably protected the so-called liberal arts, doctrine still remained the foundation, because religion was, after all, a tool for winning the people's hearts.

---

75 [Special Editor's Note] Augustine (Aurelius Augustinus, 354–430), Bishop of Hippo in North Africa, known as a "Father of the Church."

76 [Special Editor's Note] Alcuin (735–804), English monk and scholar, favored by Charlemagne, managed education for Charlemagne.

Due to the influence of Charlemagne and Alcuin's advocacy for education, roughly three stages of education were formed: (1) Elementary education was taught by parish priests; (2) Secondary education was connected to cathedrals or taught in monasteries; (3) Higher education was limited to "private tuition."

While the power of the Roman Church dominated all of Europe, on the one hand, majestic Gothic cathedrals towered everywhere; on the other hand, poems praising mysterious superstitions were sung everywhere. By the 11th century, the official learning of Scholasticism developed to prove the miracles of the Bible and the creation of heaven and earth. This philosophy attempted to use logic or dialectics to provide proofs for religious beliefs, attempting to give a rational basis to the previously mysterious, world-fleeing monastic worldview. Therefore, while on one hand it showed a tendency to reject ecclesiastical authority and emphasize reason, in reality, it was like Charlemagne's revival of ancient learning in the 8th century, utilizing grammar and rhetoric for the Church. Scholastic philosophy's study of theology also utilized Greek philosophy to address church problems. Originally, at this time, the eastern Islamic faith was advancing aggressively, and the Christian Church was in a defensive position. To counter this, it reluctantly had to bow to grammar, rhetoric, and logic, which it had previously regarded as hindrances to faith, and temporarily enlist them as weapons. Scholasticism arose in response to this opportunity.

Although the universities that emerged in the late Middle Ages originated from the demands of social life and possessed the character of independent academic institutions, because the Church still held supreme power at that time, a theology faculty had to be established. Even outside universities, theological research was extremely active. Although universities also had law and medical faculties, famous ones like the University of Paris and Oxford University emphasized theology as their main subject. In the latter half of the 12th century, schools supervised by Christian bishops implemented theology-centered education. Other episcopal and church schools did the same.

Education so thoroughly dominated by Christian doctrine naturally lacked what is called the scientific spirit. Conversely, all scientific research, pursuit of knowledge, and even the raising of questions were regarded as sins. Those who violated the prohibitions were severely punished by the Inquisition. People only needed faith and prayer; all problems were to be solved by God's omnipotence. Thus, by this time, the organizational function of the early Church had ended, its past role as a storehouse of knowledge was lost, and it had now become the source of the most obstinate thought representing medieval darkness and conservatism.

Other schools under the control of the Christian Church included grammar schools and song schools. Grammar schools taught Latin, while song schools taught singing and reading. After the 14th century, many schools were attached to small monasteries. Wherever two monks lived together, one would teach at the grammar school level and the other at the song school level (i.e., lower grades). These schools dominated elementary education in the 14th and early 15th centuries. Therefore, even by the 15th century (i.e., 500 years ago), the Christian spirit remained a central focus of education.

Women's education at that time took place in convent schools[77], learning music, handicrafts, Latin, etc. After graduation, they received secluded, isolated cultivation in ladies' private chambers, still not escaping the character of medieval Christianity.

---

77 [Special Editor's Note] Convent schools were schools attached to nunneries.

Another type of education for the Ruling Class was chivalric education. But this was education opposed to Christian ecclesiastical power, aiming not to train clergy as a form of labor power but to train knights as a form of labor power.

After the feudal system began to be implemented among the Germanic peoples, knights appeared alongside the princes, ready to serve the king in times of trouble. Although the Germanic peoples were influenced by the Christian Church and embraced Christianity, their barbaric nature was not easily subdued by world-weary ecclesiastical power. Moreover, after the Dark Ages of the 10th century, Charlemagne's empire had already fragmented, and the Christian Church was thoroughly corrupt. Thus, the worldly, enterprising "savagery" of the Germanic peoples became even more dissatisfied with the reclusive power of the Church. The so-called education of knights subsequently flourished alongside the development of the feudal system.

Regarding the relationship between knights and monarchs at that time, it was bound by close obligations. That is, the monarch had the responsibility to support and protect his vassals, and the knights had the obligation to be loyal and to serve the monarch. Furthermore, because the Germanic peoples still had remnants of matrilineal systems, preserving a custom of respecting women (the habit of respecting women among Europeans today is a legacy of that time), the aim of chivalric education was to serve the lord and protect women. The subjects taught were the seven skills of riding, swimming, archery, fencing, hunting, chess, and poetry, also emphasizing the practice of social intercourse and the encouragement of a sense of honor. Its nature was directly opposite to Christian education and was beyond the reach of religious influence. However, because the Christian Church's secular authority was, after all, long established, even in chivalric education, it was necessary to study doctrine and swear to protect

Christianity.

Yet, it was precisely this chivalric education that was truly necessary for the feudal class itself. Moreover, being a knight was an honor that could be conferred upon young nobles. Sometimes commoners could hope for this honor if they performed exceptional military feats.

As for university education, it did not originate from the class domination of the Church or the state. Before the emergence of universities in medieval Europe, higher educational institutions could only be found in monastic schools. But these were not adapting to the demands of general society; they were merely institutions for training clergy. After Eastern civilization invaded Western Europe, and the industry and commerce of the Muslims developed globally, the educational institutions of the Church could no longer meet the demands of real social life. Thus, naturally, academic educational institutions responding to social needs emerged in various cultural centers. Although this organization, born from social control, had to submit to Church control to avoid persecution, it was by no means the successor to monastic schools; on the contrary, it took an oppositional stance towards the Church. Therefore, the nature of university education was quite consistent with the purpose of broad social production. The subjects established in universities, such as medicine and law, stood completely outside the scope of Christian education, and scholars were extremely enthusiastic.

Finally, civic education, i.e., the education of merchants and artisans. Originally, wherever feudal lords' castles and church buildings were located, specialized artisans and traders dealing in local products appeared, forming permanent markets, which eventually developed into the new commercial cities of the later Middle Ages. Especially after the failure of the Crusades, the

Pope's authority gradually declined, and the knightly class also tended to decline, while on the other hand, the restoration of traffic with the East led to the influx of various new knowledge into Western Europe. As a result, alongside the development of the aforementioned independent universities, there was the simultaneous rise of cities everywhere. The merchants and artisans in the cities, because they did not receive adequate legal protection, formed guilds for mutual aid and promotion of their trades. Therefore, the establishment of guilds placed them in an oppositional position to the state and Church of the time. This shared the same social dynamic as the medieval universities becoming independent organizations. They used city funds to establish a special kind of school, specifically teaching practical knowledge to their children. These schools, relative to monastic schools, were called civic schools. However, due to interference from the clergy, they failed to develop fully. Their types included writing schools and Latin schools, while the guild apprenticeship system, which continued into modern times, can be regarded as the more organized educational system for practical life and action at that time.

To summarize, education in European feudal society exhibited the following characteristics: (1) Church-dominated education held the most power. (2) The peasant masses were serfs, somewhere between slaves and free people; they were tied to the land and sold along with it; they lived a monotonous life season after season, year after year, in the same lonely and squalid villages, the same cold and dark huts, eating the same black bread and salted meat. Such a bleak peasant life naturally received no cultural enrichment. Even if they could read and write, it was only for the convenience of accepting Christian doctrine, to win God's favor and pray for rewards in the afterlife, offering no real benefit to their actual lives. (3) The so-called anti-ecclesiastical chivalric education was exclusively enjoyed by the feudal nobility and served their interests. (4) Although universities emerged as independent social groups opposing the Church, they were limited to a group of intellectuals persecuted by Christianity due to religious reasons and had little to do with the interests of the peasants at that time; moreover, later, many universities were founded or supported by feudal nobles, and with the emergence of modern nation-states, universities came under state control and lost their independent character. (5) Only civic education represented the education of the emerging merchant and artisan class opposing the feudal Ruling Class, but it was merely in its infancy, its full development awaiting the future.

Such education, although class-based, was no longer education for all humanity and society. In other transformation education can be found everywhere.

Now, let us examine education in Chinese feudal society.

Education in Chinese feudal society can more clearly be said to be exclusively for the nobility, education emphasizing rituals and music, and education for training ruling personnel.

The legendary Xiang, Xu, Xue, etc., were merely places for supporting the aged and educating the sons of nobles.

After the feudal system was established, peasants cultivated their allocated fields while also cultivating the public fields; their wives and children also worked alongside them. They had no opportunity for education.

Books like the Rites of Zhou, forged by Han dynasty scholars, are certainly unreliable. But even according to these forged records, it is evident that those receiving education were still nobles. For example, the Rites of Zhou states:

"The Master... taught the sons of the state; all the sons of nobles studied there. The Grand Master of Music mastered the methods of the Chengjun school to administer the educational administration of the established state and unite the sons of the state. The Grand Director kept the register of scholars, awaiting the summoning of the various sons."

Also, the King Wen as Son and Hei chapter in The Book of Rites says:

"In all learning, the heir apparent and the scholars must do so at the proper seasons."

Here, the terms "sons of nobles," "sons of the state," "various sons," and even "heir apparent and scholars" all refer to the sons of princes, ministers, and officials.

The legendary subjects were: rites, music, archery, charioteering, writing, and mathematics. From the ancient saying, "Three hundred dignified ceremonies, three thousand rules of etiquette," we can know that the content of education at that time was only moral education, only education for "strictly upholding the distinction between superior and inferior" to maintain the feudal social order.

Women's education, according to the Pattern of the Family, was roughly as follows: at seven, girls did not share a mat with boys; at ten, they did not go out the door; they learned the womanly virtue of gentle obedience, practiced sericulture, spinning, weaving, and other women's work, and also learned the rituals for wine, vessels, cooking, and ancestral sacrifices. At fifteen, they had their hair pinned (signifying adulthood); at twenty, they married. As for noble women, they received education in the palace or ancestral temples. The important subjects for women's education were womanly virtue, womanly speech, womanly appearance, and womanly work.

But we cannot believe these records are reliable. Because under corvée labor, peasants and their wives and children had no opportunity for education, let alone women's education?

The purpose of education at that time was to train governing personnel. Consider this saying from the Analects:

"When engaged in official service, one should, time permitting, pursue learning; when engaged in learning, one should, time permitting, undertake public service."

Confucius's reply to Fan Chi more clearly proves the separation between education and actual productive labor at that time:

"Fan Chi asked about grain. The Master said, "I am not as good as an old farmer." He asked about gardening. The Master said, "I am not as good as an old gardener." Fan Chi went out. The Master said, "What a small man Fan Xu is! When those above love ritual, the common people dare not be disrespectful; when those above love righteousness, the common people dare not be disobedient; when those above love trustworthiness, the common people dare not be insincere. If it were like this, the people from all directions would come carrying their children on their backs—what need is there to talk about grain!"

By the Warring States period, there were statements like that of Mencius:

"Some labor with their minds, and some labor with their strength. Those who labor with their minds govern others; those who labor with their strength are governed by others."

And the living conditions of the so-called laborers at that time were just as Mencius described: "... We are barely able to save the dying, fearing we cannot meet the need; how could we possibly have any leisure to attend to rites and righteousness?" They certainly did not receive education, nor did they need this kind of ornamental education that "does not fill the belly nor warm the body."

From this, it can be seen that during the Zhou Dynasty, and the Spring and Autumn and Warring States periods, i.e., the era when the feudal system prevailed and began to disintegrate, education was already an unequal education distinguishing the noble from the base, and was already education far removed from social labor. Yet now some people say "... the Chinese people have historically been equal," and "At the same time, every early spring, people in the villages, regardless of gender or age, go to school to listen to lectures from early morning until returning late at night, also emphasizing universal education"[78]. Others believe that Zhou Dynasty education aimed at "cultivating the complete person," that it was "commoner education" that "transformed the people with virtue"[79]. Is this not an incorrigibly major error?

By the Han Dynasty, Emperor Wen began establishing Erudites. Emperor Wu rejected the Hundred Schools of Thought and revered Confucianism. Emperor Wu established the Imperial University, appointed Erudites for the Five Classics, set fifty disciples, and also ordered commanaderies and principalities throughout the empire to establish schools. Emperor Zhao selected worthy and talented scholars of letters, increasing the disciples of the Erudites to one hundred. Emperor Xuan

---

78 Shu Xincheng, General Theory of Education, Zhonghua Book Company, pp. 19–51.

79 Fan Shoukang, Discussion on Zhou Dynasty Education, History of Education, Commercial Press.

increased the number of disciples of the Erudites to two hundred. Emperor Yuan, favoring Confucianism, set the number at a thousand. Under Emperor Cheng, the disciples of the Imperial University increased to three thousand. Emperor Guangwu built the Imperial University and appointed Erudites for the Five Classics. Under Emperor Zhi, the number of itinerant scholars increased further, reaching over thirty thousand. Who were these so-called disciples of the Erudites and Imperial University students? Certainly, the children of officials and nobles constituted the majority. As for the children of peasants who "... serve the government offices, provide corvée labor... furthermore suffer from floods and droughts, harsh exactions and tyrannical violence... sell their fields and dwellings, and even their children and grandchildren..." (as described by Chao Cuo), they were clearly excluded.

"The thirty thousand Imperial University students of the Eastern Han dynasty spoke boldly and debated deeply, not concealing the faults of the powerful; high officials avoided their criticisms." (Huang Zongxi). This shows that the purpose of the Imperial University students' studies did not deviate from the path of "governing."

During the reign of Emperor Taizong of the Tang Dynasty, schools were greatly promoted. A Confucian temple was established in the National University, Confucian scholars from across the empire were extensively recruited to serve as academic officials, and 1,200 additional school buildings were added to nurture the worthy and capable of the empire. The school system at that time included, in the capital, six schools and two institutes like the School for the Sons of the State, the Imperial University, and the Chongwen Institute. The subjects included the Book of Rites, Spring and Autumn Annals, Book of Songs, Book of Documents, etc., also including law and mathematics. Enrollment was limited to sons of high officials and outstanding individuals among the commoners. Local areas had fixed quotas for students based on prefecture and county. Local officials and commoners could all enroll, and the subjects were entirely based on the various classics.

The School for the Sons of the State in the Song Dynasty was exclusively for the sons of officials. The School for the Sons of the State in the Ming Dynasty was for both outstanding sons of officials and commoners. The Clan Schools, Imperial University, and Directorate of Education in the Qing Dynasty were all for the sons of officials.

After the Han Dynasty, there were systems of recommendation and imperial examinations. These served two purposes: one was to select officials and also to control scholars; the other was to absorb social forces, thereby helping to maintain social order.

In the early Han Dynasty, scholars were selected through three methods: Worthy and Virtuous, Filial and Incorrupt, and Disciples of the Erudites. The commanderies and principalities would carefully assess the learning and conduct of Confucian scholars to decide selection. During the Wei period, this was changed to the Nine-Rank System, where a Rectifier in each commandery and city would evaluate individuals and assign them a rank from top-upper to lower-lower, before sending them to a Grand Rectifier for assessment by the same method. Its malpractices led to "no humble families in the upper ranks, no noble clans in the lower ranks." By the early Sui Dynasty, the method shifted to selecting scholars through poetry and rhapsodies, and policy questions. In the Tang Dynasty's imperial examinations, scholars, regardless of wealth or poverty, could take the examinations administered by the prefectures and counties. At that time, they tested both poetry/rhapsodies and "memorization of the classics," neither of which met the actual needs of society. This trend peaked in the late Tang and the Two Song Dynasties, leading to the situation where "the drawback of poetry and rhapsodies led to frivolity and ostentation; the drawback of memorization led to rote learning." Furthermore, malpractices like bribery, smuggling cribs, and collusion had already emerged in the Tang Dynasty. The Northern Song Dynasty selected scholars entirely based on mastery of the classics and policy discourses. By the Ming and Qing Dynasties, the eight-legged essay on the Four Books and Five Classics became the examination method. This proves that Ming and Qing society still required Confucian doctrine to maintain social order. And since Confucian doctrine precisely represented the consciousness of feudal society, it further proves that Ming and Qing society still preserved the remnants of the feudal system.

After the mid-Qing Dynasty, influenced by European capitalism, the examination system introduced categories like Vast Learning and Vast Words and Special Category for Statecraft. In 1898 (the 24th year of the Guangxu reign), new measures were implemented, such as establishing schools, abolishing the eight-legged essay, and using current affairs and policy discourses in examinations. In 1901, academies across the country were converted into schools at various levels; however, the curriculum still focused on the Four Books, Five Classics, and the core principles of the Three Bonds and Five Constant Virtues, supplemented by historical mirrors and Chinese and foreign political arts. In 1905, the imperial examinations were completely abolished, and the following year, the educational aims were proclaimed as loyalty to the sovereign, reverence for Confucius, emphasis on the public good, emphasis on martial spirit, and emphasis on practical studies. In an edict issued that year, it was explicitly stated:

Schools shall take Chinese learning as the foundation and Western learning for its practical application; they shall cultivate general talents, prioritizing moral education; and they shall determine their orientation based on loyalty to the sovereign, reverence for Confucius, emphasis on martial spirit, and emphasis on practical studies.

Not only was this true for late Qing education, but even the educational aims announced by the Ministry of Education in the first year of the Republic of China (1912) was still "to focus on moral education, supplemented by utilitarian education and military-citizen education, and to complete this morality through aesthetic education." The educational aims issued by Yuan Shikai in the fourth year of the Republic of China (1915) was "patriotism, emphasis on martial spirit, reverence for practicality, following Confucius and Mencius, stress on self-governance, and caution against rash advancement." It particularly emphasized:

All heterodox doctrines and violent acts that can initiate the beginnings of rebellion must be rejected unheard, avoided like a torrent, and detested like a sparrowhawk chasing small birds.

Even recently, we can still often hear phrases like "restoring ancient morality." Some primary schools even persist in using books like the Four Books, Five Classics, Classic for Girls, Hundred Family Surnames, Thousand Character Classic, and Dragon-Lashed Steed as textbooks[80].

---

[80] The Shanghai Republic Daily, December 16, 1929, reported: "The Anhui Department of Education yesterday issued an order to all counties to ban the use of the _Four Books_ and _Five Classics_ in primary schools. The text stated: '...According to reports from our department's inspectors, while many primary schools in our province do use approved textbooks according to regulations, there are also numerous instances where Four Books, Five Classics, Classic for Girls, Hundred Family Surnames, Thousand Character Classic, Dragon-Lashed Steed, etc., are used as textbooks. These books are either too

As for privately established academies and private schools after the Song Dynasty, although they were considered relatively widespread institutions for popular education, few common people actually attended them, and the "curriculum" was biased towards classical meaning, based on the standards set by the imperial examinations. Especially in private schools, the readings were always the Three Character Classic, Poems of the Prodigy, Young Learner's Forest of Words, and the Four Books and Five Classics, all books transmitting feudal morality. The highest achievement was merely knowing some "loyalty, filial piety, chastity, and righteousness."

In essence, judging from China's educational systems (including schools and selection mechanisms) and educational spirit since ancient times, they were indeed everywhere imbued with feudal meaning, with the general populace having little opportunity for education. The educational content emphasized morality, as Xunzi said, "Confucians model themselves on the ancient kings and exalt ritual principles"; the Analects said, "It is rare for one who does not like to cause disorder to be fond of transgressing against superiors." Using recent legal terminology, this is called "still venerating the Confucian classics." The purpose of this education was to train officials and local gentry—the "scholar-officials"—to assist the feudal class in carrying out exploitation and maintaining order.

Without eliminating feudal forces, feudal concepts in education cannot be eradicated. Therefore, revolutionary educators should participate in the struggle to sweep away all remnants of the feudal system—naturally, this must be linked to the struggle

---

profound in language and unsuitable for primary school teaching materials; or their meanings are obsolete and out of keeping with the contemporary currents; some are utterly meaningless and only useful for rote memorization. If their use is allowed to continue, the harm to children will indeed be profound...'"

against imperialism.

Questions

1. Discuss the relationship between education and social classes in medieval Europe.

2. What is the nature of Christian education? Critically evaluate the current missionary education in China.

3. How did universities originate in medieval Europe?

4. Chinese history often describes the Zhou Dynasty as an era of fully developed culture and institutions. Do you find this credible? Were the Chinese people truly equal in history?

5. Your hometown likely still has many private schools. Can you investigate what they actually teach children?

6. What are the feudal concepts in education? Provide concrete examples.

SECTION 7: EDUCATION IN CAPITALIST SOCIETY

An Overview of Capitalist Society – Comparison with Feudal Education – The So-Called Characteristics of New Education: 1. Integration with Labor; 2. Scientification; 3. Socialization; 4. Neutralization; 5. Internationalization – Our Critique – Two Major Transformations: 1. Monopolization; 2. Commercialization – Three Major Contradictions: 1. Between Individualization and Commercialization; 2. Between Labor and Education; 3. Between Free Research and Dominant Ideology – Questions

Capitalist society is the society we all live in now—referring to the whole world. This society is also called bourgeois society because its pillars are the capitalists, while the extras are the laborers. These are the two fundamental classes; it is a society where the bourgeoisie and the the proletariat stand opposed. It is also the era in which the form of class struggle has become the most acute in all history, and thus an era in which a dramatic change is destined to occur in history, moving from class society towards the elimination of classes and the formation of a human society.

The characteristics of capitalist society, stated succinctly, can be listed as three points: (1) commodity production; (2) monopoly of the means of production by a few capitalists; (3) wage labor. A detailed explanation of these points should be left to the _New Economics_ in this series and will not be elaborated here.

What needs to be addressed promptly now is what is particularly distinctive about education in capitalist society, and to what stage its Transformation has progressed.

First, we can discuss the differences between education in capitalist society and that in feudal society, as these two societies followed closely one after the other.

In Section 3, discussing "Several Distortions of Education," I already mentioned them. First, in the feudal era, no education was provided to the common people, whereas in the capitalist era, compulsory education is implemented for all nationals. Second, education in the feudal era was almost solely moral education, while education in the capitalist era expanded its scope to include the transmission of knowledge and skills for daily life. Naturally, there are other differences that could be listed, but these two are fundamental and most important. Why such differences? I also offered an explanation there. Namely, the reason for the first point is that in the feudal era, where agricultural production was the main social industry, the common people had no need to study learning. But within the capitalist economic organization, this economic structure itself requires literacy; hence, the universal education is solely for cultivating the labor power of the nation, not for the happiness of the nationals themselves. The reason for the second point is that the feudal system was one that respected ritual propriety, hence education emphasized morality to cultivate law-abiding, good subjects. But in capitalist society, on the one hand, the economic organization itself requires knowledge and skills; on the other hand, to win the hearts of the laborers, it is also necessary to emphasize labor education.

Naturally, there is no need here to add much explanation. However, regarding the reason for imparting necessary knowledge and skills for daily life, a few supplementary words can be added. It is because capitalist society is a society of naked exploitation, utterly devoid of sentiment. Therefore, what it needs is precisely this kind of knowledge and ability, not morality.

And please recognize the face of capitalist society:

The bourgeoisie has played a most revolutionary role in history.

Wherever it has got the upper hand, the bourgeoisie has put an end to all feudal, patriarchal, idyllic relations. It has pitilessly torn asunder the motley feudal ties that bound man to his "natural superiors," and has left remaining no other nexus between man and man than naked self-interest, than callous "cash payment." It has drowned the most heavenly ecstasies of religious fervor, of chivalrous enthusiasm, of philistine sentimentalism, in the icy water of egotistical calculation. It has resolved personal worth into exchange value, and in place of the numberless indefeasible chartered freedoms, has set up that single, unconscionable freedom — Free Trade. In one word, for exploitation, veiled by religious and political illusions, it has substituted naked, shameless, direct, brutal exploitation.

The bourgeoisie has stripped of its halo every occupation hitherto honored and looked up to with reverent awe. It has converted the physician, the lawyer, the priest, the poet, the man of science, into its paid wage laborers.

The bourgeoisie has torn away from the family its sentimental veil, and has reduced the family relation to a mere money relation. (The Communist Manifesto)[81]

81[Special Editor's Note] The above quotation is translated today as:

The bourgeoisie, historically, has played a most revolutionary part.

The bourgeoisie, wherever it has got the upper hand, has put an end to all feudal, patriarchal, idyllic relations. It has pitilessly torn asunder the motley feudal ties that bound man to his "natural superiors", and has left remaining no other nexus between man and man than naked self-interest, than callous "cash payment". It has drowned the most heavenly ecstasies of religious fervour, of chivalrous enthusiasm, of

Think about it! With such a cruel and merciless face, could it possibly need to stress hypocritical morality? Therefore, the reason why education in the capitalist era emphasizes "necessary knowledge and skills for daily life" is abundantly clear.

Earlier, when discussing the Transformation of education, I listed five characteristics and have already discussed them one by one. Those five characteristics are particularly apt and prominent when observed in the education of capitalist society. There is no need to reiterate them here with citations. However, eulogistic discourses praising capitalist education often reach our ears, indeed causing many educators and ordinary people to develop superstitions and erroneous understandings. This is something that must be dissected to clarify the truth.

The eulogistic discourses for capitalist society's education are precisely the eulogistic discourses for modern new education. Here, five main arguments can be listed.

The first argument is the so-called integration with labor, or integration with life.

---

philistine sentimentalism, in the icy water of egotistical calculation. It has resolved personal worth into exchange value, and in place of the numberless indefeasible chartered freedoms, has set up that single, unconscionable freedom — Free Trade. In one word, for exploitation, veiled by religious and political illusions, it has substituted naked, shameless, direct, brutal exploitation.

The bourgeoisie has stripped of its halo every occupation hitherto honoured and looked up to with reverent awe. It has converted the physician, the lawyer, the priest, the poet, the man of science, into its paid wage labourers.

The bourgeoisie has torn away from the family its sentimental veil, and has reduced the family relation to a mere money relation. (See Selected Works of Marx and Engels, Vol. 1, People's Publishing House, 1995 edition, pp. 274–275.)

As mentioned before, since the division of society into classes, education separated from labor, becoming one characteristic of Transformation education. Education in feudal society was precisely such education separated from labor. But when it came to capitalist society, especially since the beginning of the 20th century, we have seen labor elements gradually incorporated into education. Needless to say, there have been notably influential facilities in the system like work-study education, practical education, and even vocational education; even in the curriculum content, scholars are no longer taught to despise labor. Consequently, some educators have stepped forward to proclaim: the old education of the past involved dead reading, while modern new education respects labor; the old education of the past was bookish and distant from society, while modern new education is practical and connected to social life. Thence emerged theories like "education is life" and the school as the center of social culture.

But does reality match what the eulogists say? Have education and labor truly reunited in modern new education? Have school education and social life truly merged into one?

Regarding this point, I believe it is worthy of study, so we might as well start from the beginning on the issue of labor and education.

In Primitive Communist Society, everyone had an equal obligation to labor, as discussed before. This obligation was not detestable. In fact, rather than calling it an obligation, it was more accurately a matter of course. Just like eating and sleeping, which are neither considered obligations nor rights, labor, in their view, was simply a necessary and proper activity. Education was a social undertaking conducted for the "preservation of the race." Therefore, labor and education, both absolutely necessary for survival, naturally stood in an inseparable relationship. In Primitive Communist Society, labor and education were thus completely combined. In other words, so-called education merely involved imparting to the youth "how one should labor for survival," making them understand it.

However, since the emergence of private property and the realization of exploiting others' labor, the concepts of disliking labor and despising labor developed accordingly. By the time state systems appeared and class domination relations became legalized in the era of Greece and Rome, the view of labor as base reached its extreme. Try turning the first page of educational history. It records the arrogant educational ideals of the Ruling Class who ensured their livelihood by exploiting others' labor. They said: "One is educated not for the means of living, but to give meaning to leisure." The Greek word _Schole_ means leisure. Their entire lives were times of leisure. On the one hand, they adorned themselves with the "golden crown of being cultured," considering themselves special, noble humans; on the other hand, they made the ruled also hold this belief and willingly remain inferior.

Thus, education and labor separated. "Education" belonged exclusively to the Ruling Class, and "labor" exclusively to the ruled class, as described in Section 2. The sole purpose of this separation was exploitation. Those bourgeois scholars actually attempt to defend this separation with the sophistry of the division of labor theory—what a waste of effort! Because the reason for the separation was confessed most honestly on the very first page of educational history.

Furthermore, educational power always remains in the hands of the Ruling Class. They consistently proceed based on the doctrine of separating education from labor. However, the result of implementing this education within the Roman Empire was the emergence of countless freemen who despised labor, ultimately leading to the decline of productive forces, a major cause of the empire's collapse. This can be considered the first outcome arising from the separation of education and labor.

In the Middle Ages, to revive productive forces, the monasticism of the St. Benedictines[82] championed the theory of "the sanctity of labor." But this call to respect labor only proved effective in consolidating the foundation of the feudal system, as recorded in educational history. And that this call was issued by the Ruling Class—which despised labor—to the ruled class, goes without saying. Consider what Christianity told the ruled class: "Since our ancestor Adam sinned and was expelled from the Garden of Eden by God, humans must labor with sweat pouring down their faces."

The result of implementing an obscurantist policy towards the productive ruled class, instilling a fatalistic mindset, was that there were neither inventions nor progress in production technology. The decline of the countryside in the late feudal period was thus inevitable. This can be considered the second outcome arising from the separation of education and labor.

How did the modern bourgeoisie deal with the separation of labor and education? From the above, we already know that the bourgeoisie, compelled by the necessities of the production organization itself, had to provide education to the laboring class as well. Consequently, some educational theorists shouted praises of the new education's integration with labor and practicality. True, from one perspective, this fact indeed proves that

---

82 [Special Editor's Note] The St. Benedictines, a religious order founded by the Italian monk St. Benedict. This order was very influential in Europe from the 6th to the 13th–14th centuries.

capitalism is the precursor system to socialism. Because the re-combination of labor and education can well be regarded as a harbinger of the return to the communist system before the emergence of domination relations, where labor and education were inseparable. Originally, exploitation relies entirely on deception. Separating education from labor was solely to facilitate deception. Now, giving education to laborers and linking education with practical labor not only makes deception difficult to practice but also easily provokes resistance against the Ruling Class. Isn't this an extremely risky venture? Yes, the **Ruling Class** is indeed aware that this is a great risk. So they devised a clever plan. That is, they aim to give the minimum of education on one hand, while extracting the maximum of labor on the other, as the price for connecting education and labor. Indeed, all the bourgeoisie's educational systems are designed to achieve the greatest effect with the smallest expenditure. Haven't you heard the open confession of those running labor education in Japan?

Yet some people, treating "a chicken feather as a warrant arrow," loudly proclaim the integration of education and labor and its practicality! Please do not be fooled. In reality, what I refer to here as the combination of education and labor is merely the minimum literacy required by the production organization, and it will not exceed this level. Therefore, in principle, it still does not depart from the stance of separating education and labor. Because this separation is the sole necessary condition for exploitation. Moreover, the bourgeoisie seizes the opportunity to use the literacy provided to make the laboring class convert to and respect the bourgeoisie, and strives to prevent the laboring class from seeing anything beyond this.

This is the truth behind the so-called integration of education with labor or socialization!

The second argument is the so-called scientification. This is a cry that rings out to the heavens, and perhaps you too find it quite pleasing to hear.

However, as discussed in the section on "Efficacy of Education" (Section 4) quoting Gongpu's passage, this is also inappropriate.

Here, what has already been said, such as that scientific education fundamentally cannot impact the the proletariat, and that the scientific method has been reduced to near impotence, naturally need not be repeated to avoid redundancy. What needs to be said here pertains to another aspect: to investigate whether education has truly been scientified, and to what degree.

We see that evolved modern states, in their monopoly and imperialism, employ very scientific precise calculations, designs, and methods, and are already implementing them step by step. However, if one consequently infers that similarly complete scientific theories and methods can be seen in the monopoly and imperialism of cultivation, then one cannot help but be disappointed. The cultivation movements of various imperialist countries have already reached a dead end; in other words, the scientific method has reached a dead end. Particularly, the cultivation movement of the dollar imperialism, the United States, which boasts of being scientific and efficient everywhere, has resulted in pure one-hundred-percent Americanism, and even produced the Monkey Trial, penalizing those who taught evolution. The Kentucky state legislature passed a bill prohibiting the use of public funds to pay the salaries of anyone teaching evolution or Darwinism (see Upton Sinclair, The Goose-step, p. 352). Such unscientific, childish actions—are they not utterly laughable! The most reactionary, yet self-proclaimed absorber of the essentials of socialism—i.e., the essentials of social science—

Mussolini's[83] cultivation movement actually stipulated in the Fascist constitution that "one must worship God morning and evening." I ask you, what scientific method is there in this? Most recently, in September 1929, Japanese imperialism conducted its so-called Total Cultivation Mobilization Movement, aiming to clarify group consciousness and revitalize the national spirit. Its implementation methods included: (1) Every morning, one must worship from afar towards the Imperial Palace; (2) Morning and evening, one must worship the gods and Buddhas; (3) One must abstain from alcohol and tobacco; (4) One must use domestic products, etc. I ask you, what science is there in this?

To be frank: cultivation (including education) in the era of modern state decline is unscientific.

Bourgeois science has long been "dead and buried." In the modern era, only the cultivation of the the proletariat can inherit the developmental lineage of science since the 18th century. The social sciences, which arose in the 19th century and had already reached an impasse by the beginning of the 20th century, only found an opportunity for rebirth through the standpoint of the the proletariat, thereby explaining the process of the collapse of the modern capitalist organization and seeking to reconstruct the organization of social existence. In cultivation, whether in method or content, only on the side of the the proletariat can there be scientific growth.

Originally, the grasp of scientific method was a feature the bourgeoisie boasted of. However, once the scientific method transferred into the hands of the the proletariat, the bourgeoisie resorted to American one-hundred-percentism and Italian and Japanese god-and-Buddha worship. This is certainly not solely an

---

83 [Special Editor's Note] Benito Mussolini (1883–1945), Italian dictator.

issue of cultivation but is connected to the fact that scientific attempts within the bourgeois structure have already become impotent. A hundred years ago, when the bourgeois state was building its new organization based on the consciousness of natural science, the church interfered vigorously, trying to exclude science from their cultivation. In the modern era, the bourgeoisie finds itself in the position of the church, strenuously refusing the study of emerging social sciences from their cultivation. A hundred years ago, the bourgeoisie, to promote the development of its own class, demanded science with all its strength, excluded ecclesiastical domination with all its strength, and overthrew compulsory church worship in various states. But now, to ensure the eternal preservation of its class domination, the bourgeoisie, as seen in America's prohibition of evolution and Italy and Japan's compulsory worship, does not hesitate to desperately adopt methods that contradict its own modern beliefs in its domination and cultivation. This clearly shows that the class structure itself has lost the support of the free scientific method. I ask you, in what aspects has modern state new education been scientified, and to what degree?

To be more concrete, when the bourgeoisie was rising and possessed revolutionary praxis, in opposition to the feudal nobility and church, it championed materialism and atheism, which were scientific. But by the latter half of the 19th century, as the bourgeoisie ceased its revolutionary praxis, bourgeois thinkers tended towards idealist, mystical, and decadent ideologies, denouncing materialism and atheism as a disgrace to humanity, and increasing the degree of conscious deception of the ruled class. In other words, the degree of being co-opted philosophy increased. Especially before the objective realities of the extreme destruction of the First World War, economic crisis, social crises, and the fateful collapse process of the capitalist system, the bourgeoisie increasingly could not help but feel despair, doubt, fear, and pessimism. Consequently, things like necromancy, spirit photographs[84], and even spiritual civilization and Eastern culture, created a complete mess, a foul and murky atmosphere. On November 24, 1929, a Shanghai newspaper even carried news about divine power healing illnesses. The original text is quoted below to illustrate a glimpse of the superstition among Americans practicing one-hundred-percentism:

"Associated Press, 23rd, Boston: In recent weeks, rumors suddenly spread that within the Holy Cross Cemetery in Malden, there was divine power that could cure illnesses, with several hundred cases already cured. This caused a sensation across the country, with over 50,000 visitors daily from various places. Consequently, Cardinal O'Connell today specifically ordered a ban on visits; hereafter, except for funerals, no one is allowed entry."

During this period, in education, there was also much talk of abstract, spiritual, empty, and mystical concepts, such as cultivating national morality, promoting world peace, "labor-capital harmony," "moderate and steady," "vast and compassionate," "filial piety, fraternal duty, loyalty, and trustworthiness"—all static, abstract concepts. The most obvious example, again, is the Japanese educational authorities who, after arresting Communists in 1928, advocated "thought guidance," and actually sought to establish university lectureships on Japanese Buddhist History, Oriental Art History, Oriental Ethics, Japanese Intellectual History, National Morality, etc., and to encourage the study of so-called spiritual sciences like philosophy, ethics, religion, and history, aiming to popularize idealist thought

---

84 [Special Editor's Note] "Necromancy," "spirit photographs": These were "spirit communication techniques" played with by "spiritualists" in modern capitalist society, claiming that the living could converse with the souls of the dead and photograph the souls of the deceased.

and expel materialist thought, which was the root of dangerous thought. This is truly a reversal tendency in modern politics, a characteristic of so-called feudal moral education.

Thus, looking at it this way, the main tendency of education in modern states is only unscientific; it cannot be seen as scientific. If one claims that pedagogy has become a science, that educational surveys, educational statistics, intelligence tests, vocational selection, etc., are all scientific methods, and that learning methods, teaching methods, etc., are all based on scientific research, then I would ask the reader to refer back to the section on "Efficacy of Education" to see how much utility scientific education actually possesses.

Merely coating the exterior with a layer of "scientific" paint, while the core remains an "unscientific" foundation, cannot be called scientification.

The third argument is the so-called popularization, or massification and socialization.

Proponents base this on the fact that in European and American imperialist countries, there is universal education, continuation education, adult education, and the gradual abolition of the dual-track system in favor of a national education that is equal for all citizens. In China recently, there has also been active implementation of literacy campaigns, mass education, and worker-peasant education. These indeed contrast with the aristocratic privileged education and official-training education of the feudal era and can be considered characteristic of the new era's education.

However, we have long known that the reason why the modern—capitalist—era implements universal education and vigorously promotes social education is, as described in the previous section, due to the demands of the capitalist economic organization itself, arising from the interests of the bourgeoisie, and not truly intended to universalize the right to education for all humanity. This we have already correctly dissected and will no longer be deceived.

Education in capitalist society is not only not popularized or socialized; on the contrary, its autocratization and monopolization are patently obvious facts.

Originally, although free competition was necessary in the early stages of capitalism, once it enters its highest—and final—stage, monopoly becomes necessary. First, there is the concentration of capital, followed by the concentration of so-called public opinion manufacturing. Apart from civilized tools like newspapers, films, and radio broadcasting being entirely monopolized by capitalists as instruments for ideological domination, educational undertakings such as schools, science, and even physical education are all controlled by capitalists. The definition of a school, besides being a place for cultivating special labor power, can more aptly be described as a factory for producing ideological products. And the latter definition is particularly apt and receives special emphasis.

Examples of the autocratization and monopolization of modern education, apart from those mentioned in Section 3 and the detailed discussion on American education later, can be briefly addressed here regarding how the ruling ideology of imperialists permeates school education.

This infusion of ruling ideology is most easily seen in the curriculum content and educational aims. For instance, primary school textbooks, especially for Ethics or Civics, often focus on cultivating virtues like diligence, thrift, saving, upholding private property, obeying national laws, and performing military service and paying taxes. In higher education, Japan serves as a good example: the University Ordinance promulgated by the Japanese government in 1918 stipulated that the purpose of universities was "to teach the theory and application of academics required by the state and to research their profundities. Additionally, attention should be paid to the cultivation of character and the nurturing of national thought." The specific mention here of "cultivation of character" and "nurturing of national thought" was not accidental; the motive was that Japan had already entered the stage of capitalist decline, with social contradictions and struggles intensifying daily. What the Ruling Class hoped for from universities was not only the production of technicians and scholars necessary for capitalist production but also the production of individuals consciously maintaining the power of the Ruling Class through "character cultivation" and "nurturing national thought." Therefore, the study of disciplines essential to constituting capitalist society, such as law, political science, economics, etc., was encouraged and actively promoted. Simultaneously, knowledge disadvantageous to it, theories that exposed its secrets, were suppressed as much as possible. Consequently, student social science research associations and left-leaning professors were disbanded and expelled. Other measures, like encouraging competitive sports and emphasizing military training, on one hand kept young students from having much time or inclination to study or participate in leftist movements, and on the other hand instilled a fixed, that is, the Ruling Class's Ideology. Thus, these also became means, directly or indirectly, for instilling the ruler's ideology.

Of course, the ideological domination of imperialists permeates not only school education but also all cultural institutions such as newspapers, magazines, lectures, libraries, theater, literature, and entertainment. The existence of measures like publication regulations, teacher certification, textbook censorship, and film inspection in imperialist countries is precisely to ensure ideological domination.

But in education, the school is the most concrete manifestation, the most systematic, and the opportunity for the comparatively longest-term instillation of the ruler's ideology. Therefore, if we carefully observe and dissect the schools of capitalist society, we can increasingly discover the true face of education in capitalist society. Hence, I venture to painstakingly translate and reproduce here in full "The School in Capitalist Society" by N. Bucharin and E. Preobrazhensky—from Chapter 10 of their The ABC of Communism.

"In bourgeois society, the school fulfills three main tasks. Namely, it teaches the younger generation of toilers the spirit of obedience and respect for capitalism; it turns the youth of the ruling class into 'cultured' disciplinarians of the laboring masses; and it serves capitalist production by utilizing science which increases technology and capitalist profits.

The accomplishment of the first task is achieved, just as in the bourgeois army, by first creating suitable 'officers for enlisting the people' for the bourgeoisie. The elementary school teachers produced for national education must learn appropriate training courses to prepare to perform the function of disciplinarians. In school instruction, only teachers deemed trustworthy from the bourgeois standpoint are employed. Moreover, they are monitored by the Minister of Education of the capitalist government. All harmful elements, i.e., socialist elements, are mercilessly expelled from among the teachers. The pre-revolutionary German elementary school, serving as a supplement to the barracks under Wilhelm II, is a good example of how the bourgeoisie and landowners, with the help of schools, cultivate loyal and blind slaves of capital. Instruction in the bourgeois elementary school is conducted according to a definite program suited to the goal of training children to be subservient to capitalism. All textbooks are also compiled in the spirit suited to this goal. For the same purpose, to make everyone believe that the capitalist social order is natural, eternal, and the best of all possible orders, all bourgeois literature written in this regard is also very useful. Consequently, students unconsciously acquire a bourgeois psychology, become infected with excitement over all bourgeois morals and with the worship of wealth, fame, and status, and immerse themselves in the spirit of careerism and the pursuit of personal happiness. The church pastors, with the doctrine of God's will (which, as a result of the close relationship between capital and the church, often becomes the bourgeois will), complete the work of the bourgeois teachers.

The second purpose, in bourgeois society, is accomplished by secondary and higher education consciously suppressing the laboring class. Education in secondary schools, especially in higher schools, requires expenses of such a large amount that laborers cannot afford them. This education requires more than ten years. For this reason, laborers and peasants, who must support their families and consequently have to send their children to the factory or farm from a very young age, or have them work at home, are unable to attend school. Secondary schools and higher schools have, in fact, become schools for the youth of the bourgeoisie. Herein, the youth of the ruling class receive various preparations to take the place of their fathers as exploiters, or as officials, or as teachers in the capitalist state. And in these schools, their instruction has a clear class character. While this is not very conspicuous in fields like mathematics, technology, and natural sciences, it manifests particularly clearly in the social sciences, which shape the students' worldview. Capitalist political economy is taught using all methods to 'annihilate Marx'. Sociology and history are taught in the same purely capitalist spirit. It is the same in other areas as well. In short, secondary and higher schools are places that impart to the children of the capitalists everything useful to capitalist society and necessary for maintaining the capitalist organization of exploitation. Even if, by chance, the children of laborers enter higher schools—usually the most talented—the majority of them, through the facilities of the capitalist school, are very skillfully detached from their class of origin. They are further imbued with a capitalist psychology, and the talents of the toilers are ultimately abused for the oppression of their own class.

As for the accomplishment of the third task, it is completed by the capitalist school using the following method. That is, in class society, due to the separation of science and labor, science not only belongs to the ruling class but also becomes the profession of a specific minority. The teaching of science and scientific research are separated from the labor process. To utilize the effects of science in production, capitalist society has to create its own research institutes to facilitate the technical application of scientific discoveries. Furthermore, it has to create many technical schools to maintain production at the same level as the effects of 'pure science'—i.e., science separated from labor. Also, the technical schools of capitalist society supply not only people with technical education but also supervisors and managers for the laboring class. Moreover, for the convenience of the commodity circulation process, commercial schools, commercial universities, etc., are established."

This is the famous "theory of the three major tasks of the school," which observes school education under the capitalist system from the standpoint of the materialist conception of history. It is also a fact that anyone can witness with their own eyes. I ask you, can one still detect the slightest trace of popularization or socialization here?

Originally, "what the history of ideas has shown from ancient times is that intellectual production transforms alongside material production. The ideas which dominate an age are always ultimately the ideas of its Ruling Class."[85] Therefore, in places dominated by the bourgeoisie, it is most natural that school education is conducted to train students in line with bourgeois thought. This holds true regardless of whether it is feudal society or capitalist society. However, as capitalism progresses to the imperialist stage, everything becomes monopolized. This monopolistic form seeks to exclude all heterogeneous elements. Consequently, whereas the monopoly of cultivation in ancient and medieval times still tolerated the existence of cultivation not controlled by the state without leading to significant particular conflicts, in modern times, this monopoly has become all-encompassing, monopolizing everything, to the point of not permitting any cultural movement free from state control. Thus, the cultural struggle also becomes one aspect of the overall class struggle.

The deeper the degree of monopoly becomes, the more it turns into the property of the Ruling Class. Thus, the so-called socialization or popularization becomes increasingly distant from reality.

The fourth argument is the so-called neutralization, or impartiality.

---

85 [Special Editor's Note] The above quotation is from Marx and Engels, The German Ideology. The modern translation reads: "The ideas of the ruling class are in every epoch the ruling ideas, i.e. the class which is the ruling material force of society, is at the same time its ruling intellectual force." (See Marx-Engels Collected Works, Vol. 5, International Publishers, 1976, p. 59). Please note that the translator has adjusted the translation here to more closely match the version of the quote provided in the original Chinese text, while also providing a reference to a standard English translation.

In all states and all eras, education has inherently never been anything but education for the Ruling Class. This should be entirely clear from the explanation in the previous section. Especially in capitalist society, although education superficially appears contrary to feudal education, which aimed only at fostering stupidity and benightedness, its underlying purpose is solely to produce loyal servants and spokespersons for the bourgeoisie. Unexpectedly, modern capitalist educators repeatedly claim that modern education completely transcends politics and class, and operates from a fair standpoint. This we must correct.

Our correction involves not only pointing out from facts that modern education's claim to be supra-political and supra-class is a lie, but also, based on the materialist conception of history, elucidating the origin of these lies.

In fact, the class and political purposes of education in capitalist society exist everywhere and require little citation for proof. One only needs to observe that in modern schools, anything beneficial to the Ruling Class, no matter how far from the truth, is compulsorily taught; conversely, anything contrary to the interests of the Ruling Class or beneficial to the ruled class is condemned as "heterodox doctrines" and rejected. Is this not extremely clear evidence?

Lenin said:

"The more cultured the capitalist state, the more subtly it deceives the people by saying that schools stand above politics and serve society as a whole. But in reality, the schools were converted completely into an instrument of the class rule of the bourgeoisie. They are thoroughly imbued with the bourgeois class spirit and aim to supply the capitalists with obedient lackeys and efficient workers."[86]

Is it not clearer than seeing fire that the education of capitalist society strenuously maintains class objectives?

But to say it is neutralized and impartial is, in a certain sense, not untrue. This point is worth our study.

What is this point? It is commercialization.

Commercialization and monopolization are characteristics of capitalist social production, and simultaneously become characteristics of capitalist social cultivation.

The monopoly of cultivation, namely the monopoly of school education, newspapers, magazines, sports, entertainment, etc., has been discussed in the previous section.

Now, let's discuss commercialization.

Commercialization has many characteristics. Here, we will mention just one: the need to flaunt "strict neutrality."

Why must capitalist commodities have this flaunting? The reason is very simple: merely to facilitate sales and make money easier. Could the shoes and hats sold in shoe stores and hat stores be labeled as liberalist or conservative? No! Absolutely not! On the contrary, they are mass-produced and sold impartially; Zhang San

---

[86] [Special Editor's Note] The above quotation is from Lenin's Speech at the First All-Russia Congress on Education. The modern translation reads: "The more civilized the bourgeois state, the more subtly it lies when it claims that schools can stand above politics and serve society as a whole. In fact, the schools were turned into nothing but an instrument of the class rule of the bourgeoisie; they have been thoroughly imbued with the bourgeois class spirit, and their aim is to supply the capitalists with obedient lackeys and efficient workers." See Lenin Collected Works (Chinese Edition), People's Publishing House, 1956, Vol. 28, p. 59.

can buy them, and Li Si can also buy them. This is "uniform pricing" and "no deception of the old or young."

This is true for the production of goods, and likewise for the production of "public opinion" or "ideas."

Take bourgeois newspapers as an example.

The initial motive for newspapers arose from the establishment of opposing groups within society. These opposing groups, each for their own group's interests, needed to promote their views, thus utilizing newspapers as a tool for dissemination, making them a means of competition between opposing groups.

But in capitalist society, where everything is commercialized, newspapers inevitably follow suit. This transformation causes newspapers, which were formerly organs for the specific demands of opposing groups, to become "strictly neutral" news outlets. Originally, the reports and advocacy of newspapers had the character of representing specific social demands; today's newspapers, however, do not lean towards any particular social stratum but adapt to common, universal demands—in other words, they take on the character of capitalist commodities.

Just look at Shanghai newspapers: some have no "current commentary"; others, though bearing the name "current commentary," are actually empty talk that avoids causing offense (not offending any side). And in their advertisements, one can always see phrases like "impartial in views," "accurate in reporting." This is just like the advertisements for medical books and cosmetics that claim to cure all diseases, be suitable for everyone, and are "a must-read for all." Their goal is merely to achieve so-called popularity.

Now, looking at education, this kind of "idea production," we can also discover its commercialized phenomena.

Elementary schools, needless to say, are like the trams in Shanghai's International Settlement with their "safe, fast, cheap, all can ride" slogan. Their enrollment advertisements might as well say "regardless of gender or wealth, all are treated equally." Although their substance is indeed, as stated in the school tasks theory above, "exclusively for the benefit of the **bourgeoisie**," their outward appearance certainly puts on a fair facade. The children of the rich and the poor pay the same tuition, read the same textbooks—a truly extraordinary equality.

In higher education, there is no propaganda for any particular party or faction; it even permanently stays out of politics, forbidding both professors and students from participating in practical movements. Why is this done? Because the highest institutions of learning are organs for academic research, they are supra-political, supra-class!

And the educational proposition to "respect individuality" is precisely a reflection of the marketplace's demand for "novel styles" and "unique designs."

The bewildering variety of academic departments and subjects is the counterpart to "a great variety of types" and "lacking no excellence."

Such commercialized education truly appears neutral and impartial. The education of capitalist society is indeed different from the "old-fashioned" and "conventional" education of feudal society.

But is this reliable neutrality and fairness?

Just as commercialized newspapers are funded by capitalists and monopolized by a few capitalists, this commercialized education, though not entirely funded by capitalists (as public educational institutions are maintained by taxes paid by the common people), is nonetheless dominated by capitalists (in China, one must add warlords, landlords, and local tyrants). The result is exactly the same as commodities serving the interests of their owners; this commercialized education naturally serves only the interests of the owners of the educational institutions. The facts are as described in the school tasks theory above.

Moreover, this signboard of "strict neutrality" is recently about to be taken down. This is because capitalist society ultimately produces within its own structure—that is, within its production organization—the class rule of the laborers, which stands opposed to the monopolistic domination of capitalism. With the progress of labor organization, this develops into two opposing social groups. Thus, just as newspapers gradually revert to their original nature, education also cannot help but reveal its true form—the naked tool of the Ruling Class.

Therefore, truly neutral and impartial education can never exist in a class society, except perhaps on the lips of bourgeois pedagogues.

The fifth argument is the so-called internationalization, particularly pacification.

Proponents argue that in recent years, witnessing the cruelty of war, people concerned with the world's path have risen together to engage in peace movements. In politics, there are organizations like the League of Nations, the establishment of the Kellogg-Briand Pact; additionally, there are the International Court, disarmament conferences, etc., all concrete manifestations of the world peace movement.

In education, there is the World Federation of Education Associations, initiated by the American National Education Association, calling together education experts from around the world to discuss methods for realizing peace. When its fourth conference was held in Geneva in July 1929, it passed many resolutions centered on international amity. According to newspaper reports, the main resolutions were: (1) To promote international understanding through education focused on an international perspective; (2) To supply the press, books, and other publications of various countries with correct and up-to-date information about education; (3) To regulate cinema from the viewpoint of international amity; (4) To include an outline of world history based on international amity in the curricula of all schools in all countries; (5) The abolition of military training.

Although educators in continental European countries did not enthusiastically participate in this American-led World Federation of Education Associations, their love for peace is no less than that of American educators. Therefore, they separately initiated the International Peace Education Campaign, establishing the League of Nations of Educational Associations in London in 1927, while simultaneously holding a "Peace Movement through Schools" conference[87] in the capital of Czechoslovakia, with various governments and pacifist groups sending representatives. The former stipulated "to lead to world peace through educational cooperation and the cooperation of all peoples," "does not require any commitment to a particular political or social form," and "guiding the education of children of all nations towards mutual understanding among all peoples is an absolute condition for permanent peace." The latter resolved to "eliminate

---

87 [Special Editor's Note] "Peace Movement through Schools" conference, i.e., a conference on "Promoting Peace through Schools".

belligerent and exclusionary teaching materials," "cultivate friendliness and a sense of solidarity through the international exchange of children," and "understand and cultivate the concept of equality between self and others through the teaching of natural sciences and the geography and history of other countries."

On September 5, 1929, French Prime Minister Briand actually delivered a speech at the League of Nations in Geneva, strongly emphasizing the importance of peace, the scourge of war, and appealing to the women of the world to do their part to eliminate war. His method was to teach their children to detest war, truly love peace, and respect other nations. (See Shanghai Republic Daily, September 6, 1929)

At the same time, a new International Children's Correspondence Club was established in London, considered a new organization of the world peace movement. Schoolchildren would correspond once a year with children from countries around the world to exchange the hand of friendship. Here is the text of the 1929 message sent by British children to children of the world:

Greetings 1929 (dated May 18 each year). We, the school children of Britain, send this greeting and all good wishes to the boys and girls of other lands. We wish you success in your lessons, joy in your play, and may everyone enjoy a happy life. And united, we send our message and good wishes to all people in the world. We British children do not know what war is, but our parents do. We pray that the League of Nations may unite the peace-loving spirit of all nations; we hope that all future inventions will help us understand each other better, building no warships, but special ships for us to visit and see each other. We devote our lives to peace, forever friends, because we all belong to one big family in this world. Let this message be the pioneer paving the way for peace. To all nations and all people. (See Shanghai Times, November 6, 1929)

The world peace movements cited above, especially the efforts in education, I can tell the reader, are all facts, and are being carried out with great seriousness.

However, I must further tell the reader that behind these facts lie other, more truthful facts that we must also recognize.

What are these more truthful facts?

They are: The League of Nations is a spoils-sharing organ dominated by the two great imperialist powers, Britain and France, a tool for deceiving and the the proletariat. Under its auspices, the Preparatory Commission for the Disarmament Conference prepared for years without yet producing a disarmament method. Conversely, it overturned the proposals for complete and immediate abolition of armaments submitted by the Soviet Union in 1927 and for arms reduction in 1928.

The Kellogg-Briand Pact is even more of a conspiracy by imperialist countries to cover up their own arms expansion, deceive workers and peasants, ease conflicts, and further unite to attack the Soviet Union. Just after the Pact was signed, the U.S. Congress passed a large-scale shipbuilding bill—their unsolicited confession.

The World Federation of Education Associations was initiated under pacifism, with the approval of the U.S. government. When the first conference was held in San Francisco in 1923, an American millionaire donated one million U.S. dollars to congratulate the conference's establishment. The Federation stipulated "absolute neutrality towards politics and religion," but when the second conference was held in Edinburgh in 1925, high clergy went to offer blessings.

The "Peace Movement through Schools" conference was held under the semi-official auspices of that League of Nations, and had government representatives in attendance. These governments, needless to say, represent the interests of capitalists and are actively expanding their armaments.

After Briand's speech at the League of Nations on the importance of peace and teaching children to detest war, we saw in the newspapers of the same month that the Japanese navy decided to begin recruiting youth aviation soldiers the following year, with volunteers required to have at least a higher elementary school education, be aged 15 to 17, and in good physical health (see Republic Daily, September 30).

As for the London International Children's Correspondence Club, having children "pray that the League of Nations may unite the peace-loving spirit of all nations" truly amounts to nothing more than a "prayer," with no other effect. To say "British children do not know what war is" is even more "deceitful boasting." British children's common knowledge about cannons, warships, military aircraft, and even the active scenes of the First World War (from films) is considerably greater than that of many Chinese adults.

We must understand that the world today presents this situation: international militarist forces have developed enormously. All imperialist countries are vigorously expanding their armaments, implementing military reorganization, shifting the main component of their armies from peasants to workers, strenuously expanding the social scope of their armies, shortening terms of military service, developing so-called "hidden armies," especially the fierce implementation of the militarization of youth and women. The militarization of industry and the development of military technology, along with the unprecedented invention of chemical weapons, have caused international militarist forces to develop to an exceptionally large scale.

Especially in 1929, the preparations for war by the great powers became even more intense. In February, the United States passed a large-scale naval expansion plan, requiring the construction of 15 new 10,000-ton armored cruisers by 1931, with funding of 274 million gold dollars. Britain's 1929 naval budget increased to 280 million gold dollars, of which 42 million was for building new ships. France dispatched battleships totaling 75,000 tons, with funding of 880 million francs. Since the signing of the Kellogg-Briand Pact, the competition in naval expansion among the imperialist powers has intensified.

Furthermore, current air power has increased twelvefold compared to the time of the last world war. At the outbreak of war, Britain, France, the United States, Japan, and Italy could immediately mobilize 13,000 to 15,000 military aircraft. France's 1929 budget for expanding military aircraft totaled 11,560 million francs. Britain worked even harder on air force expansion, establishing networks of military air stations between South Africa and Australia, and between India and Iraq. The United States also passed funding of 8 million gold dollars to build military airfields with a capacity of 65 million cubic meters and began establishing four large aircraft depots. Japan decided to build a second large military aircraft carrier, with a cruising range of up to 6,000 kilometers. As for the invention of chemical weapons, it is even more astonishing, but many are secret and not easily known to the outside.

Additionally, the great powers are adopting all methods to implement the militarization of the people and industry. Before the war, military service in various countries was mostly two or three years; now it is universally shortened to eight months or one year. Military training has been added to schools and social organizations, and the intensification of youth militarization, in particular, has become a common phenomenon. Some countries, like France, Poland, and Bulgaria, also provide military training for women. The reserve armies of the great powers are increasing extremely rapidly, reaching at least over 20 million people.

Now, let's specifically discuss the militarization of children and youth, as this is directly related to our education.

The militarization of children and youth is currently being carried out on a large scale, aiming to establish a reserve force with a military or semi-military organizational form among the youth, obtaining many young people who can be mobilized immediately for war.

The main methods of militarization are:

Providing military training and discipline to children within official or semi-official children's organizations.

Short-term compulsory conscription into the army and navy.

Compulsory army training (not conscription).

The organization of official or semi-official youth volunteer corps.

Military training for children is prevalent in most imperialist countries. Some countries (like Japan, Italy) have only government organizations to train children, but most countries unite schoolchildren to provide military training. For example, British schools have fixed weekly hours for organized games and physical training. Some countries organize student corps with a strong military nature. As for organizations like the Boy Scouts and Girl Guides, governments of various countries provide special facilities to facilitate their development. They also use funding and encouragement methods to make children eager to join such organizations. Governments further organize military camps and travel teams, dispatching military instructors to guide their training work. In short, using such methods, the work of militarizing children has already been established in most capitalist countries.

This work is also frequent among youth. Some countries like Japan and Italy have government youth organizations that provide military training to youth and compel all young workers to join (e.g., Japan's Youth Training Centers).

Japan, France, and many other European countries adopt the method of compulsory military service (conscription). After completing the service period, individuals move from the active army to the reserves but must still perform annual drill obligations. In countries like Australia and New Zealand, conscription is not implemented, but youth within a certain age range are forced to undergo military training. These youth must undergo several large-scale drills and short periods of barrack and tent life each year.

In other countries, especially Britain and the United States, there is no system of compulsory conscription or training[88]. However, this does not prove that youth militarization there is not intense. Britain has a Territorial Army, nominally voluntary, but in fact requiring participation in several large-scale drills each year and a two-week camp life. In the United States, during the 1924-1925

---

88 [Special Editor's Note] Britain and the United States previously relied on voluntary enlistment, but since the Second World War, both have implemented conscription and compulsory military service. Britain passed the _National Service Act_ in 1948, the United States passed the _Universal Military Training and Service Act_ in 1951.

academic year, over 226 schools implemented military training; Congress appropriated more than $3,818,000 for the Reserve Officers' Training Corps (ROTC), with the number of students receiving military training reaching over 125,500.

Furthermore, within every country, there are dozens of youth organizations funded by the government and capitalists, conducting military training under various pretexts. These clearly reflect the frantic war preparations of imperialism.

Simultaneously, the ideological preparation for war among youth is developing extremely rapidly. This process of ideological militarization is achieved directly and indirectly through a thousand and one methods. Besides history, geography, and other subjects being filled with virulent patriotism, all schools are strenuously disseminating bourgeois ideas preparing for war. Lectures on patriotism, displays of military maps, guiding entire schools to visit military exhibitions, organizing "superior" children's groups to tour warships, forming student corps to participate in army exercises—these are just a few examples among many methods. Magazines and films for youth and children propagate patriotism and war preparation. Youth groups funded by the government and capitalists use every method to carry out persistent and clever pro-war propaganda.

Did the aforementioned World Federation of Education Associations and the "Peace Movement through Schools" conference protest against this kind of war-preparatory education or engage in any anti-war propaganda? No, they did not protest, nor did they conduct anti-war propaganda. They simply follow the imperialists' intentions, on one hand covering up the facts of this arms expansion, and on the other hand singing the praises of vague, passive pacifist anti-war theories. This is because the anti-imperialist forces are actively engaged in the struggle against militarism and a major war. The imperialists know well that a large portion of youth can be influenced by such pacifist anti-war rhetoric but will not be swayed by general pro-war propaganda, and they know even better that this portion of youth is most susceptible to the anti-war propaganda of revolutionary groups. Therefore, in recent years, they have paid more attention to this segment of youth, attempting to utilize pacifist anti-war discourse to overcome the revolutionary groups' anti-war propaganda.

The highest expression of this deceptive propaganda was the World Youth Peace Congress held in the Netherlands in 1928. Fortunately, thanks to the enthusiastic participation of revolutionary youth groups, the hopes of the imperialists—to use this conference to conduct propaganda against the revolutionary groups' anti-war efforts—were thwarted. But we must recognize that behind the mask of "peace," the crisis of war is intensifying daily, and consequently, the revolutionaries' task of opposing war naturally becomes more serious.

In this period of developing militarist forces and growing danger of a major war, the fact that the peace movement in our education is precisely being pursued with particular effort allows us to easily discern its true purpose.

To say that modern education is internationalized and pacified supposedly adds luster to modern education. But this kind of international peace theory does not lead to genuine peace; rather, it promotes cruel war. If you don't believe it, wait until the next world war breaks out soon; these educational groups currently calling for world peace will certainly be the first to advocate "defending the fatherland" and urge youth to enlist enthusiastically. Just wait, I am not lying!

Alright, the virtues of modern education praised by bourgeois pedagogues, in our eyes, all turn out to be deceptive boasts. We acknowledge that modern education indeed has novelties and progress compared to medieval education. However, we must further acknowledge that these novelties and progress are precisely consistent with the novelties and progress of modern commodities; they do not serve the interests of the whole society or all humanity, but rather the interests of a particular special class. We must also acknowledge that the education of capitalist society remains Transformation education, possessing all the characteristics of Transformation education.

However, the Transformation of education in capitalist society, besides the five characteristics mentioned initially, requires the addition of two more characteristics: monopolization and commercialization.

This monopolization corresponds to the process of capitalist monopolization and the transformation of liberal states into imperialist states; hence, it can also be called "imperialism" in education. It differs from the monopolistic forms of cultivation by previous ruling classes, which still tolerated the coexistence of the ruled classes' cultivation, by being absolutely exclusionary, truly deserving the sign "the only shop in town." This point has been mentioned earlier, and the facts of this monopolization have also been discussed.

The characteristics of commercialization include mass production, rapid manufacturing, patenting of knowledge, "fair trade" (the so-called strict neutrality mentioned above), valuation by money, and more. Here, due to space constraints, we will leave the detailed discussion for the later section on "Education and the Economy."

However, there is one point that must be mentioned in this section: the contradictory phenomena in capitalist societal education. These are not uninteresting, so I will write them for the reader to see.

These educational contradictions can generally be seen from three aspects: (1) The contradiction between the development of individuality and compulsory uniformity; (2) The contradiction between "enlightenment" and obscurantism; (3) The contradiction between academic research and ideological dictatorship.

The emphasis on individuality in education is indeed a characteristic of progress. Although this emphasis is a manifestation of the demand for "novelty and innovation" in commodity production, allowing the "unique talents and abilities" possessed by individuals more opportunity for development is still praiseworthy. Yet, simultaneously, mechanisms of enforced standardization such as the class system and the grade system make schools truly resemble factories—sites of mass production and batch manufacturing. Consequently, education itself takes shape as a series of departments laboring for the market, which clashes sharply with the innate drive for individual development.

On the other hand, the development of individuality is demanded by the production organization of free competition; hence, individualism holds an absolutely major position. For instance, the issues considered by bourgeois literature and art are only about individuals, only about personal struggles, fate, etc. Yet, under common compulsory curricula, class, and academic year systems, there are elements that hinder this individual development. Furthermore, the propaganda and inculcation of patriotism and ruling ideology are also sufficient to suppress the growth of individualism.

In essence, a contradiction clearly appears here between individual development and enforced measures. This contradiction, in other words, is the contradiction between individualization and commercialization.

The bourgeoisie, on one hand, needs the masses to be literate, educated, clever, and intelligent; on the other hand, it needs the masses to obey bourgeois laws, believe that capitalist society is the optimal social order, and not let them doubt or hold hostility. As stated at the beginning of this section, as education and labor gradually recombine, there is also the fear that education will provoke the laboring class's will to resist the Ruling Class. Therefore, they can only impose various restrictions, striving to ensure that the education received by the laboring class does not become poison that kills them. The Ruling Class encounters a major difficulty in this matter: given the general trend, labor (and merchant and peasant) education naturally cannot be avoided. But once provided, it inevitably causes much anxiety. "You want the horse to run fast, yet you don't let it graze." How can things in the world be all benefit and no drawback for oneself? But today's bourgeoisie feels extremely troubled by the matter of mass education. This is the contradiction between "enlightenment" and obscurantism, which is essentially still the contradiction between education and labor.

The third contradiction is as follows: Academic research, which championed freedom as its core principle, was originally a product of capitalist society. This is because the bourgeoisie's "dominion" can be said to have been acquired not solely "from the saddle" (i.e., by sheer force), but also by demanding science and freedom of thought. Now, many university professors or specialized scholars still meticulously pride themselves on "liberalism." In Japan, the dignified terms "university autonomy" and "independence of scholarship" are still prevalent. However, because the class struggle has become extremely severe, reaching a final life-and-death juncture, the walls of the highest institutions of learning are gradually being shaken by the shouts from outside.

Consequently, left-leaning professors arise in response, and radical students are ready to climb over the walls and leave. The Ruling Class, alarmed, has no choice but to act impolitely, dismissing university professors and expelling university students. Institutions of higher learning, whose fundamental duty is free academic research, actually forbid the study of social sciences—is this not another contradiction?

Furthermore, on one hand, academic research is encouraged, with provisions like scholarships and grants; on the other hand, there are so-called invention patents, which prohibit the public application of new benefits from scholarship, and there are even those who sell their inventions to big capitalists. How are they sold? Does the purchaser acquire the right to use his invention and disseminate it globally for the benefit of all humanity? No, he sells the right to suppress such an invention, preventing humanity from applying it for decades! (See Upton Sinclair, The Goose-step, p. 380)

Is this not a significant contradiction?

Civilization has progressed to capitalist society, yet there are actions that destroy civilization and hinder progress—isn't this somewhat inconceivable?

But having these or those contradictions in capitalist society is not inconceivable. It is its "destiny" to be so. Let us wait and watch its decline!

"The East is red!" As the Japanese left-leaning professor Kawakami Hajime once began saying this phrase from the podium, he was ordered to "stop!" by the police officer monitoring the event. I will borrow his words to end this section.

Questions

1. Please critique my "Critique of the New Education."

2. Provide facts illustrating the "concentration of public opinion production."

3. Critique the theory of "Educational Socialization" in Chinese education.

4. Science does not acknowledge the existence of "God," yet Christianity, which primarily sells "God," expresses welcome towards science. What do you think?

5. What are your thoughts after reading the "Theory of the Three Major Tasks of the School"?

6. Investigate the current state of worker-peasant education and mass education in China, and explain the impact of this education on the worker-peasant masses.

7. Chinese senior high schools and above are currently implementing military education. What is your critique?

8. Are you aware of the current struggle against a world war? What attitude do our educators take towards this struggle?

9. What opinions does your pedagogy teacher express regarding the "World Federation of Education Associations"?

10. Is there an organization for social science research in your school? Can you hold meetings and conduct research freely?

SECTION 8: EDUCATION IN SOCIALIST SOCIETY

An Overview of Socialist Society — Marx's Views on Education: 1. From the Manifesto; 2. From the Critique of the Gotha Programme — The Nature of Education in the Transitional Period: Still Class-Based, but Different from Capitalist Society — Key Elements of Education in the Transitional Period — Questions

These words should pertain to the time after "the East is red."

Now, the "East" cannot be considered fully crimson; there is only a glimmer of dawn. I can only rely on this glimmer and what is indicated by the emerging social sciences to write a little.

Socialist society is the social organization destined to succeed capitalist society. The characteristics of this society are the public ownership of all means of production, the abolition of private property, and the cessation of the coercive apparatus of power, namely the state.

Morgan once wrote a passage describing future society; upon reading it, you should be able to envision a general picture:

Since the advent of civilization, the growth of property has been so immense, its forms so diversified, its uses so expanding, and its management for the owners' benefit so ingenious, that it has become, to the masses, an unmanageable power. The human mind stands bewildered in the presence of its own creation. A time will come, however, when human reason shall rise in mastery over property, and define the relations of the state to the property it protects, as well as the limits of the rights of owners.

The interests of society are paramount to individual interests, and the two must be brought into just and harmonious relations. If progress, as in the past, remains the law of the future, the mere pursuit of wealth is not the final destiny of humanity. The time which has passed away since civilization began is but a fragment of the past duration of human life, and but a fragment of the ages yet to come. The dissolution of society bids fair to become the termination of a historical course where property is the sole and ultimate aim, because such a course contains the elements of self-destruction. Political democracy, social fraternity, equality of rights and duties, and universal education, foreshadow the next higher plane of society to which experience, intelligence, and knowledge are steadily tending. It will be a revival, in a higher form, of the liberty, equality, and fraternity of the ancient gentes. (Ancient Society, p. 552)

However, from the standpoint of the materialist conception of history, this future society is not something fantasized in the mind of this or that individual, but is inevitably destined to arrive following the laws of social evolution. For example, the modern capitalist system is itself a product of historical necessity. The capitalist system is by no means an institution designed by the imagination of a few geniuses; rather, just like the feudal system of a previous era, it necessarily unfolded through the operation of history's wheel. Thus, the future society succeeding capitalism is also by no means reliant on the fanciful designs of geniuses; rather, like the emergence of capitalism itself, it must necessarily unfold along its path due to history's wheel running on the capitalist track. What we can do, and must do, lies not in fantasizing about what kind of society to create, but in foreseeing the society that is inevitably demanded, so as to facilitate the smooth and agile operation of history's evolutionary wheel.

Then how can we foresee the future society? This is achieved by dissecting and analyzing modern society to discern within it the sprouts of the new society. "The new society incubates under the wing of the old society." Therefore, Marx knew that the society succeeding capitalism would be socialist society.

The discussion of social evolution must be based on this materialist conception of history, and the discussion of educational issues must also be based on this materialist conception of history.

We cannot be like utopian educational revolutionaries, who merely clamor that modern education is bankrupt, yet cannot propose practical opinions or methods of implementation. These people are the so-called utopian socialists. They curse the dark present society and fantasize about a bright future world, yet completely lack scientific methods. In their discussion of education, they also regard education as a separate undertaking, detached from the social organization. How could they not go astray?

Previously, I have analyzed education in capitalist society from the standpoint of the materialist conception of history. This education, "in a word," serves only the interests of the bourgeoisie itself.

Now the question arises: How should we deal with this education from a Marxist standpoint?

On the one hand, there is the proletarian educational movement within capitalist countries; on the other hand, there exists the educational enterprise of the contemporary sole socialist state, the Soviet Union. However, I will reserve these two points for separate discussion below. Here, I wish first to introduce Marx's own discussions on education. Fortunately, both the proletarian educational movement and the Soviet educational enterprise are based on Marxism.

Marx did not publish specialized, systematic treatises on educational issues; here, we can only gather his relevant statements concerning education.

Regarding the bourgeois accusation that communism does not recognize individuality, he said:

In a word, you reproach us with intending to do away with your property. Precisely so; that is just what we intend.

From the moment when labour can no longer be converted into capital, money, or rent, into a social power capable of being monopolised, i.e., from the moment when individual property can no longer be transformed into bourgeois property, into capital, from that moment, you say, individuality vanishes.

You must, therefore, confess that by "individual" you mean no other person than the bourgeois, than the middle-class owner of property. This person must, indeed, be swept out of the way, and made impossible. (Communist Manifesto, p. 34)[89]

Regarding the accusation that communism abolishes culture, he said:

---

89 [Special Editor's Note] The above quotation is from Marx and Engels, Communist Manifesto. A contemporary translation reads: "In a word, you reproach us with intending to do away with your property. Precisely so; that is just what we intend." "From the moment when labour can no longer be converted into capital, money, or rent, into a social power capable of being monopolised, i.e., from the moment when individual property can no longer be transformed into bourgeois property, into capital, from that moment, you say, individuality vanishes." "You must, therefore, confess that by 'individual' you mean no other person than the bourgeois, than the middle-class owner of property. This person must, indeed, be swept out of the way, and made impossible." See Selected Works of Marx and Engels, Vol. 1, People's Publishing House, 1995 edition, p. 288.

All objections against the communistic mode of producing and appropriating material products have been extended to the production and appropriation of products of the mind. Just as the abolition of class property is, in the eyes of the bourgeois, the abolition of production itself, so the abolition of class culture is for him identical with the abolition of all culture.

That culture, the loss of which he laments, is for the enormous majority a mere training to act as a machine. (In the same book, p. 35)[90]

Regarding the accusation that communism destroys family relations, he said:

Do you charge us with wanting to stop the exploitation of children by their parents? To this crime we plead guilty.

But, you will say, we destroy the most hallowed of relations, when we replace home education by social.

And your education! Is not that also social, and determined by the social conditions under which you educate, by the intervention, direct or indirect, of society, by means of schools, etc.? The communists have not invented the intervention of society in education; they do but seek to alter the character of that intervention, and to rescue education from the influence of

---

90 [Special Editor's Note] The above quotation is from Marx and Engels, Communist Manifesto. A contemporary translation reads: "All objections against the communistic mode of producing and appropriating material products have been extended to the production and appropriation of products of the mind. Just as the abolition of class property is, in the eyes of the bourgeois, the abolition of production itself, so the abolition of class culture is for him identical with the abolition of all culture." "That culture, the loss of which he laments, is for the enormous majority a mere training to act as a machine." See Selected Works of Marx and Engels, Vol. 1, People's Publishing House, 1995 edition, p. 289.

the ruling class.

The bourgeois clap-trap about the family and education, about the hallowed co-relation of parent and child, becomes all the more disgusting, the more, by the action of Modern Industry, all family ties among the proletarians are torn asunder, and their children transformed into simple articles of commerce and instruments of labour. (In the same book, pp. 36-37)[91]

Among the measures generally applicable in the most advanced countries, those relating to education are:

8. Equal liability of all to labour. Establishment of industrial armies, especially for agriculture.

9. Combination of agriculture with manufacturing industries; gradual abolition of the distinction between town and country, by a more equable distribution of the population over the country.

10. Free education for all children in public schools. Abolition of children's factory labour in its present form. Combination of education with industrial production, &c., &c. (In the same book,

---

91 [Special Editor's Note] The above quotation is from Marx and Engels, Communist Manifesto. A contemporary translation reads: "Do you charge us with wanting to stop the exploitation of children by their parents? To this crime we plead guilty." "But, you will say, we destroy the most hallowed of relations, when we replace home education by social." "And your education! Is not that also social, and determined by the social conditions under which you educate, by the intervention, direct or indirect, of society, by means of schools, etc.? The communists have not invented the intervention of society in education; they do but seek to alter the character of that intervention, and to rescue education from the influence of the ruling class." "The bourgeois clap-trap about the family and education, about the hallowed co-relation of parent and child, becomes all the more disgusting, the more, by the action of Modern Industry, all family ties among the proletarians are torn asunder, and their children transformed into simple articles of commerce and instruments of labour." See Selected Works of Marx and Engels, Vol. 1, People's Publishing House, 1995 edition, p. 290.

p. 42)⁹²

The above represents Marx's thoughts on education. The tenth item listed last particularly exemplifies the Marxist view on education. Readers, please contemplate coherently (1) the equal obligation of all to labour, (2) free public education for all children, (3) the combination of industrial production with education, and (4) the gradual abolition of the distinction between city and countryside, etc. It should not be difficult to envision what kind of society would be realized under Marxist education.

Furthermore, in the Critique of the Gotha Programme, we can also see Marx's opinions on education:

In a higher phase of communist society, after the enslaving subordination of the individual to the division of labour, and therewith also the antithesis between mental and physical labour, has vanished; after labour has become not only a means of life but life's prime want; after the productive forces have also increased with the all-around development of the individual, and all the springs of co-operative wealth flow more abundantly—only then can the narrow horizon of bourgeois right be crossed in its entirety and society inscribe on its banners: From each according to his ability, to each according to his needs!⁹³

---

92 [Special Editor's Note] The above quotation is from Marx and Engels, Communist Manifesto. A contemporary translation reads: "8. Equal obligation of all to work. Establishment of industrial armies, especially for agriculture." "9. Combination of agriculture with manufacturing industries; gradual abolition of the distinction between town and country, by a more equable distribution of the populace over the country." "10. Combination of education with industrial production, etc." See Selected Works of Marx and Engels, Vol. 1, People's Publishing House, 1995 edition, p. 294.

93 [Special Editor's Note] The above quotation is from Marx, Critique of the Gotha Programme. A

Compare the text following "the antithesis between mental and physical labour has vanished" written here with the discussion on the combination of labour and education in the previous section on capitalist education. What reflections will you have?

The following text in double quotation marks is from the Gotha Programme; Marx criticizes the text within double quotation marks to express his own opinions:

"The German Workers' party demands as the intellectual and moral basis of the state:

1. Universal and equal elementary education by the state. Universal compulsory school attendance. Free instruction."

Equal elementary education? What idea lies behind these words? Is it believed that in present-day society (and it is only with this one has to deal) education can be equal for all classes? Or is it demanded that the upper classes also shall be compulsorily reduced to the modicum of education—the elementary school—that alone is compatible with the economic conditions not only of the wage workers but of the peasants as well?

"Universal compulsory school attendance. Free instruction." The former exists even in Germany, the second in Switzerland and in the United States in the case of elementary schools. If in some

---

contemporary translation reads: "In a higher phase of communist society, after the enslaving subordination of the individual to the division of labour, and therewith also the antithesis between mental and physical labour, has vanished; after labour has become not only a means of life but life's prime want; after the productive forces have also increased with the all-around development of the individual, and all the springs of co-operative wealth flow more abundantly—only then can the narrow horizon of bourgeois right be crossed in its entirety and society inscribe on its banners: From each according to his ability, to each according to his needs!" See Selected Works of Marx and Engels, Vol. 3, People's Publishing House, 1995 edition, pp. 305-306.

states of the latter country higher education institutions are also "free," that only means in fact defraying the cost of the education of the upper classes from the general tax receipts.

In regard to school regulations, at least, one should have demanded something like this: technical schools (theoretical and practical) in combination with the elementary school.

"Elementary education by the state" is altogether objectionable. Defining by a general law the expenditures on the elementary schools, the qualifications of the teaching staff, the branches of instruction, etc., and, as is done in the United States, supervising the fulfillment of these legal specifications by state inspectors, is a very different thing from appointing the state as the educator of the people! Government and church should rather be equally excluded from any influence on the school. Particularly, indeed, in the Prusso-German Empire (and one should not take refuge in the rotten subterfuge that one is speaking of a "state of the future"; we have seen how matters stand in this respect)[94] the state has need, on the contrary, of a very stern education by the people.

"Prohibition of child labour!"[95] Here it is absolutely essential to

---

94 In the earlier part of the Critique of the Gotha Programme, Marx observed that the German Empire, like other civilized nations, was built upon modern capitalist society, yet it had failed to achieve a level of democracy comparable to that in Switzerland and the United States. Particularly noteworthy is Marx's first use in this work of the term "the revolutionary dictatorship of the proletariat."

95 [Special Editor's Note] The above quotation is from Marx's Critique of the Gotha Programme. A contemporary translation reads:

"The German Workers' party demands as the intellectual and moral basis of the state:

'1. Universal and equal elementary education by the state. Universal compulsory school attendance. Free instruction.'

state the age limit.

A general prohibition of child labour is incompatible with the

---

'Equal elementary education?' What idea lies behind these words? Is it believed that in present-day society (and it is only with this one has to deal) education can be equal for all classes? Or is it demanded that the upper classes also shall be compulsorily reduced to the modicum of education—the elementary school—that alone is compatible with the economic conditions not only of the wage workers but of the peasants as well?

'Universal compulsory school attendance. Free instruction.' The former exists even in Germany, the second in Switzerland and in the United States in the case of elementary schools. If in some states of the latter country higher education institutions are also 'free,' that only means in fact defraying the cost of the education of the upper classes from the general tax receipts.

In regard to school regulations, at least, one should have demanded something like this: technical schools (theoretical and practical) in combination with the elementary school.

'Elementary education by the state' is altogether objectionable. Defining by a general law the expenditures on the elementary schools, the qualifications of the teaching staff, the branches of instruction, etc., and, as is done in the United States, supervising the fulfillment of these legal specifications by state inspectors, is a very different thing from appointing the state as the educator of the people! Government and church should rather be equally excluded from any influence on the school. Particularly, indeed, in the Prusso-German Empire (and one should not take refuge in the rotten subterfuge that one is speaking of a 'state of the future'; we have seen how matters stand in this respect) the state has need, on the contrary, of a very stern education by the people.

Prohibition of child labour! Here it is absolutely essential to state the age limit.

A general prohibition of child labour is incompatible with the existence of large-scale industry and hence an empty, pious wish. Its realization—if it were possible—would be reactionary, since, with a strict regulation of the working time according to the different age groups and other safety measures for the protection of children, an early combination of productive labour with education is one of the most potent means for the transformation of present-day society."

See Selected Works of Marx and Engels, Vol. 3, People's Publishing House, 1995 edition, pp. 316, 318.

existence of large-scale industry and hence an empty, pious wish. Its realization — if it were possible — would be reactionary, since, with a strict regulation of the working time according to the different age groups and other safety measures for the protection of children, an early combination of productive labour with education is one of the most potent means for the transformation of present-day society.

From the collected words of Marx above, we can derive his consistent thought, which is essentially the fundamental issues of "the combination of education and labour," "public and free education for all children," "specialized schools (theoretical and practical) in combination with the elementary school," etc. When readers see the educational enterprise of the Soviet Union below, they will know how Marx's thought is being realized.

However, such a new society cannot be fully realized overnight. The transition from capitalism to socialism necessarily requires a transitional period. This period is called the period of the dictatorship of the proletariat[96]. During this period, classes and the state still exist; but it is moving towards a classless, stateless socialist society[97], and it is moving consciously and actively towards socialist society.

Education during the period of the dictatorship of the proletariat is, of course, like education in capitalist society, also class-based. The difference is that during this period, educational authority resides with political power, not in the hands of the capitalists,

---

96 [Special Editor's Note] Proletariat is a phonetic transliteration of the French word prolétaire (proletariat), meaning the working class.

97 [Special Editor's Note] The socialist society referred to here means its higher stage—communist society.

but in the hands of the proletariat. Education in capitalist society aims to cultivate faithful servants for the capitalists; education under the dictatorship of the proletariat aims to cultivate loyal fighters for the proletariat and thereby prepare for the future classless society. Furthermore, the former must conceal the class character and political nature of education, while the latter openly declares itself to be class-based and political.

What results does education with such aims produce for the proletariat?

In capitalist society, although there are also workers and peasants who receive an education, under the influence of capitalist education, they gradually become estranged from their class of origin. Once they become officials or engage in other intellectual work, they naturally betray their original class and adopt a hostile attitude. Such occurrences are not rare under the capitalist educational system. Moreover, capitalist education even takes such occurrences as its primary task.

In contrast, proletarian education seeks to raise the class consciousness of the proletariat, to unite them with the vanguard, conscious segment of their class, thereby cultivating organized, revolutionary proletarians and faithful supporters and comrades among the peasants. The education in the Soviet Union today takes this as its most important task.

Several key points regarding the aims of education during this period of dictatorship can be outlined. (Generally found in The ABC of Communism, Chapter 10, "The School and Socialism," sections 77-87)

First, regarding the school question, as with all other spheres, there is not only a constructive task but also a destructive one. That is, everything within the school organization of bourgeois society that makes the school an instrument of class domination for the bourgeoisie must be universally destroyed. In bourgeois society, higher-level schools become the possession of the exploiting classes; these schools should be reorganized. Teachers in bourgeois schools, who implement bourgeois education and deceptive work, must also be mercilessly expelled from the new schools. In the old schools, textbooks compiled according to the bourgeois spirit are used, and educational methods beneficial to the class interests of the bourgeoisie are adopted; all these will be completely eliminated from the new schools.

Second, in the new schools, the school should be utilized as an instrument for implementing socialist education and enlightenment. The first priority is to strive to elevate all backward toiling masses to a higher stage of socialist consciousness. The bourgeoisie uses schools to enslave the workers; the proletariat, on the contrary, uses schools to liberate itself and to fundamentally eradicate all traces of slavish mentality existing in the consciousness of the workers. The bourgeoisie admits proletarian children into its own schools to instill bourgeois spirit; the task of the new school, however, is to educate bourgeois and petty-bourgeois children with the proletarian spirit. In essence, the socialist school must perform the task of transforming bourgeois society in the spiritual realm, in the human psyche, adapting the consciousness of adults to new social relations, and especially educating youth who possess a psychology based on the new society.

Third, there will be a major shift in the concept of children. In bourgeois society, children are largely considered the property of their parents. When parents say "my children," this not only signifies the existence of a blood relationship but also implies the right to educate their children. However, from the socialist viewpoint, this right is completely unfounded. This is because each individual does not belong to himself, but to society, to humanity. Only when society exists can all individuals live and develop. Therefore, children belong to society (they can rely on societal support to live within society) and are definitely not the property of their parents. The most fundamental right concerning children's education should also belong to society. The demand, through family education, to impart the parents' own narrow-mindedness onto their children's minds should be rejected from the socialist standpoint.

The ability to educate children is not as universal as the ability to produce them. Out of a hundred mothers, perhaps no more than one or two can fulfill the tasks of an educator. Therefore, in socialist society, family education must be abolished and social education adopted. Only social education can offer socialist society the possibility of educating the next generation of humanity with the least effort and means and with the greatest effectiveness.

Social education is considered necessary not only from an educational perspective but also for its immense economic benefits. With the realization of such social education, will not hundreds of thousands, even millions, of mothers be liberated for their own cultural development and productive work? Therefore, teaching institutions like kindergartens and nurseries must be established everywhere to facilitate pre-school education.

Fourth, from age 8 to 17—according to current Soviet regulations—is the period when all children and youth receive equal and free public education. The schools providing this education should be unified labour schools.

The term "unified" carries the following meanings: (1) Abolition of separate education for boys and girls; (2) Abolition of the poorly coordinated educational sequence of primary, secondary, and higher levels; (3) Similarly, abolition of the distinctions between primary schools, secondary schools, and higher schools as general schools, specialized schools, or vocational schools, as well as class-based schools and status-based schools; (4) Not only can all students pursue studies, but they should also be able to study continuously from the lowest stage, kindergarten, up to the highest stage; (5) Both general education and technical education should be received by all students.

This unified school not only represents the ideal of all progressive educators but is also the only possible school model for socialist society or a society aiming for socialism. Although educators in bourgeois society also cherish the hope of creating a unified school, this type of school can only be realized under socialism.

Furthermore, there are several important reasons why the new school must be a labour school, practically combining education with labour and depending on labour to conduct education.

1. It is considered for the effectiveness of teaching itself. What children understand most easily, fundamentally, and happily is learning not reliant on books or teachers' instructions, but grasping lessons through the combination with their own experiential labour. Although, as mentioned before, progressive bourgeois schools have begun implementing this. However, within the nature of bourgeois society, which deliberately fosters parasitic elements and forcibly separates mental and physical labour with an insurmountable gap, this cannot be fully accomplished.

2. Labour is also necessary for the physical development of children and for the comprehensive development of their abilities. According to practical experience, the time spent on labour in school, far from hindering children's progress in acquiring diverse

knowledge, actually promotes it.

3. The labour school is even more directly essential for socialism itself, because all citizens of socialist society must, at least in general, know about all occupations. In this society, there will presumably no longer exist groups of people stubbornly attached to their own specialized, fossilized professions. Even the most talented scholar must simultaneously be a skilled physical labourer. To students about to leave the unified labour school, socialist society might offer the following advice: "You do not necessarily have to become a professor, but you have the obligation to be a valuable producer." Starting with games in the garden, children unconsciously progress from the continuation of play to labour. And through this method, from the very beginning, labour is not regarded as unpleasant or as punishment, but as the natural, independent expression of innate abilities. Labour thus becomes a desire akin to eating and drinking. Only such a desire can be aroused and developed in a socialist school.

In socialist society, due to the rapid progress of technology, huge and rapid shifts of labour power among various industrial sectors will inevitably follow. At such times, it becomes necessary to allocate and organize the labour force for various industries. Moreover, in socialist society, all workers must be capable of performing this not only within a single sector but across many sectors. In bourgeois society, this situation can only be remedied by utilizing the industrial reserve army, i.e., the masses of the constantly unemployed. As for socialist society, unemployment will not exist. The reserve for all production sectors lacking labour power can be supplemented by the capabilities of workers from other sectors. Only the unified labour school can cultivate workers capable of fulfilling various functions in socialist society.

Fifth, youth acquire from the unified labour school the entirety of theoretical and practical knowledge necessary for all citizens of socialist society. However, schooling does not end here. Beyond general knowledge, specialized knowledge is also required. The scope of the most essential sciences has expanded to a degree that no single individual can fully grasp it all. Hence, the necessity for specialized study arises. The unified labour school does not inherently exclude specialized education; moreover, in its final years, students inevitably begin to show inclinations towards one profession or another. To accommodate this natural demand and enable the possibility of learning the foundations of various sciences, it is necessary to provide education with a specialized character during this period.

However, formal specialized education should commence only after the age of 17. There are additional reasons for setting this age limit. Youth in the labour school before age 17 should be considered students rather than workers. The primary task of the labour process within the school lies not in the production of value or the increase of state finances, but in education. Upon reaching 17, the student becomes a worker. He must share the obligation to labour and must participate in the production of goods for human society. He must first fulfill his duty to society before he can receive specialized education. Therefore, youth aged 17 and above typically pursue specialized studies only outside of their working hours. With the advancement of technology, working hours can potentially be reduced to 8 hours, 7 hours, or even less than 6 hours. Thus, through this method, all members of socialist society have ample time available for specialized education. For those with exceptional talent, or when deemed necessary from a societal perspective, they may naturally be exempted from labour for two or three years or have their working hours further shortened, allowing them to engage in scientific research and education.

Sixth, under socialism, the precise nature of specialized institutes or universities cannot yet be accurately predicted. What can be said is that the student body will primarily consist of workers, thereby making technology and science the common property of the working class, and all distinctions between professors and students will also be eliminated.

Seventh, besides schools, there are various adult education institutions and recreational facilities, such as libraries, museums, art galleries, radio broadcasting, theaters, music, cinema, travel, etc. These will not only be universal but also completely open to the public, allowing all cultural instruments to become objects commonly owned and shared by the masses. Furthermore, the socialist spirit will be allowed to permeate the hearts of the masses.

Originally, in capitalist society, talent is regarded as the direct property of its possessor and serves as a means for personal enrichment. The products born of talent, in this society, are commodities that can be sold at various prices, or even forced to be sold; consequently, such products become the possessions only of those with the most money. Works of genius, which possess great social significance and are, in essence, collective creations, can be purchased by people like America's Morgan, and by the same token, these individuals have the right to alter or even destroy them. According to the laws of capitalist society, no one can penalize them for this. Items like artworks or manuscripts, through private trade, largely become the monopolized possessions of the exploiting classes, and the general populace does not even have the right to view them.

In socialist society, it is imperative to declare all artworks, collections, libraries, etc., as public property, and all theaters and film enterprises as state-owned. Only in this way can the scientific and artistic works created by the sweat and blood of the labouring masses be returned to the hands of their true owners.

Finally, in the transitional period from capitalist to socialist society, not only do schools have the task of propagating socialism, but all institutions of the entire state apparatus must also undertake the task of propagating socialism.

The primary means of this state propaganda are: (1) the nationalization of the printing industry; (2) the monopolization of news and publishing enterprises; (3) the state operation of large-scale film enterprises, theaters, etc.; (4) the full utilization of all means of "mental production" that have become state-owned, for the broad political education and general education of the working class, and for building a new socialist culture on the class basis of the proletariat.

In essence, the state propaganda of socialism is the means for eradicating all traces of bourgeois consciousness and a powerful weapon for creating a new consciousness, new thought, and a new worldview.

Questions

1. Why is the arrival of socialist society inevitable?

2. Where do the erroneous roots of utopian educational revolutionaries lie?

3. How does class education in the transitional period differ from that in capitalist society?

4. What are the main educational tasks during the transitional period?

5. What changes will occur in the status of children in socialist society? Consequently, what changes will follow in education?

6. What will the relationship between labour and education become at that time?

7. Will the aforementioned types of educational [Transformation] still exist then? Why or why not?

8. What tasks must the entire state power perform in the cultural sphere during the transitional period?

CHAPTER 3: AN OVERVIEW OF EDUCATION

SECTION 9: EDUCATION AND THE ECONOMY

The General Relationship between the Economic Base and the Superstructure — The Interaction between Education and the Economy — Several Characteristics of the Commodification of Education — The Economic Movement and the Educational Movement in the Late Capitalist Period — Questions

According to the materialist conception of history, the economic structure of society is the base of the superstructure; that is, the superstructure is determined by this base.

From political phenomena right up to philosophical phenomena, encompassing the entire system of the superstructure, within society, as a necessary link in the chain of social phenomena, [it] is connected with the economic base of that society and with its technical system. (Bucharin, Historical Materialism)

This explains the relationship between the economic structure and the superstructure. However, this does not imply that the former is the most important or the latter is unimportant. It is like the left hand and the right hand, or a gear and a spring: between them, there is only a kind of mutual relationship, with no difference in importance whatsoever. When it comes to importance, both sides are "relatively important"; the difference lies merely in the function performed by each mechanism.

Bucharin provides a clever explanation on this point:

All differences are differences in function. Production management and production itself each have their own tasks. That is, production management serves to eliminate friction, prevent contradictions, organize and regulate the various elements of labour. In other words, it establishes a certain "order" for the labour force. The same holds true in other spheres. For example, among humans, moral habits and all similar regulations serve to adjust human beings, to bring them into certain categories, to prevent the constituent parts of society from disintegrating. What about science? Science is also the same. In this sphere of labour, (if it is natural science) it ultimately serves to indicate the course of the production process, enhance its effectiveness, regulate its progress, and establish its order.

Just as production management arises from production itself, philosophy arises from science. In this sense, philosophy is not primary but secondary; not an original but a derivative phenomenon. But on the other hand, philosophy can, to a certain extent, dominate science; because it has already provided science with a "common viewpoint" or "method."

From these examples, one can probably sufficiently understand the fundamental significance of distinguishing between material production and the labour of the superstructure. For the mutual relationship between these two exists in the form of ideological labour, which is on the one hand a derivative quantity and simultaneously a regulative principle. To the extent that it relates to the totality of social life, the difference ultimately lies in the difference of function.

In essence, although the productive forces of society's economic relations form the real base when viewed from the superstructure, the superstructure itself also has an effect on society's economic relations and productive forces. That is, it can sometimes promote the development of the productive forces, and at other times constrain the development of economic relations. Among the various social phenomena, there continuously exists—a process of interaction: cause becomes effect, and effect becomes cause.

Based on the above exposition, let us examine the relationship between education and the economy.

First and foremost, education, as part of the superstructure, naturally takes shape according to the economic structure and changes along with economic development. To cite some simple examples, nations with backward economic development inevitably become nations with backward cultural development. Furthermore, as mentioned before, feudal society emphasized etiquette, capitalist society emphasizes knowledge, and socialist society emphasizes the unification of education and labour—all of these serve as clear evidence of education's dependence on the economy. Even Confucius's saying, "First make them wealthy, and then educate them," and Mencius's statement, "The people are so busy saving themselves from death that they fear they haven't enough; how can they have leisure to practice propriety and righteousness?" are not without reason in this sense.

Another example is the current class-teaching method, which was advocated by the Czech[98] educator Comenius (1592–1670) in the 17th century. However, it was not widely adopted until after the Industrial Revolution in England at the end of the 18th century. Later, as capitalism developed further, the power of capital extended into various aspects. Cultural phenomena that were previously considered relatively unaffected by economic forces

---

98 [Special Editor's Note] Comenius was a Czech educator. Because the Czech lands were then part of the Austro-Hungarian Empire, he is referred to here as an "Austrian."

gradually came under the sway of capital. In recent times, the commercialization of newspaper and magazine operations and the operation of schools as businesses are notable examples. Undertakings such as news and schools originally placed superior importance on human elements, but now economic elements such as facilities and funds are gradually replacing them.

Another striking example is the impact of industrial rationalization on the educational world. In England, due to educational rationalization, expenditures were greatly reduced and teachers were laid off. As a result, many elementary schools were closed, and many teachers lost their jobs. In Japan, the implementation of industrial rationalization increased unemployment, caused school disputes to surge, and worsened the difficulties of entering school and finding employment year after year. These insoluble contradictions, although inevitable products of the rationalization process, must be driven forward relentlessly in imperialist Japan. Thus, capitalism ultimately has no choice but to head down the path of decline.

We mentioned earlier the commodification of education; let us now explain it in more detail.

The first characteristic of the commodification of education is the valuation of education in monetary terms. For instance, one might say that primary education is worth a certain amount of money, and secondary education is worth another. In society, salary levels are indeed determined by one's level of education. Take Japan as an example: in April 1928, the average starting salary for graduates who found employment was 68.83 yuan for university graduates, 56.22 yuan for specialized school graduates, and 37.38 yuan for secondary school graduates—according to a survey by the Central Employment Bureau.

In a certain large company in Shanghai, China, the starting salary standards were: 200 yuan for graduates from Western universities, 150 yuan for graduates from Japanese universities, 60 yuan for graduates from domestic universities and specialized schools, and about 30 yuan for secondary school graduates.

An even more blatant example is the United States, the dollar imperialist proud of its one hundred percent pragmatism. An article titled "Does Education Pay?" in the Boston Journal of Education on February 18, 1926, stated that E. W. Lord, head of the Business Administration Department at Boston University, had found a clear answer to this question. According to his research: those without secondary education training had to rely on physical strength to earn money, but their capacity diminished after age 30; their maximum average annual income was no more than $1,200 (U.S. dollars, same below), and their lifetime earnings (from age 14 to 60) amounted to only $45,000. A secondary school student spent at most $2,000 during four years of education, but within seven years after graduation (age 18), they could recoup this cost and surpass the maximum annual income of the untrained. Their maximum annual income could reach $2,200, and lifetime earnings could total $78,000—spending $2,000 more but earning $33,000 more than the former. A university or specialized school student, although spending more money, could, from graduation at age 22 to age 28, have an income equal to that of a secondary school graduate at age 40; their maximum annual income could reach $6,000, and lifetime earnings could total $150,000—$72,000 more than a secondary school graduate. Therefore, Lord said: four years of secondary education are worth $33,000, and a university diploma is worth $72,000.

Furthermore, many universities and specialized schools in the United States are merely of a "vocational school" nature. For instance, the University of Cincinnati even had students study in the morning and work in factories, department stores, and banks in the afternoon. As for Washington University in St. Louis, it frankly advertised how it could enhance students' money-making ability. (See Upton Sinclair, The Goose-step, pp. 331-332)

This is the theory of educational value held by efficiency-obsessed, scientific Americans. But is this situation unique to the United States?

The second characteristic is mass production. Using the class system and following a fixed curriculum, students are required to complete their studies within a set timeframe. How is this different from operating several machines according to a fixed mold to manufacture large quantities of goods? The similarity is particularly striking in terms of "anarchic production." Capitalist production, because it does not calculate social needs or purchasing power, but involves competing production by individual capitalists, leads to overproduction, crises, mass unemployment among workers, and other phenomena: this is called anarchic production. Similarly, in education, without considering the employment prospects of graduates, schools simply admit new students batch by batch and send them into society, resulting in the difficulty of finding employment: this can also be called "anarchic production." For example, in Japan, according to a Home Ministry survey in June 1929, unemployed members of the intellectual class nationwide had already reached 100,000 people. According to a Central Employment Bureau survey in November, the employment rate for graduates of public and private universities and specialized schools was 64.7% of the total number of graduates in 1927 (Showa 2), 53.9% in 1928, and 52% in 1929. Furthermore, the hiring rate (of those who registered) was 68.3% of the total graduates in 1927, 54.2% in 1928, and only 46% in 1929. This decreasing trend of pessimistic figures already exposes the bankruptcy of the modern education system. In April 1929, there were still 10,000 graduates without a "market"; by April 1930, over 20,000 new graduates would be "produced," making a total of 30,000 people to enact a battle for jobs. Is this not a kind of "crisis"?

The third characteristic is the factory-ization of schools. In countries with developed capitalism, there are many public and private factories engaged in the manufacture of commodities; similarly, there are many public and private schools engaged in mental production. They employ hundreds of thousands or even millions of education workers, who daily produce vast quantities of ideological goods for millions or tens of millions of students, the raw materials or consumers of educational labour. In capitalist countries, these massive quantities of ideological products are just as indispensable for the reproduction of capitalist social relations as the massive quantities of capitalist commodities in material production.

As for the quality of the ideological products produced or reproduced for the daily consumption of millions or tens of millions of consumers from these thought factories, it is as described earlier in the "Discussion on the Tasks of the School," so there is no need to elaborate here.

The fourth characteristic is the so-called "fair trade" mentioned above, striving to be "accessible to the masses" to attract widespread patronage.

The fifth characteristic is the patent rights for inventors, treating inventions entirely as commodities that can be bought and sold with money. In the modern era of economic rivalry among the imperialist powers, an embargo policy on inventions and research is even implemented in economic strategy. Look at the number of patent applications in various countries in 1927:

United States   87,545

Germany   63,003

Great Britain   35,469

France   23,067

Japan   12,607

Furthermore, with the implementation of the "Utility Model Law" in Japan and Germany, the results for the same year were:

Germany   126,728

Japan   40,282

More patents mean more monopolies, meaning knowledge becomes increasingly privatized. As for the previously mentioned case of American large corporations buying up new inventions only to suppress them, depriving the masses of the opportunity to benefit, this is even more vicious. Why do they do this? Because a new invention might affect their monopolized machinery business; if it fell into the hands of another independent entrepreneur, it might cause a significant loss for the big corporation. So they buy it with money and have the right to destroy it, thus a great inventor is turned by this social system into a kind of scientific plunderer. (See Upton Sinclair, The Goose-step, p. 380)

The sixth characteristic is the commercialization of sports. On page 371 of Sinclair's same book, it is stated that all universities have alumni committees who scout for the best athletes, investigate the sports activities of various schools and other universities, and use various means to entice those "tough guys." Although the use of money is supposedly prohibited, no university fails to break this rule. Tickets are sold during competitions, and various staff are employed. One student in charge of intercollegiate track and field received $800 for this role. Harvard University's annual sports budget exceeds one million dollars, and football games alone can cover this expense. First-class coaches receive annual salaries of $20,000, and graduated managers also receive high salaries.

More recently, on October 23, 1929, the Carnegie Foundation for the Advancement of Teaching in the United States issued a report strongly criticizing sports in American universities and specialized schools. Because sports today have become commercialized, and the subsidization of athletes lowers student morality. When recruiting new students, all universities and specialized schools invariably use various pretexts to lure sports stars from secondary schools. First-rate universities like Harvard, Princeton, Columbia, Pennsylvania, and New York all use scholarships and other names to subsidize athletes' tuition and give them special treatment. The report listed 130 universities and specialized schools, among which "there was no evidence that athletes were not subsidized." Furthermore, according to a report in Cosmopolitan magazine: during the 1928 football season (i.e., November), the total gate receipts from football games in the United States amounted to 50 million U.S. dollars. Of this, Yale received 1 million, Harvard 420,000, Princeton 300,000, and Michigan 625,000. The income of ordinary corporations could not match theirs.

In fact, this "business" of competing for athletes is not only prevalent in the United States; even Japan is not immune. And as for our China, while we may lag behind in other areas, in the preferential treatment of athletes, I'm afraid we are not falling behind!

Other aspects, such as "individuality development" as an expression of modern individualism and liberalism, also serve as an example of commodification. Because the commodity itself manifests the following social relations: (1) society is an individualistic economic organization based on the principle of private property, (2) there is an extensive division of labour within society. This division of labour is not just a segmentation of tasks within one industry, but a specialization across all industries.

The above all illustrate how economic forces dominate education.

Now, does education also sometimes influence the economy? Yes, it does.

Take science as an example. We just stated that natural science is "used to indicate the course of the production process, enhance its effectiveness, regulate its progress, and establish its order." This is the impact of science on the productive forces and economic relations. Capitalist society particularly encourages the study of natural science precisely because such research can contribute to the development of production. The industrial rationalization that has become popular in recent years is a product of scientific research. While the application of machinery, the division of labour, and the development of factory industry certainly promote the development of various types of industrial education; the development of various industrial educations, in turn, enables more efficient control over production activities, improves the effectiveness of technology, and achieves the goal of capital accumulation.

Recently, we have encountered an instance where the economic movement actually requires the assistance of the spiritual movement. That is the "Total Spiritual Mobilization" implemented by Japanese imperialism after September 1929, mentioned earlier. Here we will provide a more detailed description and critique. According to the directive issued by the Japanese Minister of Education:

Our country is facing many difficulties, and although there are numerous matters requiring remedy; the shaking of national thought and the distress of public finance and the economy are truly the most worrisome... To overcome these difficulties and achieve the prosperity of the national fortune is the urgent task at hand. Examining the origins of the current maladies, the relaxation of the national spirit is the greatest cause. Once the spirit relaxes, a trend of frivolity and self-indulgence arises, consequently thought loses its correctness, life leads to self-indulgence, resulting in today's state of affairs. The method to remedy the current difficulties... fundamentally lies in clarifying the concept of the national polity, revitalizing the national spirit, and seeking to improve economic life, thereby fostering national strength. Hence, the current spiritual mobilization.

From this, it can be seen that the practical significance of the Total Spiritual Mobilization lies precisely in the issues of public finance and the economy. Although "shaking of thought" and "relaxation of spirit" are mentioned, it is only because they lead to a self-indulgent, uneconomical, non-austere lifestyle that requires remedy. The so-called "clarifying the concept of the national polity, revitalizing the national spirit" is actually still for the purpose of "improving economic life, fostering national strength." For such a spiritual movement originating from economic motives, the implementation methods they set were:

The preparations for the Total Spiritual Mobilization in Tokyo City were scheduled for November 3rd, Meiji Festival, under the auspices of the Tokyo Federated Youth Corps, featuring a grand parade for austerity and savings propaganda, with a brass band at the forefront playing the "Austerity March." The Austerity Committee for all metropolitan elementary schools set the implementation method for the Total Spiritual Mobilization as: every morning before elementary school classes begin, the entire school holds a worship ceremony towards the imperial palace, striving to promote the spirit of revering the imperial family and the national polity. Also, the City Education Bureau coordinated with various movie theaters, requiring that before screening films, the national flag (Hi-no-Maru) must be projected and the national anthem "Kimigayo" must be played.... The Tokyo Federated Youth Corps also issued a spiritual mobilization notice in the name of its leader: (1) Worship towards the imperial palace every morning; (2) Worship the gods and Buddhas morning and evening; (3) Must abstain from alcohol and tobacco; (4) Must use domestic products. (Tokyo Asahi Shimbun, evening edition, October 9)

Originally, a feudal state's economy required frugality of consumption to maintain its limited productive capacity for a militaristic economy. As for a capitalist state's economy, it should encourage flourishing consumption to develop production and achieve "the prosperity of the national fortune." But in Japan's case, they actually resort to means like "propagating frugality," "revering the imperial family," "promoting the concept of the national polity," and "worshipping gods and Buddhas" to remedy the "distress of public finance and the economy." Isn't this a strange thing?

But upon careful thought, this is neither accidental nor strange. The necessity to seek help from the spiritual movement in the economic movement is a characteristic unique to the late stage of capitalism. In the early stage of capitalism, namely the 18th and 19th centuries, economists and philosophers strove to exclude the spiritual movement from the economic movement. Not only in the 18th and 19th centuries, but in no era has the economic movement been so closely linked with the spiritual movement as in the period of capitalist decline today. The original purpose of capitalism was to reject the spiritualist state and establish an economist state; hence, it vigorously rejected the spiritual movement, just as mechanics does not calculate the weight of the soul, aiming to liberate itself from under the spirit, which served as the starting point of the modern economic movement. Even if there were so-called spiritual movements at that time, they were none other than spiritual movements based on the "spirit" of the evolutionists of the time, aiming to liberate themselves from under the spirit.

However, by the late stage of capitalism, the vigorous revival of the spiritual movement is a result of the capitalist state losing its liberalist structure, with external peaceful commercialism turning into militaristic imperialism, and internal democracy turning into fascism. Materialistic monistic capitalism, in its final stage, has reverted to a dualistic life of matter and spirit. Those engrossed in material life should, in principle, disregard spiritualism, but due to the current instability and insecurity of their material life, their fear has awakened the inherited spirit, leading them to try to save matter through spirit. Although they know through modern science that chanting prayers cannot save a ship in distress, when the actual ship is in distress, they cannot help but utter "Amitabha Buddha," which contradicts modern knowledge.

Therefore, this is a symbol of the degeneration of the modern state. It seeks, like the old states that hindered its predecessors' endeavors, to use the spiritual movement to prevent the emergence of the new era. This spiritual movement aims to hinder the evolution of human economic action. But in reality, this is merely "reactionary and perverse," because in the real world, disasters cannot truly be saved by prayers.

Questions

1. What are the characteristics of the commodification of education? Try to cite examples from Chinese educational facts.

2. How do economic forces influence education? Can education break free from economic influence?

3. Why does the late capitalist period require spiritual movements to remedy economic difficulties?

4. Can examples of this degenerative phenomenon of modern states be found in recent Chinese politics and education?

5. Can education alone improve a country's economy?

SECTION 10: EDUCATION AND POLITICS

The Politicization of Education — Historically, There Has Never Been Education That Transcended Politics — Instances of Modern Political Domination over Education (Japan) — The Cultural Struggle as a Medium for Political Struggle — Political Education and Education Preparing for the Construction of Socialist Society — Questions

Now let us examine the relationship between education and politics.

Politics itself is also conditioned by the economy; in other words, politics is also one part of the superstructure, with the economic structure of society as its real base. The essential meaning of politics is the concentrated expression of the economy, i.e., the activity of power. In a given society, there exist political relations corresponding to its economic relations (ruling class and ruled class, capitalist state and workers), and consequently, there exists a political organization, i.e., a political system, corresponding to the economic organization.

As for education, although it is also part of the superstructure like politics, it is even more secondary, even more derivative. Because it is determined not only by the production process but also by the political process.

Just as education and the economy interact, education and politics also interact. First, let's discuss the power of politics over education. In a class society, politics dominates the general spiritual life process of society, and education is certainly no exception. Changes in the meaning of education manifest themselves during historical periods of change in social class relations. Throughout history, there has never been education divorced from political relations. No matter what kind of education system, it ultimately exists only by and for the ruling class.

Education can be broadly divided into two categories: that which is subordinate to politics, and that which transcends politics. In the era of autocracy (including constitutional forms containing autocratic elements), educators follow the government's policies to standardize education, often being purely subordinate to politics. In the republican era, educators can establish standards from the standpoint of the people, thus achieving education that transcends politics. (Cai Yuanpei's "Opinions on New Education," see Shu Xincheng, Modern Chinese Educational Historical Materials, Vol. 4, p. 26)

These were Cai Yuanpei's views held in the first year of the Republic (1912). By the current Party-State era, they might have changed. However, this view of education transcending politics must indeed be considered an extremely common one. Therefore, we still find it necessary to critique it.

In fact, based on our discussions in the previous sections, there is no education that is not subordinate to politics. Even education in the republican era (presumably referring to the era of the bourgeois state after the French Revolution) never transcended politics. Let's take France itself as an example.

France was the first to advocate the politicization of education.

France underwent a change at the end of the 18th century, becoming a republic... Although the form of government changed repeatedly, the educational policy was almost consistently politicized.

The Constitution following France's first establishment as a republic in 1791 contained the following provision: "The state shall create and organize a system for educating all citizens; all knowledge necessary for humankind shall be provided free of charge by the public. Schools of various levels shall be distributed throughout the country to meet demand. Schools shall have holidays commemorating the French Revolution, the spirit of mutual fraternity among citizens, and obedience to the constitution, the state, and all laws." This is probably the earliest provision concerning education in any national constitution... In 1792, the separation of religion and education was decreed... From 1794 to 1795, the National Assembly passed a bill for national educational facilities...

During Napoleon's sixteen-year dictatorship, he vigorously promoted secondary and higher education, pioneering the system of using the university as the central administrative organ for national education... Simultaneously, he proclaimed the educational aims as: (1) promoting Roman Catholic doctrine; (2) loyalty to the royal house that works for the people's welfare and to the Napoleonic dynasty that guarantees French unity and constitutional articles; (3) obedience to the unified education, producing a corps of teachers for the church, the state, and the family (i.e., the University) as stipulated by law. (Zhuang Zexuan, The Evolution of Western Educational Systems and Their Background, pp. 202-205)

The claim here that France was the first country to advocate the politicization of education is not factual—even in Zhuang's same book, it is stated that "several small German states had already established statewide educational systems in the 16th and 17th centuries," and "Prussia had compulsory education laws as early as 1716." However, it is sufficient to fully demonstrate the incredulity of the statement that "in the republican era... one can achieve education that transcends politics."

Educational history records that in the 8th century, Charlemagne advocated that education should cultivate patriotism and even ordered clergy to abandon Latin and use the vernacular for sermons. In China, since Emperor Wu of Han (over 2,100 years ago) dismissed the hundred schools of thought and revered Confucianism, and also established the selection system (for officials), education subordinate to politics has been implemented continuously without interruption.

Zhuang also states:

As for education in Britain and America, it had not been politicized in the 19th century. In terms of the rate of educational popularization, Britain and America lagged behind France. In terms of educational administration, Britain did not establish a Ministry of Education until the early 20th century, while the United States still has no Ministry of Education to this day. (In the same book., p. 208)

I feel this statement is overly constrained by the formal aspects of educational politicization. It must be understood that the fact of educational politicization does not depend on whether there are constitutional provisions or a central educational administrative body. As long as it is education dominated and utilized by the ruling class in a class society, the "aims" and "policies" of this education inevitably align with the political relations of the time. Chinese education since the Han Dynasty has revered Confucius and Confucian classics; Japanese education throughout its history has worshipped the Emperor and respected the Imperial Household. Can these not be cited as instances of educational politicization?

Even regarding 19th-century British and American education,

traces of "politicization" can be found.

For example, from the late 18th to early 19th centuries, Adam Smith, Jeremy Bentham, Robert Owen[99], and others advocated the necessity of universal education. Adam Smith, in his 1776 The Wealth of Nations, advocated using minimal public expense to implement the most fundamental part of education for all citizens. Bentham, in his 1802 Principles of Penal Law, argued that education should be an action of the government, and where parents neglected it, the state should step in. Owen, in his A New View of Society published between 1812 and 1816, also advocated universal elementary education from early childhood, believing that a good government must have the best possible national educational organization. Apart from such proposals for state-run education, the government—the organ exercising political power—in the 1802 Factory Act, restricted child labour and stipulated the obligation for apprentice education, which can be seen as the origin of state-provided universal education. In 1833, Parliament passed a grant of £20,000 to subsidize schools of the British and Foreign School Society and the National Society[100]. This increased to £30,000 in 1839. By 1870, the famous Forster Act[101] was passed. This act is the foundation of today's educational organization: (1) compulsory local education

---

99 [Special Editor's Note] Robert Owen (1771-1858), British utopian socialist.

100 [Special Editor's Note] The "British and Foreign School Society" and the "National Society" (full name: "National Society for Promoting the Education of the Poor in the Principles of the Established Church").

101 [Special Editor's Note] The Forster Act, commonly known as the Elementary Education Act 1870, was a fundamental English education law. Passed in 1870 under the sponsorship of MP William Forster, its main aim was to advance mass education.

rates (taxes); (2) establishment of local authorities[102] everywhere; (3) proclamation of compulsory education. The law further required children aged 5 to 13 to attend school. The grant money reached £562,000 that year. Even private denominational schools received subsidies, thus bringing all elementary education under government supervision. The 1891 Act abolished tuition fees, and the 1899 Act provided for special education. In 1899, the Central Board of Education was established in the central government, also having the power to inspect secondary education, further showing the progress towards national educational unification.

In the United States, by the latter half of the 19th century, most states had also established public education systems and tuition-free arrangements.

In essence, the educational system throughout history has always been one formulated by the ruling class. When modern states explicitly proclaim laws for universal or public education and use state funds to supply schools, it indicates that "politicization" has reached a level of formal openness. How can one still say it is "not politicized"?

We openly declare — the so-called school that transcends life and politics is nothing but deception and falsehood.

We can firmly believe Lenin's words without doubt.

However, it is true that in modern states, the politicization of education is more thorough and stringent than before. Especially in the imperialist stage, the educational policies of the ruling class

---

[102] [Special Editor's Note] "Local authorities" refers to the division of areas into school districts, organizing school boards to supervise education in their district.

become more profound and thorough. Here, we will detail the cultural policy (including educational policy) of Japanese imperialism to illustrate one aspect of educational politicization.

Recently (1929), Japan's cultural policy was based on three major political central issues: preparation for imperialist war, capitalist rationalization, and anti-Soviet policy.

First, the crisis of imperialist war. Japan's aggressive encroachment on Manchuria and Mongolia in recent years, military expansion, and consecutive large-scale army and navy exercises indicate the intensity of Japan's war preparations. Simultaneously, in the cultural sphere, we can observe the following facts: (1) Compulsory military training in schools above secondary level; establishment of youth training centers for working youth, strictly implementing military education; (2) Scientific research on warfare, striving to utilize scarce material resources effectively; (3) Propaganda of war ideology, utilizing novels, plays, etc., as propaganda tools; (4) Concentrating all bourgeois demonstrations on war preparation, such as mobilizing national reservists and youth corps during the "Imperial Accession Ceremonies", and having students participate in military exercises.

Secondly, capitalist rationalization is the most practical issue for Japan, having suffered two major blows: the post-WWI panic and the 1923 Great Kantō earthquake. Bank mergers, dissolution of small companies, development of large corporations, etc., are all manifestations of rationalization. According to methods recently published by the Resources Bureau, these include: (1) Cultivation of the national intellectual and physical strength and training for social service; (2) Perfection of various experimental research on science and technology; (3) Encouragement of industrial inventions and designs; (4) Establishment of employment agencies; (5) Thorough popularization of correct national defense concepts; (6) Allocation of resources for military and civilian needs; (7) Wartime resource control and operational organs... The manifestations of this rationalization in the cultural aspect include the following: reforming the examination system, making it a monopoly of knowledge for the bourgeoisie; popularizing rationalization ideology, making it a facade for social reformers; upgrading specialized schools, eliminating the distinction between universities and specialized schools; employment agencies providing labour education to cultivate loyal, skilled workers, while also creating permanent unemployment, etc. Among these, the rationalization of education and the cultivation of privileged workers are the most noteworthy.

Thirdly, the manifestation of the anti-Soviet policy includes arresting Communists, proclaiming death penalty decrees, and constantly propagandizing that domestic communist movements are related to the Soviet Union. Its manifestations in culture are twofold: (1) Hindering the import of Soviet culture, such as banning films, preventing troupes from landing, confiscating proletarian cultural publications, etc.; (2) Direct slander and counter-propaganda against the Soviet Union, such as attempting to negate the Russian Revolution itself to obliterate its true significance. Additionally, many anti-communist publications are issued.

The Japanese bourgeoisie, following the above three policy directions, implements its reactionary cultural policy. As for the organs through which these cultural policies are implemented, they are described below.

The organs utilized for this reactionary policy are very systematically organized. Besides utilizing state organs, they also utilize all other peripheral organizations.

The state administrative organs include the Resources Bureau and the Decorations Bureau within the Cabinet. The former seeks to control the national economy and culture, the latter provides a material basis for state ideology. Within the Home Ministry, there are the Shrine Bureau, Police and Security Bureau, Health Bureau, and Social Bureau. Under the Police and Security Bureau, there are the Nutrition Research Institute, Sanitation Experimental Station, and Publication Censorship. Under the Social Bureau, there is the Central Employment Bureau. The Patent Bureau under the Ministry of Commerce and Industry is the organ for the propertization and monopolization of knowledge. The Ministry of Education is the cultural administrative organ, housing the Specialist School Affairs Bureau, Ordinary School Affairs Bureau, Vocational School Affairs Bureau, Textbooks Bureau, Religious Affairs Bureau, Infectious Disease Research Institute, Japan Academy, Japan Art Academy, and all other cultural control organs.

Under these administrative organs, there are other direct and indirect educational institutions, all operating for the benefit of the ruling class.

First, one can point to the highest organs of bourgeois ideology, namely research institutes. These include universities, the Institute of Physical and Chemical Research, the Nutrition Research Institute, the Kitasato Institute[103], the Infectious Disease Research Institute, etc. Beyond these, there are various learned societies like the Engineering Society, the Industrial Policy Society, the Japanese Social Academy, etc., which are also groups that unify specialists, give them bourgeois objectives, and promote the progress of bourgeois science.

---

103 [Special Editor's Note] The Kitasato Institute, located in Tokyo, is a famous Japanese medical research institute.

Second, there are the schools at all levels, which are organs for disseminating completed bourgeois science or for training specialists. These can be considered the most directly under government jurisdiction among cultural institutions and the ones most meticulously managed by the bureaucratic ruling class. The task of higher-level schools is to produce individuals suitable for government organs, qualified leaders for the social labour process, namely state officials, local government public servants, scholars, teachers, technicians, doctors, lawyers, journalists, etc. Students receiving higher education are mostly children of the bourgeoisie and petty bourgeoisie. In other words, higher-level schools are monopolized by the bourgeoisie, realizing the strange phenomenon where ownership equals the right to education, while the children of workers, poor peasants, and proletarian citizens are confined to a state of ignorant slavery. Lower-level schools provide education for the impoverished masses under the name of compulsory education; their task is entirely to prepare children to qualify as exploited individuals, developing the industrial efficiency desired by the bourgeoisie. Currently, Japan has a total of over 45,480 schools nationwide, with a total student population reaching 11.79 million. Beyond these, the various Youth Training Centers, established in 1926, under the control of absolute authoritarianism and militarism, unify the education and organization of the entire youth mass, aiming to enhance labour capacity and prepare them to serve as reactionary troops in "emergencies." Organizations like the Greater Japanese Culture Association are even more purely reactionary in purpose. Also, to control the teachers responsible for this education, organizations such as the Imperial Education Association, the International Education Association, the National Vocational Education Association, and the National Elementary School Women Teachers Association have been formed.

Third, among the government-affiliated organizations and those of a similar nature are the Reservists Association, the Patriotic Women's Association (1.44 million members), the All-Japan Federated Youth Corps, the Boy Scouts of Japan Federation, the Tokyo Federation of Girls Youth Corps (the above are officially run), the Greater Japan National Essence Society, the Japan Justice Group, the Black Dragon Society, the Great Unity Society, the National Essence Society Headquarters (the above are violent groups), the Nogi Association, the Central Patriots Group, the Central Repaying Virtue Association, etc.

Fourth, there are educational groups claiming autonomy, not directly guided by the government, such as autonomous youth corps, girls youth corps, and boy scouts. The total membership of these three groups is 4 million (including officially run youth corps). Others include the Society for the Dissemination of Scientific Knowledge, the Japanese Esperanto Association, etc.

Fifth, there are the so-called social work organizations. The largest is the Japanese Red Cross Society, with over 2 million members. Others include the Sakura Kaede Society (aiming for social reform movements), the Kōsai Society (medical relief), the Saisei Society, the Children's Protection Society, the Hoosei Society (prisoner protection), orphanages, etc. Also, employment agencies recently organizing various vocational guidance meetings and training courses can be included in this category. Special among social work organizations are public and private libraries.

Sixth, there are industrial groups that simultaneously conduct educational movements. For example, industrial cooperatives not only engage in economic activities like industrial finance but also serve as consumer cooperatives. Organizations like the Greater Japan Agricultural Association and the Imperial Agricultural Association, aiming to improve agricultural practices, hold various agricultural training courses; their role as deceptive educational organs is even greater than their original role as economic organs.

Seventh, there is so-called physical culture; all sports organizations belong to this category. These groups include the National Student Track and Field Federation, the All-Japan Track and Field Federation, the Greater Japan Athletic Association, the Greater Japan Swimming Federation, the National Student Swimming Federation, the Greater Japan Basketball Association, the International Submarine Club, the Japan Tennis Association, the Japan Softball Association, the Tokyo Metropolitan Girls' School Sports Federation, the Imperial Horse Racing Association, the Meiji Shrine Sports Association, the Kōdōkan (Judo Institute), the Greater Japan Martial Virtue Society, etc. The encouragement and promotion of these competitive sports superficially aim to enhance physical strength and cultivate perseverance and fortitude, but actually have three other purposes: (1) to display the might of Japanese imperialism to the world; (2) to prepare a large pool of human resources available for mobilization in case of external or internal "emergencies"; (3) to exploit youths' desire for fame and competitiveness, diverting their attention to the sports field, hoping to keep them away from, or even isolated from, the "movements" in factories and rural areas. Furthermore, it serves to instill the ruling class's ideology, giving them no reason or time to study emerging social sciences. Among these, organizations like the Kōdōkan (membership over 2.23 million) and the Martial Virtue Society (membership over 39,000) are particularly rich in feudal consciousness, adhering to the bushido spirit; they are also opponents of emerging forces and the source of East Asian fascism.

Eighth, there is education conducted through art. The groups in this field aim more at cultural monopolization than at propaganda and education. In painting, from the Imperial Fine

Arts Academy down, there are the National Art Association, the Pacific Painting Society, the Japan Fine Arts Academy, etc.; in traditional Japanese music, there are the Kanze School, Hōshō School, Kiyomoto Society, Nagauta Kensei Society, etc.; in Western music, there are various groups for amateurs and professionals; in theatre, most troupes themselves are incorporated into capitalist organizations, and Kabuki and Shimpā actors have formed the Tokyo Actors Association; in literature, although there are no specific bourgeois groups, most publishing outlets are capitalized.

As for organizations like theaters, film companies, music, and radio broadcasting, they are naturally not openly accessible to the masses. High-priced tickets and long performance hours make them inaccessible to ordinary workers, peasants, and citizens. But on the other hand, there are also cheap, short-term entertainment venues specifically for the masses. The content performed there invariably promotes militaristic ideas and emperor worship, all aimed at obliterating emerging class consciousness.

Ninth, there are various religious groups. The religion most closely connected with the state religion, almost considered a state religion itself, includes from the Grand Shrine of Ise down, the Meiji Shrine, and various government-supported and nationally funded shrines. Although these don't have direct followers, they exist everywhere nationwide, and their powerful propaganda organs are the schools. Next, there is Shinto, including Kurozumikyō, Tenrikyō, etc., with over 16.57 million followers. Buddhism has over ten sects like Tendai, Shingon, Jōdo, Rinzai, etc., with about 31.6 million danka parishioner households and about 8.54 million direct followers. Christianity is divided into Old and New churches, etc., with 220,000 followers.

These religions not only have shrines, mission stations, temples, churches, and other institutions but also run various social work organizations, educational institutions, and schools.

Finally, one can cite publications as propaganda and research organs for bourgeois culture. First are newspaper companies, then magazine publishers, and finally, publishing houses. In this era of capital's omnipotence, the operators of these enterprises are, of course, the owners of the means of production, the political rulers. With the development of printing technology, the scholars, writers, and journalists they can mobilize are increasingly able to perform the work of mass spiritual control on a large scale.

The most popular magazines piled up in bookstores nationwide, if not about feudalism, emperor-centrism, or militarism, are about religion, love, and sexuality, having a hypnotic effect. Magazines claiming liberalism, like Chūō Kōron and Kaizō, practice their "commodification," including almost anything. Thus, they sometimes carry rather leftist discourse, and at other times exhibit extremely rightist reactionary thought. Several major newspaper companies, like the Osaka Asahi Shimbun and Mainichi Shimbu, and the Tokyo Hōchi Shimbun, etc., to practice "commodification," all flaunt "class and political neutrality" and "social fairness." But in reality, they are all connected to bourgeois political parties.

From this, it can be seen that organs for the production and propaganda of Japanese bourgeois culture exist in all aspects. The items listed here, although not belonging to the same category or series, suffice to illustrate how culture and politics are skillfully combined, providing us with ample understanding.

Now let's see how the Japanese ruling class, through these various organizations, produces, propagates, and defends culture.

First, the production of bourgeois culture. Is the bourgeoisie capable of creating culture? Of course, it is. Isn't the bourgeoisie continually increasing material and spiritual wealth? However, three points are noteworthy: First, the producers of culture are not the bourgeoisie themselves, but intellectual labourers; second, the production of bourgeois culture gradually shifts from expanded reproduction to simple reproduction, and from simple reproduction to shrinking reproduction; and third, the production of reactionary culture does not increase wealth in any way.

In bourgeois society, when a scientist makes a discovery, this intellectual wealth itself does not benefit the scientist. Because this knowledge is useless if it does not enter the production relations. But if the scientist's research funds are supplied by the bourgeoisie, then the fruits of this science also do not belong to the scientist. Look at the "Regulations Concerning Inventions, Utility Models, and Designs Made by Staff" of the Institute of Physical and Chemical Research:

Article 2: When a staff member makes an invention in the course of their duties at the Institute, the right to receive a patent shall be inherited by the Institute...

Article 7: When a staff member, in the course of their duties at the Institute, makes an invention eligible for a patent regarding matters listed in Article 3, Nos. 2 or 3 of the Patent Law, the Institute shall have the exclusive right, for a material invention, to manufacture, use, sell, or distribute the article; for a method invention, to use the method and to use, sell, or distribute articles manufactured by that method.

Therefore, here arises a class opposition between scientists (intellectual labourers) and the bourgeoisie. The bourgeoisie becomes the exploiter of science.

Consequently, in bourgeois society, cultural production is necessarily greatly restricted. When the bourgeoisie attacked feudal society and played a revolutionary role, all newly produced culture served their interests. But when the bourgeoisie loses its progressive character, becomes an obstacle to social progress, and turns reactionary, the scope of cultural production must inevitably shrink. Recently, the policies of various research institutes, universities, or the fundamental policies of the Industrial Policy Society and the Engineering Society are entirely determined by the bourgeoisie's three major policies: preparation for imperialist war, capitalist rationalization, and the rejection of proletarian culture.

This, furthermore, affects the scientific methodology of the bourgeoisie, driving it into a complete dead end. The result manifests as idealism. From the standpoint of dialectical materialism, Lenin once deduced its recent effects in the field of natural science, particularly in physics, and made the following observation:

"A minority of modern physicists, influenced by the great discoveries which led to the breakdown of the old theories, influenced by the crisis in physics which demonstrated the relativity of knowledge with particular force, and unable to rise straight away to dialectical materialism, have slipped by way of relativism into idealism. The idealism of the modern physics, like the idealism of the modern physiology, is a reactionary, transient phenomenon."[104]

---

[104] [Special Editor's Note] The above quotation is from Lenin's Materialism and Empirio-Criticism. A contemporary translation reads: "The 'physical' idealism of our day, like the 'physiological' idealism of yesterday, merely signifies that one school of natural scientists in one branch of natural science has slid into a reactionary philosophy as a result of an inability to rise directly and at once from metaphysical materialism to dialectical materialism." See Lenin Selected Works, Vol. 2, People's Publishing House, 1995

From this perspective, so-called reactionary culture does not represent an expanded reproduction of culture but is, in fact, a gradual narrowing of the cultural sphere. A reactionary cultural policy is nothing other than a policy that deprives society of all progressive culture. The content of reactionary culture is an accumulation of past culture; while its appearance may seem to take on new forms, in reality, it only differs slightly in the manner of combination.

Then, by what methods is it propagated and popularized?

Observing from the content, some are blatantly reactionary, some wear the mask of liberalism, and still others put on the guise of socialism. Here, besides the bourgeoisie colluding with feudal remnants, social democracy also becomes part of bourgeois reactionary culture. Furthermore, in terms of quality, the bourgeoisie simply utilizes everything. For example, in literature, they exploit everything from so-called high literature down to popular ballads like Naniwa-bushi and Yasugi-bushi[105].

Finally, speaking of the defense of bourgeois culture, it can be "summed up in one phrase" as the suppression of its opposing culture, namely proletarian culture. First, from a legal perspective, they use the Public Peace Police Law, the Peace Preservation Law (with its death penalty provisions), the Publication Law, the Newspaper Law, etc., to deprive people of the freedoms of speech, assembly, association, publication, performance, film screening, and exhibition. Second, they utilize violent groups to carry out cruel persecution. Third, there is passive defense,

---

edition, pp. 211, 215.

105 [Special Editor's Note] Naniwa-bushi and Yasugi-bushi are both types of popular Japanese narrative songs.

restricting the producers and propagandists of bourgeois culture. Examples include high tuition fees, the abolition of examination systems to favor the children of the bourgeoisie, and obstructing the children of the proletariat.

From the Japanese example cited above, we can see how closely imperialist cultural policy is integrated with general policy. Within the sphere reached by culture, political power follows everywhere, so closely intertwined that they are as inseparable as form and shadow. If anyone still claims that modern education "can transcend politics," or believes that running education can be separate from politics (as seen in Tao Xingzhi's "Our Creed," see The Transformation of Chinese Education, pp. 113-116), it is frankly illogical.

Then, does education also have an effect on politics? Yes, it does. This can be seen from the struggle against reactionary culture.

In the struggle against reactionary culture (including the educational movement), three points must be noted:

First, this cultural struggle cannot be separated from the political struggle. This is not only because cultural policy is determined by general policy but also because cultural and political organs are skillfully interconnected. As described above, when observing the bourgeois cultural organizations systematically, attacking them one by one must ultimately transform into an attack on the central political apparatus. Otherwise, it will achieve no effect. However, from this perspective, attacking them one by one can indeed become an attack on the central political apparatus. In other words, the cultural struggle must proceed alongside the general revolutionary struggle; only then can this cultural struggle become truly effective.

Second, in the organization of the proletariat, it should also encompass all aspects of culture, such as opposing world war, opposing militarism, carrying out school struggles, developing proletarian sports organizations, art movements, publishing ventures, and even creating proletarian culture. The most important among these is introducing emerging sciences, etc. It is through this cultural struggle that the main task of political transformation is to be achieved.

Third, the so-called cultural struggle is not merely a struggle within culture. In countries where political transformation has not been completed, all struggles should be regarded as a medium for mobilizing the masses towards the political struggle. Lenin emphasized the educational significance of political transformation and discussed the rapid growth of mass consciousness during the revolutionary period. Therefore, within all economic and political struggles, a kind of educational activity must be carried out. In all struggles surrounding commemorative days, opposing war, opposing military exercises, and opposing social democracy, the educational significance of all propaganda and agitation must be highly evaluated.

As for countries where political transformation has been completed (like the Soviet Union), they still require political education. Apart from general schools being political, there is specific political education for adults. Its purpose is to prepare for the construction of socialist society. As for Soviet schools and party schools, they also exist to enable the construction work of the Soviet state to proceed more rapidly and correctly; in other words, they use education to promote the task of building socialist society.

Questions

1. Citing examples from Chinese educational history, provide instances of the politicization of education.

2. What kind of education should the Chinese labouring masses receive at the present stage?

3. Why must the cultural struggle be linked with the general revolutionary struggle?

4. Please pay attention to the educational discourse published in newspapers and magazines: how much of it discusses politics, and how is politics discussed?

5. Criticize the current cultural movement in China and discuss the tasks it should have at present.

SECTION 11: THE TEACHERS

The Teacher's Responsibility at the Present Stage — The Inevitability and Possibility of Teacher Association, etc. — The Organization and Function of the Soviet Union's Educational Workers' Union — Questions

The content of this section[106] will be limited to the following two points: the teacher's responsibility and the teacher's association movement.

First, let's discuss the teacher's responsibility.

In the present stage of social transformation, the mission borne by educators is naturally very significant. This is not to say they have the power to save or build the nation single-handedly, but rather that within the cultural sphere, they indeed have the possibility and necessity to fulfill a part of the revolutionary task. In the section on "The Efficacy of Education," I already mentioned the relationship between education and politics, stating that education before the revolution is used for struggle, being one of the weapons aimed at seizing political power. In the previous section, I just discussed how the "cultural struggle serves as a medium for the political struggle," a struggle that should be centrally conducted within all political and economic struggles, and the educational significance of all agitation and propaganda should be fully evaluated. This is the understanding that educators should foremost have regarding educational work, and it also becomes the preparation they should make for

---

[106] [Special Editor's Note] Part of the content in this section was previously published under the title "The Political Mission of Educators," using the pen name "Gongpu," in The Education Magazine, Vol. 20, No. 9, September 1928.

themselves.

Secondly, educators (especially primary school teachers) must recognize where their mission lies regarding the children who are the objects of their work. Aren't the children that educators spend their days with overwhelmingly the sons and daughters of the petty and middle classes? They are the oppressed; they demand liberation in all aspects: politically, economically, legally, socially, and even educationally. Whether they can find the path to liberation, or remain subjected to the dominant forces without seeing the light of day, depends on how educators educate them today. If you teach them to "know their place and keep to it," not to involve themselves in any struggle, then they will gain no benefit, although actual living conditions will inevitably provide them with practical political education. Conversely, if you teach them to understand the local political environment, the local economic situation, and how these relate to their own interests, guiding them at all times to approach reality and participate in work, then this kind of education is truly relevant to their lives.

Furthermore, educators also have responsibilities towards the general populace. It is well known that revolution requires the strength of the masses to succeed. The Chinese revolution is not yet complete, and the need for mass movements is extremely urgent. In this regard, educators should not confine themselves to the narrow world they currently see and inhabit; they should recognize themselves as a major road connecting culture and the masses. Educators should never consider their duty fulfilled by being confined within school gates, studying theories, teaching textbooks, merely maintaining their personal livelihood and satisfying personal desires. The worldview and educational outlook of educators should not be limited to the individual but opened up to society. Educators bear a social mission; they should liberate themselves from the lectern, move towards the social masses, participate in, or even lead, social mass movements. In the future, schools should not merely be schools for children, even less should they remain "no admittance except on business" institutions; they should become the central points of local culture, the sources from which the local masses draw cultural resources. They should engage in the movement to eliminate illiteracy, in mass political training movements, and use various revolutionary anniversaries for expanded agitation and propaganda movements. They will be the great headquarters for campaigning against superstition and breaking old customs, and the great assembly halls for mass entertainment and gatherings. Therefore, future educators should be the propagators of national culture, and schools should be the lighthouses of national culture. The more enlightened the culture, the more effective the work of political struggle will be. Naturally, as we already know, such effects are difficult to obtain satisfactorily within this bourgeois society. But is resigning oneself to inaction due to difficulties really the attitude that conscious educators should have?

Moreover, teachers, especially primary school teachers, mostly come from impoverished social strata. It seems rare for the sons of the privileged and wealthy classes to aspire to become primary school teachers and receive teacher training. However, this so-called teacher training does not meet the needs of the teachers themselves, nor the little citizens they will educate in the future, but rather serves the needs of the ruling class. Therefore, for a primary school teacher from an impoverished class to speak words that do not serve the impoverished class to primary school children of the impoverished class is truly a miracle under heaven. Thus, the living conditions of educators and the general masses are, in reality, consistent. By helping the suffering masses and seeking solutions to their suffering, educators are actually seeking to relieve their own hardships. Once educators understand this point, I believe they will certainly strive harder to carry out all practical educational work for the general masses.

Children need to receive education about the things they must inevitably live through, the masses also need to receive education about the things they must inevitably live through, and educators themselves also need to receive education about the things they must inevitably live through. In summary, they must all work to remove oppression and strive for freedom, and educators have the responsibility to prepare themselves and train children and the masses.

However, educators cannot possibly fulfill this responsibility with isolated, scattered strength. They must fully gather the strength of their own group, forming a kind of social force, on the one hand to protect their own interests, and on the other hand to devote themselves to the work of social transformation. Thus, the teacher association movement becomes an important current issue.

The following will discuss the teacher association movement.

Teachers in China, whether in universities, secondary, or primary schools, have formed groups before, and many still exist today (e.g., the Staff and Workers Union of Peking University). They have taken actions such as strikes and issuing manifestos to fight for salary increases, oppose incompetent educational authorities, and protect their own positions. However, according to newspaper reports in September 1928, when the Legislative Yuan drafted the Trade Union Law, Article 3 stated: "Personnel and employed staff of state administrative organs... educational undertakings... may not invoke this Law to organize trade unions." So, under the Nationalist Government, teacher association becomes problematic. Because typically, teacher associations aim "to enhance knowledge and skills... improve labour conditions and life." (Trade Union Law, Article 1)

For now, let's set this aside and only discuss the nature and consciousness of the teacher association movement. As for how to proceed, it depends on the efforts of the education workers.

First, the significance of teacher association. The teacher association movement is largely similar in nature to the trade union movement. This is because the lives of educators are close to those of general labourers. Here, educators refer mainly to primary school teachers. Look at the low monthly salaries, mechanical work, and schools repeating the same tasks—aren't these roughly similar to low wages, mechanical work, and factories repeating the same tasks? Naturally, there are many differences between educator organizations and labourer organizations, but we must acknowledge the many inevitabilities of teacher association existing as association.

Second, the inevitability of teacher association. In terms of facts, the teacher association movement is very evident in Britain, Germany, France, the United States, and especially in Russia. Theoretically speaking, there are actually the following necessary prerequisites:

1. They receive salaries rather than grant them; that is, they belong to the ruled class, not the ruling class. But the question of which class educators actually belong to is often raised. Some seem to say that educators are gramophones consciously played by the ruling class, and they also possess the so-called privilege of knowledge. Yes, in capitalist society, everything is commodified, or at least calculable in monetary terms. For example, during Cao Kun's era, a bribe-taking parliamentarian was worth 5,000 yuan[107];

---

107 [Special Editor's Note] Refers to the scandal in 1923 when the Beiyang warlord Cao Kun, to get himself elected as "President," bribed 590 members of parliament with 5,000 silver yuan per vote to vote

the position of a Japanese political party president was worth 500,000 yuan; and a neutral parliamentarian was worth 100,000 yuan (the price during the Tanaka cabinet in 1928), etc. In such an era, indeed, there is no product that is not advantageous to the owning class. Jewelry merchants and fashionable women certainly exist for the owners; even things like warships and cannons are entirely manufactured for them. Again, things like Invincible Brand toothpowder might be considered daily necessities needed by ordinary people, but since it is a commodity, at least 50% or more of its price ends up in the capitalist's pocket. Furthermore, some believe that rice is independent of the owning class, but given the phenomenon that those who produce rice themselves cannot get rice to eat, to insist that rice does not belong to the owning class is ultimately rather unconvincing. Now, perhaps some might still say that education is neutral, eternal, and independent of capitalist society. We have already thoroughly refuted the incredibility of such statements earlier[108]. Therefore, in this society, it is not an overstatement to say that all people stand on the side of the rulers, for the benefit of the rulers. Our educators are no exception. Moreover, as we said before, school teachers in capitalist society implement capitalist education and deceptive work. However, in terms of their relationship of interests, they are, after all, like other labourers, surviving under the control of others. Consequently, they, like other labourers, ultimately cannot escape the status of being ruled.

2. Another reason for viewing educators as standing on the side of the rulers is that educators possess the so-called privilege of

---

for him.

108 [Special Editor's Note] See Section 3 of this book, "Several Distortions of Education." That section refutes one by one distortions such as the sanctity of education, the purity of education, the neutrality of education, and the independence of education.

knowledge. But this privilege does not seem to bring great profit when sold; at most, it only exchanges for a license, giving priority for teaching positions. Besides, the salaries received by primary school teachers nowadays are frankly, in many cases, less than those of skilled workers, even not reaching those of chauffeurs or rickshaw pullers[109]. True, there was a time when these people enjoyed privileges above their living expenses; but that has become an old tale, and now they cannot even speak of being well-fed and clothed.

3. That educators do not stand on the side of the rulers, but rather occupy a position equivalent to wage workers, is actually because there are several points of commonality. The first point of commonality is the so-called mechanical work. Factory workers have absolutely no choice over their own products; they only need to enter the factory owned by the factory owner and sell their labour power all day long in exchange for sustenance. They stand beside the machinery that has been set up, obeying the commands of the machinery to manufacture a certain product. Once dismissed by the factory, they can hardly dispute it.

What about teachers? They first spend a number of years adding certain skills and proficiency to their own labour power by going to training grounds called teacher training schools. After the

---

109 [Special Editor's Note] According to a declaration made by the Jiangsu Provincial Secondary School Federation to the government and society in September 1929: primary school teachers' monthly salaries were only ten-plus to thirty-plus yuan, their year-round diligence insufficient to support parents, wives, and children; secondary school department heads and staff received at least 20 yuan, at most 80 yuan. According to the budget stipulated by the Executive Yuan of Central University, the academic dean of a first-class secondary school had a monthly salary of 80 yuan, less than a clerk in an administrative organ. Teaching remuneration was at most 7 yuan per hour per month. A Chinese language teacher had to teach three classes, correcting 130-140 essays weekly to earn 120 yuan, less than a section member in a county or city government.

training period, they become skilled workers and are hired by workshops called schools (not necessarily guaranteed employment). There, they have ready-made textbooks, teaching materials, teaching methods, and other machinery, requiring them to apply techniques to produce the people needed by the state. If they dare to impose ideas and training beyond the regulations on students, they will be expelled from this school workshop. In short, the point of becoming a "mechanical person" who cannot discover anything of their own reveals a major commonality between factory workers and teachers.

Some might say this comparison is somewhat excessive. They think education is much freer and more effective; how can they be placed together? True, the object of education being lively humans certainly makes it more interesting than dealing with inanimate objects. However, from the perspective of becoming a "mechanical person," we dare say there is not much difference between educators and factory workers. This mechanical sense lies in completely obliterating individual personality; it's not about not moving, but that such movement is also mechanical movement. Take the most obvious example: the timetable. The length of class periods is fixed, textbooks and teaching materials are fixed, teaching methods are almost fixed, and the size of classrooms and the number of students per room are largely fixed. Within this fixed time, the progress of the curriculum is also fixed. Therefore, some say that in France, with its uniform system, one could check a fixed schedule to know what subject was being taught from a certain time to another. Others say that if you cut off Japanese schools at a certain moment and examined this cross-section, you might even find them all on the same word or sound. How much does this differ from making soapboxes of the same size? If the box you make deviates slightly from the specification, your livelihood will be endangered. Three or four years ago, a secondary school teacher in a certain U.S. state taught evolution to students, which interestingly led to the so-called Monkey Trial, ultimately resulting in a court fine. A primary school student in Tokyo Prefecture, Japan, was said to harbor socialist ideas, which was considered the responsibility of the head teacher, who was then transferred elsewhere. Probably these two teachers, similar to the worker who made the box two or three fen longer, were therefore deemed to have transgressed the norm and had to be disciplined.

4. The second point of commonality between educators and factory workers is that both are wage workers. Neither of them possesses means of production; they have no other way to make a living besides relying on selling their labour power. The teacher's license received by educators is only effective in places recognized by the state as schools.

Previously, those with "teacher qualifications" could still set up their own private schools, own their means of production, and even slightly impart their own color to their processed products. But in modern times, unless hired by state-run or individually founded capitalist schools to sell their educational-skilled labour power, they have no means to find a livelihood. If they arbitrarily exert their labour power, such as running a private school, because it is not a school workshop, the processed products coming to them for processing won't be plentiful. Moreover, the state refuses to affix a completion or graduation label to such processed products. Therefore, their processing can only end up meaningless (without a market). This means that educators, unless employed by state or state-approved schools, have no other means of production available to them.

5. Therefore, educators cannot have any other means of livelihood besides being employed by state-run school workshops, manufacturing standardized products according to state-

prescribed machinery. This point places them within the same category as wage workers. Certified teachers are skilled workers, assistant teachers are semi-skilled workers, substitute teachers are unskilled workers, female teachers are female workers—their types are similarly categorized. Only, factory workers' wages are in principle daily, while teachers' are monthly. Teachers' status is relatively more respectable, what common parlance calls the "long-gown class."

Another point: schools are run by the state, while the majority of factory workers labour in privately owned factories. Here there seems to be some difference. But actually, there is no major point of difference, nor can any major point of difference be found, between teachers, who can be called public service workers, and workers labouring in privately owned factories.

6. From the above description of teachers' lives, we can see they indeed have the possibility of association:

Educators' workplace is a collective of many people called a school. Ordinary trade union organization requires many people engaged in the same industry or occupation. Speaking of our primary schools, although rural schools may have only two or three teachers, urban schools generally have around ten. If teachers in one locality unite, the number becomes considerable. Therefore, the possibility of association is quite sufficient in terms of numbers.

Educators have no other way to make a living besides selling their labour power as salaried workers, and moreover, they are "mechanical persons." This is the reason why they can possess the consciousness of the oppressed class and stand at the forefront of the oppressed class movement. In this regard, educators are much closer to industrial workers than to peasants when compared.

The above explains the inevitability of teacher association in great detail. But in fact, educators, who are so rich in the inevitability of tending towards association, often have an inclination to avoid association. What is the reason for this? Now we will discuss this point, namely:

The repelling tendency[110] against teacher association. Originally, educators have their particularities, which can be listed in three items:

As mentioned above, educators have the so-called privilege of the teacher's license. Having obtained this privilege, it seems their livelihood is somewhat more secure, their working hours are relatively shorter, and there might be seniority-based raises, pensions, and other preferential treatments. Relying on this privilege, they find a position in the school workshop, and regardless of the external economic situation, they are rarely directly affected. So, when periodic or aperiodic crises arrive, although many unemployed factory workers wander without recourse, their workshop is rarely affected. However, on the other hand, when the economic situation is very good, while others may be thriving, they inevitably remain shabby, or even feel desolate compared to their surroundings.

This viewpoint, we know, does not suffice to explain how secure or superior teachers' lives are, and in fact, they are in quite the opposite position. But that is another issue. What I am explaining here is simply that this privilege is sufficient to create an obstacle for them regarding association, which is also a fact.

Another reason hindering teacher association is that their salaries are issued by the state or local authorities. The target of their

---

110 [Special Editor's Note] It means obstacles or resistance.

demands after association is often the government, not a specific capitalist. Consequently, difficulties in achieving their demands and hesitation in putting them forward inevitably follow. Moreover, because of this, the nature of the association easily shifts from the scene of economic struggle to that of political struggle. This is the difficulty of teacher association, but also what makes it meaningful.

The third difficulty in association stems from the consciousness of teachers. The social classes from which teachers originate (referring specifically to primary school teachers) are mostly lower-middle classes like middle peasants, small merchants, and minor clerks. Therefore, families that wish their children to become teachers mostly adhere to the life creed of safety first—knowing their place and keeping to it. They believe that those who are "teachers of men" must be well-behaved, gentle, and refined. Unfortunately (?), the institutions where they receive training are teacher training schools, which are like windless zones. These schools are the only ones that waive tuition or reduce board fees. When our teacher trainees have just graduated from primary school and begin to have many questions about society, they are forced to receive education for "being a teacher to others," education where all teaching materials and methods are pre-arranged, allowing you only to imitate, not to hold many opinions. Within the roots of this bureaucratic nature and pedantic nature lies the feudal ideology inherited unchanged for thousands of years. Especially in China, where feudal remnants are still prevalent, this bureaucratic and subservient mentality is all the more rampant.

Besides nurturing feudal ideology, adding admonitions like being a "teacher of men" or a "model for others" forms a teacher's nature of seeming inviolable. Making people with this nature engage in association movements is not an easy task.

The manifestation of this feudal ideology is strict adherence to master-servant relationships; it is the so-called "a gentleman's thoughts do not go beyond his position in action," the so-called "he who is not in any particular office has nothing to do with plans for the administration of its duties," the so-called forbidding "unemployed scholars recklessly criticizing." Using a common term, it is the lack of "freedom of speech... etc."

An example of this kind of thinking can be seen in contemporary educational magazines. Although there are many educational magazines, what percentage of their content discusses political, social, and economic issues? The vast majority is limited to the narrow scope of so-called professional education, never daring to "transgress the norm." For instance, during the Beiyang warlord era, educational magazines (and other magazines too) regarded the word "revolution" as taboo, going to great lengths to avoid it. This shows how teacher consciousness becomes an obstacle to the association movement (Note! This is a general statement; there are certainly many teachers with revolutionary consciousness, who should be considered exceptions).

But overall, teacher association is ultimately possible. Consider the following:

Third, the possibility of teacher association. Considering the task of teachers and the trends of society, we can see that the aforementioned repelling tendencies will be like a candle flame before the wind, unable to withstand even a slight breeze; and the possibility of teacher association will vigorously unfold.

Above we have already discussed the responsibilities educators should fulfill at the present stage. Now, let's add a few words explaining the fundamental social task of educators. The fundamental social task of educators is to cultivate talent. Since it is cultivating talent, it is necessary to establish the goal of cultivation. And this goal can only be established by correctly understanding the evolutionary process of human society.

The talent we want to cultivate should be capable of adapting to contemporary and the near-future society, and simultaneously must be talent with the ability to realize [goals]. But in real society, we see many defects; each educator must first possess the conviction and strength to reform these many defects, must first equip themselves with the insight to perceive social evils and the passion to implement reforms.

How to gain this insight, how to exert this practical ability, is an actual important problem. But right here lies the necessity of teacher unity, the significance of teacher association.

Among modern professions, few professionals occupy a position like educators, who have the intelligence to discern the times and strive for its realization. The children and youth who are the objects of their work are the players who will break the shell of modern society and enter the new era. Therefore, it is a great contradiction to say that the educators cultivating such talent are the most conformist and appeasing social stratum.

What attitude should educators who are aware of this new mission adopt? First, they should know the historical role of modern society, use sharp eyes to observe the social facts occurring among the various social strata, and then grasp the future society that is the inevitable conclusion of social evolution. Next, they should pay attention to translating this kind of observation and grasp into their own lives and influencing children with it.

But when doing this, many difficulties naturally arise: first in research, second in practice. To resolve these difficulties, the need to rely on the strength of the multitude becomes even more apparent. With associations and meetings, teachers can pool collective wisdom and strive for implementation. Once the will of the majority of educators is formed, social power can naturally arise. Therefore, teacher organization is most essential for bringing out the essence of education. Conscious educators must engage in the teacher organization movement; that is the right path.

The above shows the possibility of teacher association from the perspective of the teacher's fundamental task. Now let's look at societal trends.

All those on the side of the ruled need an organization as a focal point for concentrating their strength. They need the power of organization to exert their "justice." Since educators are social animals, they also easily form this or that kind of group. For example, the various educational associations are one instance. However, such groups do not necessarily reflect the will of the educator masses, so truly conscious educators should organize groups that can realize the true mission of educators.

Fourth, the organization of teacher groups. Thus, looking from the ideal side, or merely from inevitability, the realization of teacher organization seems quite easy. But looking from the realistic side, the effect of repelling tendencies quite hinders the progress of the association movement. Here we see the particularity of teacher organization and consider it an important point for those engaged in the association movement to consider. Now, let's discuss how teacher groups should be organized.

The biggest difference between teacher groups and trade unions or peasant associations lies in the more diverse and complex employment relationships of teachers. For example, in trade unions, the employer is the factory owner; in peasant associations, the employer is the landlord. Although, due to capitalist development, governments enact regulations to hinder the movement, leading to phenomena like general strikes and intensifying into a situation where the two fundamental classes confront each other politically, the primary economic struggle ultimately targets the factory owner or landlord.

But for teachers, the employment relationship is extremely complex. Due to various legal provisions, general teachers are actually controlled by several levels: the school principal, the city/township, the province/county, and even the state. Among these, the school has the most direct relationship with daily life, while the state has the greatest overall relationship. Therefore, the target for educators, after all, is not as independent and specific as a single capitalist or landlord, but has connectivity and universality.

All teachers in state-administered primary schools (whether national, provincial, county, or township-established) lack individual particularity. They receive similar salaries and handle similar affairs. As long as state decrees remain unchanged, no school can undertake distinctive activities or receive significantly higher pay. Although differences in treatment exist between urban and rural areas, or between commercial hubs and remote villages, these are never unique to individual schools but are, at minimum, common to an entire locality. As for restrictions in their work, there is no distinction between urban and rural areas or elsewhere.

Therefore, the organization of primary school teachers, possessing this unified profession and structure, should also form a large, unified association on a broad scale. In the initial stage, those with the potential for organization should take the lead, connect with existing organizations, and gradually merge into a single entity, or be organized as branches to realize a unified collective. Through this process, local associations form county-level federations, county federations form provincial federations, and finally advance towards a single national organization possessing coordinated power. Although establishing this central organization is not easy, the rationale for advocating it lies elsewhere. As mentioned in the previous paragraph, the consciousness of many teachers today still retains feudal elements. Many of these teachers cling to the empty ideal of 'education for education's sake' and dare not make this or that demand. If the majority can unite, acting with collective strength can be sufficient to exert influence and correct teachers' consciousness. However, since the masses are local, the movement must also be conducted locally. Crucially, this movement must not be seen as separate local movements but as part of the whole; this must be clearly recognized.

As for the basic unit of teacher organization, it should be the school, as half of a teacher's life is spent there. Yet, as mentione before), teachers' actions are often common to a locality. Movements such as demands for salary increases necessitate the union of all teachers in a city or school district. Therefore, the next level should be local organization, centralizing the local teacher masses to conduct movements as a local collective, followed subsequently by county federations and then provincial federations.

Fifth, the aspects of the teachers' association movement. Considering China's current situation, there seem to be three key aspects requiring attention in the organizers' movement: (1) Ideologically, a critical attitude must be adopted to thoroughly sweep away feudal ideas and reformist ideas; (2) Politically, various freedoms must be struggled for to relieve the oppression of authority; (3) Economically, the stability of livelihood must be guaranteed to achieve a humanized daily existence. In essence, the goal of the educators' movement can be said to be the fight for thorough democracy, securing freedom of criticism, and stability of life.

For the readers' reference, let me discuss here the social status of Soviet teachers and their organizations.

In the Soviet Union, teachers are regarded as genuine activists politically, socially, and intellectually. This is even more pronounced in the villages. There, sometimes the teacher is almost the sole intellectual leader, and thus the real leader. For instance, in one village, the teacher is a representative in the village soviet, chairman of the cultural committee, an active member of the cooperative, a correspondent for the peasant news, an instructor for radio telephony, and also takes turns serving as an official. In another village, he manages agricultural propaganda, organizes model gardens cultivated by a group of peasants. Examples like this are everywhere. It is evident that Soviet teachers are precisely the ones who can genuinely fulfill the fundamental social tasks of education.

The Educational Workers' Union of the U.S.S.R. boasts 800,000 members, making it the largest and most powerful teachers' organization in the world. Its membership includes, besides various teachers, school doctors, librarians, village club staff, and all workers related to education. It is one of the 23 major industrial unions in the Soviet Union and operates as part of the working-class movement. Consider the program announced by the Union's Central Executive Committee:

Although we form an entity within the Union, we are not an isolated group of workers. We are an integral part of the entire Soviet working class. All issues raised by our Union are considered from a single perspective – that our goal is the ultimate goal of the entire working class.

The Union's work maintains close relations with the People's Commissariat of Education (the administrative body). All educational laws and regulations are carefully considered by the Union before approval. When the Union holds its annual conference, members of the People's Commissariat of Education's committee must attend to report and answer questions.

The Educational Workers' Union has two major functions: one towards teachers, and one towards society. The former uses collective methods to protect its members (in terms of salary and treatment) and to raise professional and cultural standards. The latter aims to raise the cultural level of the local community by enhancing educational standards and improving social organization.

Educational workers have a club in every major center. These clubs, like those organized by other trade unions, serve as bases for the cultural work and social activities of the teachers' union. They are managed by committees of the local teachers' union. The committee elects a manager specifically responsible for operations, who receives a salary. Each club typically has at least one lecture hall (in regular use), a library, a dining room, classrooms, a games room, and a notice board regularly preparing for sports meets and excursions.

(Regarding the organization of Soviet educational workers, it is best to consult Chapter 10 of Nina's Education in Soviet Russia)

Questions

1. What kind of consciousness should teachers possess in the revolutionary work of the present stage?

2. How should primary school teachers implement education related to the lives of children and the masses?

3. If teachers truly cannot obtain the right to organize, or are unable to freely exercise the rights of association and assembly, what attitude should they adopt and what actions should they take?

4. What necessity exists for teachers' associations? What obstacles exist? How should these obstacles be overcome?

5. Criticize the current teachers' association movement in China and discuss the difficulties in association and the methods to realize a teacher organization charged with a revolutionary mission.

SECTION 12: STUDENTS

Examining Students from a Political Standpoint — The Recent Living Conditions of Chinese Students — The Sorrows of Students — The Revival of the Student Movement — Misconceptions and Illusions Regarding the Student Movement — The Tasks and Program of the Student Movement — Student Organizations in the Soviet Union — Questions

Discussions about students in educational texts are common in books like 'General Introduction to Education'. However, my motivation for discussing students in this book does not stem from a purely educational standpoint, but rather from the position students occupy in present-day China – that is to say, a political standpoint.

Fundamentally, so-called students do not constitute the entirety of the educated. Before school age and after graduation, society should provide multifaceted and continuous education for all children and adults. Using educational terminology, for the former, pre-school education or kindergarten education should be implemented; for the latter, adult education or mass education should be provided. This is because the venues for education are not limited to schools, hence the educated are not limited to in-school students. However, given the current situation, in-school students indeed form the main body of the educated, and schools have always been regarded as the most widespread manifestation of education. Consequently, this book's discussion of students is limited to those studying in schools, temporarily setting aside those who should receive pre-school education and post-graduation education.

Based on our understanding of education – that education is

political and class-based – and according to the principle of 'learning by doing', it is unquestionable that students should participate in political work. That students should engage in political movements thus becomes the starting point of this discussion and the premise for all following exposition.

Let us first look at the current predicament of Chinese students. I will only write based on what has been disclosed in newspapers:

First, students' burdens are too heavy. Compulsory education ought to be free, and should even supply learning materials, yet many primary schools in China charge tuition fees. Families unable to afford these fees have no choice but to keep their children out of school. Normal schools, which waived tuition and board fees a decade ago, can no longer offer such preferential treatment nowadays. Those receiving university education also lament the heavy burden. Consider the petition from the joint session of student association representatives from various colleges of National Central University:

> The number of students requesting fee exemptions due to financial difficulties is increasing daily, while the tuition burden is uniquely heavier than that of other domestic universities. With the cost of living in the capital rising year by year and personal expenses growing, impoverished students scarcely have the opportunity to study; those barely managing are also subjected to economic pressures, unable to focus on their studies... The university authorities also seem acutely aware of the students' plight; they stipulated a financial aid method, but due to failure to raise the fund, it remains a dead letter, unrealized to date. In the 17th year (1928), fee-waiver quotas were established, but the number is too small and based purely on academic performance. Economically well-off students, with a professor's certification, can receive full fee exemptions, while those from poor families,

truly diligent in their studies, are left out in the cold. (From Shanghai Times, August 31, 1929.)

This shows that even students from the petty bourgeoisie and above, who receive university education, feel the hardship of economic pressure, and the nominal fee-waiver quotas merely serve to whitewash the situation.

Second, opportunities for advancing to higher education are too few. According to a public declaration by the Jiangsu Provincial Secondary Schools Federation to the government and society:

> Primary schools urgently need expansion, while junior secondary schools, under the current situation, already require expansion by more than sevenfold, and senior secondary schools require at least a threefold expansion. In recent years, provincial secondary school admissions have been excessively crowded; some even resort to connections seeking to become auditing students. The public, unaware of the importance of education, necessitates legislation to compel it and various means to promote it. Now, the people pay for education, yet face insurmountable barriers, leading their children to wander helplessly outside the gates. What could be more lamentable than this?

Furthermore, according to a survey by the Secondary Schools Federation on admissions for the first semester of the 1929 year, the total number of applicants was 12,913, with only 3,768 admitted. This shows an admission rate of merely 29.2%. This only considers those with the financial means to advance their studies; those who graduate from primary or junior secondary school but do not apply due to inability to afford further education are naturally not included.

Although we lack statistics for university admission rates, factual inference suggests that they certainly do not admit all secondary school graduates who wish and have the means to pursue higher education.

Having the money but no place to study – how can this not be a disheartening phenomenon!

Third, many are deprived of education due to warfare and natural disasters. A Xi'an dispatch from September 11, (1929), carried by Shanghai Republic Daily, stated that education in Shaanxi Province has been affected by various factors in recent years, leading to a gradual decline in educational affairs, with countless out-of-school youth. On the student side, due to severe disasters and difficult family finances, many have suspended their studies; those able to strive for education number no more than seven or eight per county. Shun Pao also reported that various secondary and higher-level schools in the Xi'an area, due to the severe drought that year, ended early in May. After the summer break, they could have opened early, but because (1) funding was unavailable, and (2) the educational sector itself was rife with internal strife, compounded by local political turmoil, the start of the school term was repeatedly postponed.

This is just regarding Shaanxi Province; other places like Henan, Shanxi, etc., also suffered disasters, and "continuous wars and calamities" persisted until the end of the 18th year (1929). Under these circumstances, with educational funds unavailable and student family finances declining, how can young people's opportunities for education not be deprived?

Other instances, such as class suspensions due to overdue educational funds or insufficient school funding, where faculty and students demand payment of arrears or increased funding, occur almost nationwide. University, secondary, and even primary school students suffer the loss of interrupted studies because of this. Whose responsibility is this?

Fourth, the harms arising from lack of teacher specialization and inadequate facilities are extremely evident. Consider again the petition from the joint session of Central University student association representatives:

> Many professors in various colleges hold concurrent posts, and those who do not are often incompetent; apart from attending classes, they never set foot in the library or research room. Since professors lack a research spirit, students naturally have little interest in studying, leading to schools becoming markets and lecture notes turning into commodities.

It also stated:

Due to financial difficulties in recent years, our university has been unable to add books and instruments or hire excellent professors. Students from poor families requesting fee exemptions cannot obtain them, yet administrative expenses consume over 500,000 yuan annually, reducing educational efficacy. The reason lies entirely in the excessive number of party members and the overly high salaries of staff... Various administrative offices in our university are overstaffed with redundant personnel who draw monthly salaries but have nothing to do.

That a university, whose function is research in advanced academics, and especially National Central University, located in the capital and under public scrutiny, harbors such blatant bureaucratic malpractices – will this not make those passionate about education, especially the "education salvationists", heave long sighs?

In fact, are the lack of teacher specialization and the inadequacy of books and instruments unique to National Central University? Readers, please investigate the schools in your respective localities; is it not the same everywhere?

Fifth, there is no freedom to research, publish, or assemble. Students in various schools spontaneously organize social science research societies, yet these are often banned; they spontaneously publish periodicals, yet these are often censored and banned; they spontaneously act against imperialism, yet are absolutely suppressed.

Sixth, there are very few employment opportunities. Whether secondary school or university graduates, once they leave school and are sent into the social labor market, how many do you think can find a way out? Unfortunately, I have no citable data here to confirm the extreme difficulty of making a living. But I can tell the reader, if you often pay attention to the newspapers in Shanghai or your locality, reporting on a certain institution recruiting a few staff and the number of applicants, you will easily discover the intensity of competition, which will simply astonish you. I vaguely remember the Shanghai Provisional Court recruiting several clerks; hundreds applied for the examination within the timeframe. Having spent one to two or even three thousand yuan on education, finally obtaining a diploma, yet still finding it difficult to be accepted by society – equivalent to an uncashed check – is this not disheartening and discouraging?

What is the nature of this difficulty in finding employment, and what are its causes? During your school years, educators do not tell you, nor do educational texts address it. As for how to solve this problem, naturally, you know even less. The education you receive is such a useless thing; the thousands of yuan spent and over a decade of time – is it not a "losing business"?

Having read the previous sections of this book, you must now understand the nature of the education you are receiving; you might be youths currently tasting the bitterness of being out of school or unemployed – so what do you intend to do?

You are young; besides the various hardships mentioned above, you may possibly suffer from others. For instance, issues of love, family problems, health issues, questions of outlook on life – these are unavoidable, personal issues for every modern Chinese youth. Have your teachers explained or guided you regarding these problems? Has the society you live in shown you sympathy and assistance? Are you perhaps cursing, "This heartless society, this cold-hearted society!" or "These irresponsible teachers, these self-deceiving teachers!"? Speaking of teachers, naturally, many are enthusiastic, brave, intelligent, and considered by you as clear guides, but are such teachers not often unable to hold their positions securely, or can they only advise you very cautiously? Ultimately, will you resent society, hate society, bitterly condemn society, or even, unwilling to live in this filthy society, throw yourself into a river? This is indeed a society that drives youth to death – how can those with insight not shed a tear of sympathy for you?

However, such passivity, such surrender to the adverse environment, is ultimately not the path that every aspiring youth should take. Look! Our student masses, who leaped up vigorously since the 'May Fourth Movement', becoming an emerging social force – despite numerous setbacks – are they not becoming active again by 1929? This trend of the student masses increasingly leaning left and becoming revolutionary is evident nationwide – even extending to students in Japan. Only such increasingly left-leaning and revolutionary struggles of the student masses represent the way out for young students to resolve the aforementioned problems. This is the positive, combative path against the adverse society, and moreover, the only correct and effective way out.

In this struggle situation, we can point out the following main characteristics:

The revival of anti-imperialism. China's anti-imperialist movement indeed went through a period of temporary quiescence since 1927. But from 1929 onwards, it has gradually revived, with young students fervently participating in this struggle.

The flourishing of social science research. Emerging social sciences are the theoretical weapon of the revolution, the ideological preparation for social change. The competition among Shanghai bookstores to publish social science series reflects the gradual ideological transformation of the student masses.

Wherein lie the reasons for this leftward shift in the student masses' struggle? Three points can be made:

Due to the intensification of the imperialist process of colonizing China, British, American, and Japanese imperialisms are more actively exploiting the Chinese people, leading to the worsening of common people's livelihoods and the increasing bankruptcy of the petty bourgeoisie.

Due to the consecutive years of natural and man-made disasters, resulting in "the people have no means of livelihood", conflicts and contradictions among social strata are 日益紧张 (increasingly tense).

Due to the instability of the students' own lives, not benefiting from education, and having to taste the bitterness of being out of school or unemployed – this forces them onto the path of revolution.

In recent years, some have believed that the revolutionary role of Chinese students has already vanished, hence there is no need to continue the student movement, or they only know how to conduct movements among a minority, unaware of developing struggles based on the interests of the broad student masses. Actually, these are erroneous tendencies, as the current leftward shift of the student movement demonstrates. Under the present circumstances, these erroneous tendencies must be severely corrected.

However, simultaneously, we should not fantasize about a unified student movement. Social conflicts among different strata have caused class differentiation within the student masses. A portion of the students have separate organizations, which we must overcome with the power of struggle. Therefore, the task of the future student movement is to develop the struggles of the student masses based on their broad interests, no longer seeking unification of student organizations from among the student masses divided by various political parties and factions.

The tasks for the current struggles of the student masses should include the following:

Expand the anti-imperialist movement, pointing out the aggression suffered by the Chinese people from foreign capitalism in recent years, with particular attention to anti-world war propaganda.

Oppose domestic warlord warfare, pointing out that the warlord system still exists. As long as warlord wars continue, exorbitant taxes and levies are unavoidable, and the livelihoods of the common people cannot be stabilized.

Strive for freedom of thought, speech, publication, research, assembly, and association; secure the freedom to participate in political gatherings, develop youth groups, run wall newspapers, organize social science research societies and discussion forums, etc.

Strive to increase educational funding, ensuring completeness of various educational facilities in schools, and oppose warlords and bureaucrats reducing or misappropriating educational funds under any pretext.

Fight for the freedom to participate in school affairs and select teachers; demand full democratic training within schools; especially oppose sacrificing student interests for the personal use of school funds and faculty positions by principals or officials.

Strive to expand mass education, raising the cultural level of workers and peasants in general.

Regarding examples of student organizations, again, none are better than referring to student organizations in the Soviet Union. For details, you can buy Education in Soviet Russia translated by Du Zhouhou from Minzhi Book Company; Chapter 9 of that book discusses student organizations. Also, Diary of a New Russian Student (translated by Lin Yutang and Zhang Yousong) and Diary of a New Russian College Student (translated by Jiang Shaoyuan), published by Shanghai Spring Tide Book Company, discuss the Young Pioneers and the Communist Youth League, providing insight into the lives of Soviet youth students. Here, I can only briefly mention a few points.

Before the October Revolution, all organizations among Russian students were often prohibited by the state. Now, student organizations are a major part of the educational system. Students at all levels learn how to live and work together through various student organizations.

Soviet student organizations mainly consist of four types: (1) Those specifically for handling student activities, such as sports, publications, maintaining student discipline, and participating in school administration; (2) Those managing and assisting academic work; (3) Economic organizations, either cooperatives or trade unions; (4) Political organizations, either in the Young Pioneers or the Communist Youth League. All these organizations are established with the help of school authorities who are experienced and well-aware of the extent to which children can participate in social activities.

Thus, although these are organizations among students, they still depend on the students' abilities. When the organizational capacity of the educated is weak, the degree of guidance from the educators' side must be strengthened; at the higher specialized school level, complete student self-government is practiced. However, it must be understood that every school always has one or several student organizations. Now, based on the report by Nina, author of Education in Soviet Russia, let us describe this more concretely.

In the lower grades of the Unified Labour School, a class secretary (meaningfully not called a class monitor) is elected with responsibility for managing the entire class, constituting the entirety of self-governing life. As grade levels increase, the scope of self-governing life expands. In the second and third years of the Unified Labour School, where a grade is divided into several classes, a grade executive committee is formed by electing one representative from each class. For children in the later period of social education (ages 12 to 15 or 17), typically three committee members are elected per class. These three members are divided into academic affairs commissioner, cultural commissioner, and health commissioner, each taking on responsibilities to realize self-government. The enforcement of discipline is an important part of student self-government. However, corporal punishment has been abolished. Students in vocational schools and higher specialized schools form intra-school trade unions according to their professions, linking with external trade unions. Daily life discipline is maintained by the respective trade unions. As many higher specialized school students are recommended by trade unions, a considerable number receive financial aid from external trade unions during their studies. But regardless of whether they receive aid, they must pay one percent of their income as dues to their intra-school trade union.

Secondly, regarding students' role in school management, from higher specialized schools down to rural primary schools, there is no student who does not participate in school management. This is simply to thoroughly implement the principle that the school exists for the students. There are two organs for school management: one is the decision-making body, the other is the executive body. The decision-making body consists of representatives from teachers, students, students' guardians, relevant trade unions, relevant political organizations (Party and State), and the trade union of school-specific workers (gatekeepers, clerks, and workers, etc.). At the school committee plenary session held once to four times a year, various fundamental policies are resolved. As for the executive body, it is generally an executive committee of five to seven members elected by teachers and students, which actually manages the school.

But student organizations are not purely for school life as described above; they also have political organizations. Depending on age and ability, they join either the Young Pioneers or become members of the Communist Youth League. In higher-level schools, there are also Communist Party members. Although not all students belong to these political organizations,

Party and League members among their peers generally play a leading role. Discipline issues in the Unified Labour School are often handled by the Young Pioneers. Under the guidance of the Youth Communists or Communist Party members, though young, they strive devotedly for the construction of Communist society, possessing greater moral courage compared to other youths, and they take pride in this. See the concluding words of Diary of a New Russian Student: "Long live our Pioneers!" How heroic!

Regarding the situation of the Pioneers and the Communist Youth League, I would like to quote and briefly translate from Chapter 11, "Youth Movement," in American Lucy L. W. Wilson's New Schools in New Russia:

The Young Pioneers had 4,000 members in 1922; 200,000 in 1923; 1,000,000 in 1925. Practically, all children from city schools aged 7 to 13, and increasingly children from village schools, belong to this organization. Almost everywhere, you can see them carrying banners, sometimes wearing various uniforms, more often using red scarves or red neckties as their only insignia, working, marching, running swiftly, singing. In summer, they go camping, protected by older Communist Youth League members, gathering around campfires, eagerly listening to stories about Lenin's youth and the October Revolution. They learn to understand nature directly. They learn methods of cleanliness, order, and drill. In these aspects, they resemble the Boy Scouts of capitalist countries in Europe and America. Additionally, they are under the direct control of the Communist Youth League, receive political education, preparing them to participate in the construction of socialist society in the future.

The age of Communist Youth League (Comsomol) members ranges from 14 to 23. Many students in secondary schools, whether urban or rural, belong to this group.

During the 1905 revolution, the children's revolutionary movement in places like Poland was very notable.

Thousands of children formed "Little Bands," occupied theatres and other public meeting places, distributed leaflets, and even participated in defensive battles. Of course, they were suppressed and disbanded. However, such experiences greatly contributed to the rapid development of the Communist Youth League after the revolution.

The function of Communist Youth League members in the progress of Soviet education has been immense and crucial. The initiation of peasant youth schools can be said to have started entirely with them, and they also greatly contributed to the development of factory schools. Pistrak (one of the Soviet education leaders) even said: "Without the assistance of the Communist Youth League, the creation of any current Soviet school would be impossible." This shows how Soviet youth students strive for the construction of a socialist society.

But these student organizations are rich in educational principles. Those of us studying education must not think these are merely political products and not educational ones; nor should we assume that because ordinary education books do not discuss student organizations, the above descriptions have ulterior motives. If you think so, you are wrong; you are truly blind followers of bourgeois pedagogy. Let me excerpt from Nina's report (original book, p. 114 ff.):

Soviet educators are now studying student organizations just as they study any other problem in pedagogy. Zaloojny[^4], Director of Educational Research at the Kharkov Education Department, speaking of the experimental and research work they can do in this area, said:

"Child study has shifted from the child as an individual to the child as a member of the community. This necessitates a complete change in attitude in the exploration of children's problems."

In a document written by Krupskaya (Lenin's wife) for the Young Pioneers, it states:

"Normal children living in proper situations will organize themselves... Clear purpose and collective life are the main conditions for children's development."

This educational principle regarding student organizations is detailed in the Scientific Pedagogy Section of the State Educational Council of the Russian Republic:

"1. The propertied classes set as the school's aim the cultivation of citizens who are obedient and have absolutely no thought of changing the existing order's main organizations. This aim determines the nature of the curriculum and the internal structure of the school."

"In such schools, the teacher is an absolute master over the class and the students. Added to this is a system of punishments and other rules. Rewards are also included, aimed solely at helping the teacher achieve his desired goals. The children are in his grasp. He can increase the workload, he can expel children from school. The children regard him as an enemy to be struck. They resist his rules, deliberately break them, and form groups for this purpose. The teacher is the representative of state power; the children's resistance to him is tantamount to resistance against the state order. This kind of struggle unites students into large groups, diminishes the authority of the administration, hinders the realization of educational aims, encourages a spirit of discontent, and fosters hostility."

"In such schools, the adoption of student self-government, aimed at eliminating the struggle between teachers and students, thereby enhancing the teacher's prestige, making children responsible for supervision, and executing the teacher's resolutions, is ultimately merely a means of forcing children to submit to the teacher."

"2. In countries where bourgeois democratic republics are firmly established (USA, Switzerland), we often see another type of self-government system in schools. Suddenly or gradually, a system resembling a bourgeois democratic republic, complete with its trappings: elections, courts, even prisons, is introduced into the school (e.g., the George Junior Republic in the USA). Students, especially youths, enjoy a degree of freedom of action under this system. Such student self-government aims to cultivate citizens loyal to the bourgeois republic."

"3. The difference between the aim we propose for the school and the aim proposed by bourgeois states exerts a decisive influence on the form and purpose of student self-government."

"4. Our school's aim is this: To cultivate useful members of human society, joyful, strong, capable of labor, possessing lively social instincts, accustomed to organized activity, understanding their place in nature and society, knowing how to connect with the progress of the times, able to firmly defend the ideals of the working class, and being powerful builders of communist society."

"5. In our schools, self-government is not a means of conveniently managing students, nor a practical method for studying the operation of systems. It is primarily a means by which students learn to live and labor well."

"6. The richer the content of student life, the more thorough the student self-government. Collective work is an immensely powerful organizing force. Unless the entire student life is invigorated by collective work, the self-government system cannot develop properly and assume the most rational and beneficial form."

"9. In its developed stage, student self-government must encompass the integration of educational groups and social activities, practically encompassing economic, recreational, artistic student work, as well as student mutual aid affairs. Students must have representation in all committees of the school."

"10. All work of self-government must be handled cooperatively by the students and teachers. The teacher's duty is to actively assist student self-government. But the teacher must allow students complete independence and not force them with his authority." (Copied from a booklet of decrees printed by the Educational Workers' Union of the U.S.S.R. — see Nina: Education in Soviet Russia, Chapter 9)

Student self-government has such theoretical foundations. Henceforth, new pedagogy books must discuss student self-governing organizations to be considered complete; henceforth, new student life must include such student self-governing organizations to be considered fulfilled.

Questions

1. Why should students participate in political struggles?

2. How many kinds of life hardships do young students suffer? Students themselves and revolutionary educators should carefully

study this.

3. How should young students prepare to struggle for their own livelihood?

4. Have you participated in any student movement? What experience did you gain? If not, how do you plan to participate?

5. What are your thoughts and opinions on the current student movement?

SECTION 13: THE EDUCATIONAL MOVEMENT OF THE WORKING CLASS

Labor Education and the Labor Movement — Ruling Class Labor Education vs. Working Class Independent Labor Education — Divisions in British Labor Education — Right-leaning: The Workers' Educational Association and Ruskin College — Left-leaning: The Plebs League and The Labour Colleges — The Theory and Practice of Working Class Education in Germany — Labor Schools in the United States — Questions

As discussed before, in class society, two types of educational rights often exist: one is the educational system of the ruling class, the other is the educational action of the ruled class. By the era of the modern state, as class antagonisms became increasingly severe, the two types of education that could previously coexist now became mutually antagonistic, even to the point of clashing. For instance, in American universities, propaganda for socialism is not allowed; professors violating this rule face dismissal; scholars from outside coming to lecture are refused entry (detailed in Sinclair's The Goose-step). Also, for example), in Japan, government authorities view student research in social sciences as "Bolshevization," dissolving research societies, dismissing guiding professors, and expelling researching students. They also forbid workers and peasants to establish their own schools. For example, in 1926, farmers in Kizaki Village, Kitaurawa District, Niigata Prefecture, recognizing that public primary schools were all organs of capitalist education, ordered all children to boycott and withdraw, establishing a proletarian farmers' primary school providing education completely not following the Primary School Order. However, shortly after its creation, it was shut down.

However, in Europe and America, just as communist parties can legally exist, the educational movement independently conducted by the working class actually manages to be somewhat public. Moreover, this educational movement of the working class is not merely substantive action but has already advanced to being organized and institutionalized. Naturally, the nature of this educational movement is anti-capitalist, hence anti-ruling class, so it inevitably conflicts with the formal educational system of modern society and is bound to suffer suppression by the authorities.

This section will describe the independent educational movement of the working class in Britain, Germany, and the United States. As for Russia's, it has already become the state's formal, sole educational system, differing from the above three countries, so I will dedicate a separate section to introduce it. The reason for the difference is naturally that the Russian working class has already seized state power.

Before describing them separately, I should explain the fundamental reasons for the emergence of this educational movement and the rationale for adding the term "independent".

The educational movement of the working class follows the entire movement of the working class. Since the establishment of capitalism, a new social group known as wage slaves has been created. The number of these wage slaves increases with the accumulation of industrial capital, and their lives sink deeper into poverty. Furthermore, due to crises and wars, they face the constant danger of unemployment and loss of life. Thus, within the capitalist social organization, from the early 19th century onwards, emerged designers who, yearning for a future society of peace and happiness, sought to experiment with their ideals;

figures such as Saint-Simon and Fourier in France, and Robert Owen in Britain, were truly the pioneers of Utopian Socialism. Additionally, there were anarchist ideas, as well as numerous literary works drawing on social issues, characteristic of this era. However, the evolution of human society is bound to break through capitalist restrictions to develop. The growth of the proletariat inevitably leads them to break free from the ideological domination of the bourgeoisie and generate their own social thought, providing theory for their anti-capitalist movement. Marx's scientific socialism is precisely the guiding theory produced by the development of the international working-class movement. The working-class education movement we are about to discuss is likewise a product of this working-class movement. Therefore, the origins of working-class education almost coincide with the origins of the working-class movement (the labor problem).

Furthermore, this working-class education is fundamentally different from the labor education given to workers by capitalists today. Working-class education is the independent education of the working class, carrying the meaning of the "class struggle in education." The purpose of this education is to liberate workers from the educational control system of the ruling class. Working-class education is fundamentally different from the education provided in ordinary universities and general schools. The education provided in current schools is essentially capitalist. It aims to praise competition and create superior individuals. In contrast, working-class education is socialist. It will uphold cooperation and produce superior social and industrial collectives. Therefore, labor education schools must "break away from the traditions and ideas of the so-called old schools" (Lunacharsky[111]),

---

111 [Special Editor's Note] Lunacharsky (Анато́лий Лунача́рский, 1875–1933), a Russian Soviet activist in public education. Served as the first People's Commissar of Education of the Russian Soviet

and base themselves on the values of their own class. I call this "independent" labor education for this very reason. However, we must also pay attention to a key point: not only do the bourgeoisie and their government have their labor education, but even within the camp of the labor movement, due to differing left and right factions, there are labor educations of different natures. Some genuinely serve the interests of the working class, while others do not. The former, standing on the position of class struggle, advocates independent working-class education, with the aim of studying the social sciences and movement theories necessary for the proletarian liberation movement; the latter is of the nature of general adult education, aiming at personal cultivation and the teaching of specific skills, and particularly emphasizes being unrelated to any political party. Originally, working-class education emerged alongside the emergence of the working-class movement and progressed alongside its advancement. When the class struggle situation gradually intensifies, differentiation occurs within the labor movement, and consequently, labor education also differentiates, which is a natural outcome. When observing labor education, we should pay deep attention to this situation so as not to go astray.

Now let us proceed to describe the working-class education in Britain.

Because Britain was the birthplace of the Industrial Revolution, the labor movement began earlier than in any other country, and thus the working-class education movement also started early. Not only that, but the divisions within labor education are particularly complex.

The earliest labor education in Britain began in the early 19th

---

Federative Socialist Republic from 1917 to 1929.

century. In 1823, the Mechanics' Institute was established, and by 1850, there were over 500 such institutes, focusing on systematic research in chemistry and mechanics, and occasionally teaching scientific principles frequently used by craftsmen like carpenters, masons, metalworkers, and dyers. However, this educational movement was not the independent education of workers, but developed under the aforementioned class-based paternalism. The People's College established in Sheffield in 1842 can be considered the pioneer of Britain's independent workers' education movement. Because it was economically independent, not receiving assistance from the government or charitable organizations. However, strictly speaking, even this school cannot be considered class-conscious. It only taught Greek, Latin, logic, civic education, etc., its purpose being merely to remedy the poverty of "knowledge". Looking at its achievements, its graduates included city councilors, aldermen, magistrates, and it even supplied the most capable mayor for the city government. This shows it was not established to cultivate talents for the labor movement.

During this time, the cooperative labor education movement gradually developed. In 1854, the Working Men's College associated with this movement was established, and later several others were founded elsewhere. But to this day, only the ones in Leicester and London continue to exist. The aim of these colleges was quite peculiar; they neither sought to elevate workers to the middle class nor aimed to instill class consciousness in workers, but rather treated all teachers and students as "Fellows," seemingly trying to break class boundaries. Therefore, this can only be called a "novel" form of labor education.

Thus, on one hand, new universities continued to appear. On the other hand, the University extension movement also began to flourish. Starting with Cambridge University in 1873, London

University, Oxford University, and others successively joined. Around 1880, this extension movement reached its peak. Eventually, due to the workers' lack of management rights, it gradually declined. By the end of the 19th century, the adult education movement had a significant influence on general worker education. Here I must mention Ruskin College, founded in 1899, a residential college for adult workers established in Oxford with donations from the American couple Walter Vrooman. It offered a 2-year curriculum, aiming to provide education in social sciences that was not biased towards any single party or faction and could contribute to the democratic working-class movement. Later, when Vrooman returned to America, the college was managed by a council composed of people from Oxford University and a few trade union leaders. Students receiving financial aid from trade unions were also sent by them. But in 1909, internal division occurred, leading to the separate establishment of the Central Labour College, which will be discussed below.

At the beginning of this century, the most notable development in British labor education was undoubtedly the Workers' Educational Association (W.E.A.), established in 1903 under the leadership of Albert Mansbridge. It set up branches everywhere, even in Australia and Canada. The most vigorous part of the Association's movement was the so-called Tutorial Classes Movement. Since the first tutorial class was started in 1908 by a committee jointly formed by the Association and Oxford University, all British universities rose to cooperate with it. By 1919, the number of classes reached one thousand eight hundred. It is said that "since this movement, on one hand, universities could reach deep into the ranks of workers, serving the majority of the populace; on the other hand, workers, constituting 6/7 of the national population, would enter the gates of universities to study together with scholars. At that time, a newspaper representing trade unions in America declared: 'We started by attacking Oxford University, now we know we were wrong, and can only end by blaming ourselves.'" (See Education Magazine Vol.21, No.8, Lei Binnan's "The Origin and Development of the British Adult Education Movement"). However, the very reason this educational movement holds no value within the labor movement is precisely because of such effects.

Now, back to the Workers' Educational Association. It was founded at a representative conference of workers and educators held in Oxford in 1903, convened out of a perceived need for workers to make contact with universities. During the Great War, the Association's activities ceased, but after the war, its scope of activities greatly expanded. It is now considered the largest labor education institution in Britain. This Association is a joint organization composed of the working class, groups and individuals related to education; local branches are established, and a central council formed by representatives from these local groups and others unifies the branches. The Association's aims are to awaken and satisfy workers' demands for education; to advocate for ideal reforms in the state education system; to provide various facilities for adult education outside schools, etc. Its main undertakings include guiding and managing the Joint Committee for University Tutorial Classes, three-year tutorial classes of university standard, one-year courses, study groups, summer schools, a central library, women's classes, etc., and publishing the monthly magazine The Highway and books for workers. This Association declares itself unrelated to any political party; regarding other organizations, except as necessary to achieve its aims through collaboration with the Education Ministry, local education authorities, universities and other educational bodies, trade unions, cooperatives, political groups, etc., it is not constrained by these bodies. Precisely because of this, it is unfit to be a truly meaningful independent workers' educational activity and can only become Britain's right-leaning workers' educational organ (the left-leaning one is the Plebs League, see below). By comparing the differences between the Labour College guided by the Plebs League and the Ruskin College belonging to the Association system described below, we can understand the differing natures of these two types of educational organs. In 1921, the Association had 317 branches, 2,896 affiliated groups, and 23,830 members.

As mentioned earlier, Ruskin College experienced an internal split in 1909, for the following reasons. Many students studying at the college had received social training; they were dissatisfied firstly because the college's management was almost entirely controlled by the Oxford faction, which sometimes disregarded student demands; secondly, because the university's educational policy was merely an extension of the old capitalist universities, tending to become an appendage of Oxford University; thirdly, because broad education was of little use to the workers' liberation movement. Thus, an atmosphere of discontent accumulated among the students. The radical students and alumni of the college subsequently organized the Plebs League in October 1908 (see below) as an independent working-class educational organ, and the following year further confronted the school with a strike, eventually splitting off to establish the Central Labour College themselves. This college later moved from Oxford to London, was renamed The Labour College (see below), and remains so today. The Labour College, following the Marxist educational policy of the Plebs League, was left-leaning. The subsequent Ruskin College, under the guidance of the Workers' Educational Association, which aimed for non-partisan adult education for workers, thus became right-leaning. However, by the 1925 British Trade Union Congress, it was resolved to place both Ruskin College and the Labour College under the management of the Education Committee of the British General Council of Trade

Unions.

Now let's discuss the Labour College. It was preceded by the Central Labour College. Guided by the Plebs League, which championed independent labor education based on Marxism, it implemented enlightening education on the means and methods used in the historical task of the labor movement. Most evidently, the college proclaimed the following items:

The foundation of this College lies in the confirmation of the conflict of interest between labor and capital.

The aim of this College is to provide education of an investment-benefit nature, opposing the ideas and theories of the capitalist class, and to impart to workers the necessary training to defend and propagate the interests of the working class.

Workers' organizations, namely trade unions, socialists, consumer cooperatives, etc., shall have their representatives manage this College.

Later the College also issued a declaration:

This college was established with the aim of supplying appropriate knowledge to workers' organizations for the accomplishment of their industrial and political tasks... Working-class education must be independent of all traditional educational authorities... It must adopt a radical form... The class most beneficial to the progress of social science, the form most beneficial to this class of science.

From this, it can be seen that the Labour College was truly "Independent Working Class Education."

This college also suffered setbacks during the Great War. However, local classes not only continued but expanded remarkably. Since its founding, it was managed jointly by the South Wales Miners' Federation and the National Union of Railwaymen, two left-leaning trade unions; by 1925, however, following a resolution of the Trade Union Congress, it, along with Ruskin College, was transferred to the management of the Education Committee of the General Council of Trade Unions. The college's curriculum was set at 2 years; besides offering special evening and daytime lectures, it also provided correspondence courses. Local labour colleges belonging to the college system now total 1,048 across the country, with 25,077 students, under the control of the National Council of Labour Colleges.

Finally, let's discuss the Plebs League. As mentioned before, it was organized in October 1908 by radical students and alumni of Ruskin College in Oxford, who broke away in opposition to the college's educational policy, with the aim of "education for workers by workers." In Britain, it and the aforementioned Workers' Educational Association form the two major camps of workers' educational organs. Its characteristic is that, contrary to the non-partisan stance held by the Association, it takes Marxism as its basis, namely: first, acknowledging the fact of class struggle; second, rejecting compromise with capitalist culture; third, believing that there can be no impartial stance in education. It further aimed "to promote interest in independent working-class education for the improvement of workers' present status, and to strive for the abolition of wage slavery." Its organization is based on individual membership; a monthly fee of 2 shillings is paid into a central fund, local branches are established, and its main activities include organizing classes for studying social sciences (maintained by trade unions, union councils, and local labor groups), publishing the monthly organ Plebs and other Plebs League publications, and guiding the Labour College and local educational organs with similar educational policies. It currently has about 2,000 members (mostly workers), with magazine circulation reaching 6,000 copies.

In essence), at present, the only powerful groups in Britain's Proletcult (Proletarian Cultural) movement are the Plebs League and the Labour College.

Next, we discuss the independent working-class education movement in Germany.

German social revolutionaries well understand the necessity of independent working-class education and are striving to discover principles for its correct application.

When the All-Russian Proletarian Cultural Conference was held in the summer of 1918, representatives from Germany attended and have since maintained close relations with Moscow and Leningrad. To realize the proletarian cultural plan, they held conferences. Although it was their first conference, its ideals were remarkable. The main points are as follows:

The class struggle in Germany is gradually strengthening, and the power of the proletariat must be mobilized in all aspects. Through this, workers can achieve victory over counter-revolution.

Publications, schools, lantern slides, churches, literature – all things called cultural groups – are merely the arsenal of the bourgeoisie. They are also nothing but soporifics that dampen the revolutionary impulse of workers. Ultimately, they are dominated by the bourgeois worldview, even within workers' own organizational groups.

The proletariat must forge the weapons necessary for the rebellion against the bourgeoisie. They must organize a proletarian culture opposed to bourgeois culture. Only when the proletariat succeeds will the people's worldview be able to become independent from the influence of capitalist poison.

For the proletariat to expect success, they must consider all questions of professional and political life from their own standpoint. Moreover, capitalist influence is seeking to interrupt the revolution from countless angles. Therefore, preparatory educational work is the most essential work for the correct application of strength.

Social revolution entails not only new methods in economics, nor merely communist organization and the dictatorship of the proletariat. It truly anticipates the construction of a new culture. It is about nurturing a cultural construction sown by the proletariat that should develop into humanity's first general culture. The dawn of this culture has already appeared. Once this culture emerges, education, ethics, art, science, and all aspects of public and private life will undoubtedly be revolutionized. The first task of the proletariat in this new cultural construction is to concentrate creative forces to achieve the unification and dissemination of the proletarian cultural movement.

Germany needs a centralized proletarian cultural collective. And this must be controlled by workers. In other words, it is necessary to unify and coordinate the forces of all groups united in planning independent working-class education.

Hence, the necessity for a collective controlled by workers.

The above outlines the theoretical aspect in Germany. Now let's look at its practical side.

Originally, Germans are capable practitioners and, simultaneously, substantial theorists. Since their theory is established, practice naturally follows. In Berlin, there is a group called the Sowjet [Soviet] or perhaps the Rote Punkt [Red Point]. The predecessor of this group was a publishing house, which gradually grew, and its activity is educational. It has a school called the Sowjet Schule [Soviet School] organized above vocational groups, and it also publishes Bolshevik textbooks. The education of this school lies not in enabling workers to acquire "general knowledge," but in equipping them with the possibility of realizing socialism.

Regarding Germany, due to limited information, we must stop here.

Finally, let us examine the independent working-class education movement in the United States.

The Rand School of Social Science, established in New York in 1906, can be considered the first workers' school in America. Initially, like Ruskin College in Britain, it was maintained by individuals (funded and initiated by Mrs. Rand). Now it relies on tuition fees and the sale of prints, etc., for maintenance. Main subjects are social sciences like history, politics, and economics. Great attention is also paid to English and Public Speaking. Textbooks are divided into several national languages depending on the type of immigrants. But this school is controlled by the Socialist Party. Compared to Britain's Labour College, it greatly lacks class consciousness and the spirit of class struggle – even though its foundation is also anti-capitalist. For example, Scott Nearing (author of the aforementioned Education in Soviet Russia) was initially associated with this school; but later, it is said he was expelled for being "too leftist." This also gives a glimpse into the school's general content.

According to the school's documents:

The Rand School of Social Science is an autonomous educational organ for socialists and the labor movement. This year (1929) is its 23rd year. It has survived several crises considered fatal, and often encountered reaction, splits, and economic shortages, etc. But due to the victory of its ideals, it will continue its work until it is no longer necessary.

The Rand School is definitely not narrow sectarianism. It does not seek to instill established beliefs into students' minds, but rather to draw out the knowledge they seek, especially to elicit their own thoughts.

Seeing such tenets, it is clear that this school is indeed not an educational organ for class struggle. That is, if not compromising, it ultimately cannot avoid being liberal.

The school's curriculum naturally also focuses on worker training. But besides regular students, it admits many auditors; this also suggests the school's lack of seriousness.

Furthermore, based on the school bulletin, the 1929 curriculum is briefly noted as follows:

Courses are divided into two main categories: Study Course and Lecture Course. Study Courses are further divided into English courses and courses in languages other than English. Listed below are subjects other than English:

American Unionism

Essentials of Socialist Economics

American Social History

Recent Sociology

Public Speaking

Appreciation of Modern Literature

Essentials of Marxism

Methods of Research

Also, lecture subjects are as follows:

The American Renascence

The Study of Human Behavior

Music of Various Nations

The World We Live In

Elements of Social Psychology

Psychology of Personality

Nations and National Problems

Labor and the Law

Labor and Social Legislation

What is Education?

America as a World Power

Philosophy and Social Thought

Symposium — Introduction to Socialism and Practice

Giants in Russian Literature

Six American Authors

Tendencies in Modern World Literature

Topics like these are inevitably rather miscellaneous.

In 1929, 107 students registered for the Training Course, 58 of whom were trade union members.

The school also offers correspondence instruction. Research results are published as pamphlets, and the American Labor Year Book is issued annually. Additionally, it engages in publishing for the proletariat.

In 1911, a Modern School was also established in New York. When it first opened, it had only one teacher and one student; all facilities were managed using Francisco Ferrer's educational principles. In 1916, it relocated to New Jersey. It is a boarding school for children's education and liberal training. At the same time, it is said to be rich in proletarian spirit. Its educational methods, influenced by discoveries in "New Psychology," are highly progressive. It is co-educational, combining mental and manual training. A monthly magazine, *The Modern School*, is published, printed successfully by the children themselves. But this naturally does not qualify as a purely proletarian cultural movement school.

In 1918, 30 trade unions in New York jointly formed the Workers' Education Bureau, with maintenance costs fully borne by the unions. Trade unions in Pennsylvania established their own educational organ (Department of Education) in 1920. The Central Labor Union of Boston organized a Business Union College after the war, entirely maintained by workers. Also, several schools in New York published the monthly magazine Cooperative Education and the weekly Cooperation.

The New School of Social Research is located in New York, but details are unknown. Here, only the Spring 1929 curriculum is listed:

Psychology of the Individual

Modern Science and Religion

Contemporary American Thought

Revolutionary Theatre in Russia

Population Problems

Society and the Individual

Intelligence and Psychological Testing

The school has no restrictions on admission. Even graduate students from Columbia University have joined, so in a bourgeois sense, it seems to be of a relatively high standard.

The only genuine labor school, at present, is actually the Workers' School in New York. Unlike the "freedom" of the aforementioned schools, it operates under the guidance of the American proletarian political party, striving with the most rigorous spirit for the propagation of Marxism. It is located on the fifth floor of the party's New York local headquarters; this year marks its seventh year of establishment.

This school not only exists in New York but also has branches in places like Boston, functioning as a national organ, actively researching under the slogan "Class struggle is the motive force of social progress." They not only regard the school as an organ for training individuals dedicated to the labor movement but also state that "the school itself is part of the movement." The school's sincere attitude can also be seen in its charter, where beneath "The Workers' School" it adds "Training for Class Struggle". The number of students was only 60 in the 1924-25 academic year, but by 1927-28 it had increased to 1,300.

According to the school's charter, the curriculum is divided into eight major categories, with subtotal under each, totaling 73 items. Here, only the main categories are listed:

English, Public Speaking, Journalism, etc.

General History (including the Chinese Revolution, the Russian Revolution, etc.)

American History (includes America as seen by Marx and Engels, the development of imperialism, etc.)

Unionism (Theory and Practice of the Union Movement, Problems of the American Labor Movement, etc.)

Economics (Marxist Economics, etc.)

Marxist Theory (Fundamentals of Communism, Leninism, Historical Materialism, etc.)

Special Problems of the American Working Class

Literature

Additionally, every Sunday from 8:00 PM, there are Open Forum public lectures and "discussions on current issues presided over by leaders of the American labor movement."

According to recent news, at the start of the new semester in September 1929, the most notable addition to the curriculum was the newly established research section on labor problems in Latin American countries. Its main purpose is to investigate the activities of American imperialism in South American countries and to study methods of struggle against them. Lecturers included I.A. Moore and Scott Nearing, among others.

Questions

1. Into how many factions can labor education be divided?

2. What constitutes true labor education?

3. Criticize the current state of labor education in China from a class standpoint.

4. Is it possible to openly conduct independent working-class education in China?

5. How can a good relationship be established between labor education and the entire labor movement?

SECTION 14: THE INTERNATIONAL ORGANIZATION OF EDUCATIONAL WORKERS

Two Types of Educational Internationals: The Bourgeois International Peace Education Movement and the Proletarian International Liberation Movement — The International Bureau of Teachers' Organizations — The Founding of the International of Educators — The World Federation of Education Associations — The International of Educational Workers — The British Teachers' Labour League — Questions

When it comes to international education movements, although there are several in name, they can be essentially categorized into two types: one that pays lip service to peace and justice but is in fact deeply tinged with capitalist colors; and another that, without pretense, raises the banner of the educational labor movement, openly declaring itself to be struggling for the proletariat.

The former can be called the International Peace Education Movement, while the latter has the specific name "Educational Workers' International".

First, let us briefly describe several international education movements, and then focus on introducing the content of the "Educational Workers' International".

The "International Bureau" of Teachers' Organizations

The initial international contact among teachers from various countries began from the end of the 19th century in Switzerland (between 1872 and 1874), Belgium (1880), and France (between 1885 and 1890). When the World Exposition was held in Liège,

Belgium in 1908, the Belgian "General Union of Male and Female Teachers" held an international "Congress on National Education" in Brussels, Belgium, and resolved to establish a permanent International Bureau for male and female teachers' organizations.

Until the World War, this "International Bureau" of the "Union of Male and Female Teachers" accomplished almost nothing. The only achievement worth mentioning is that, besides the Belgian "Teachers' Union", it added the "British National Education Union", the "Dutch Teachers' Association", the "German Teachers' Union", the "French Teachers' Union", etc., totaling about 390,000 members. In the pre-war era of rampant [militarism/nationalism], it was already suppressed by the authorities. When the war broke out, it was further enveloped in an atmosphere poisoned by mass slaughter. Later, the British "National Education Union" suggested to Secretary-General Knut in Belgium to reorganize the bureau on its pre-war foundation. But Knut replied, "We do not wish to share a platform with German lackeys." Thus, Britain turned towards the dollar republic, namely the United States. Because America was planning, under the protection of capitalist morality and economics, to organize a World Federation of Education Associations (the present World Education Conference).

Subsequently, Knut published accounts concerning the international solidarity of teachers in the annual reports of unions from various places, and sought to reorganize with the help of the League of Nations (Germany had not yet joined at that time). But this provoked indignation among teachers throughout Central Europe, and thus the "International Bureau" fell into a state of complete inactivity.

The Founding of the "International of Educators"

The iron fist of the Great War shook the educational world. A portion of educators were trapped in the most cowardly silence, but another portion rose in passionate protest. While pacifist activists in the victorious countries were cowed by the might of victory, the surge of worker and peasant education in Central Europe liberated teachers from the educational policies of state and religious authority (though later, some teachers participated in the proletarian mass movement, while others showed no sympathy). Among them, in nationalist countries like Finland, Hungary, Czechoslovakia, and especially Bulgaria, and Fascist countries like Italy and Spain, a segment of teachers continuously rose up against their governments' exploitation, falsehood, and enslavement, and continuously suffered penalties such as fines, imprisonment, exile, persecution, drowning, shooting, and hanging.

However, even in democratic countries, some relied on the victory of the militarists to stem the revolutionary tide. France, a democratic country, is one example. The international movement of French teachers started very early, and before the war, it achieved victory in the struggle for secular schools. But now, it shows loyalty to the imperialist government.

Nevertheless, a very small number of ardent individuals, based on pre-war struggle experiences and the experience of the great European war turmoil, became an increasingly fierce revolutionary force.

During the war, the French "Teachers' Union" secretly or openly conducted anti-war movements. Its organ magazine, L'École Émancipée (The Liberated School), was truly the only magazine in France that most courageously protested the war. But these male and female teachers who joined the organization for the pacifist movement were successively arrested and imprisoned, and after the war, suffered further persecution, losing their positions.

Stimulated by the supreme ideal of opposing war and the pre-war revolutionary realist syndicalism, the "Teachers' Union" called for the construction of a teachers' international in 1919. At the Tours Teachers' Congress (April 1919), the renowned thinker Anatole France[112] delivered the following speech, which the International of Educators used to propagate to the world:

Burn! Burn books that teach all hatred! I wish, from the bottom of my heart, that the teachers' committees of all nations would immediately join the International of workers, jointly formulate a common global curriculum, sow the seeds of ideals that produce world peace and a common human spirit into the souls of the young, and consider the possibility of this... Only the solidarity of workers can bring peace on earth.

At the end of this congress, Madeleine C. Martel laid the foundation for building the International of Educators and drafted a general plan for the movement as a resolution. The following year, at the Bordeaux Congress (August 1920), attended by Renata, a committee member of the Italian "Teachers' Association", the "International of Educators" was established. Albert Brizard and F. W. N. Veldkamp were elected as secretaries. Several months later, branches were established in six countries: France, Germany, Italy, Hungary (exiles in Czechoslovakia), the Netherlands, Spain. Later, individuals from Luxembourg, Belgium, Portugal, Russia, Scotland, Japan, and China also participated. Veldkamp was elected secretary because he was an

---

112 [Special Editor's Note] Anatole France (1844–1924), French novelist and thinker, Nobel Prize laureate in Literature. Joined the French Communist Party in his later years, sympathized with the workers' movement.

Esperantist.

Thus, the "International of Educators" was born from the cry against war and the current social system that causes war.

Coincidentally, in the United States at this time, there was also a thinker, a fighter against American imperialism, who called the international solidarity of educators worldwide a historical necessity. This is an extremely interesting matter, and a coincidental correspondence that is not difficult to understand. He was Upton Sinclair. In the conclusion of his famous work The Goslings, he calls out to male and female teachers:

Educators are workers, useful workers. Therefore, the field of struggle for educators is alongside all their class brothers. Educational workers of the world, unite! By this, you will lose nothing but your chains, and conversely, you can make the whole world yours.

Since its founding, the "International of Educators" has continuously exposed militarism latent in schools and all other aspects. The demands and rights of educational workers are linked with those of other oppressed classes. It proceeded along two lines: peace education against war for children, and the syndicalist movement for decisive struggle among teachers' organizations worldwide.

3. The World Federation of Education Associations (The San Francisco International Peace Education Movement)

In Europe, pacifist discourse fell completely silent after the war, or merely issued cowardly sighs amidst the intensifying class struggle. The bourgeois social order, extremely fearful of educators joining the struggle and becoming a purposeful movement, lacked the power to create a direct environment leading to the dissolution of the "Educational Workers' International". However, in the post-war period, a very powerful American capitalism continuously watched the world situation. Even in education, it recognized the necessity of aiding the revived capitalism in Europe. Consequently, the National Education Association of the United States, under the protection of the U.S. government and under the signboard of pacifism, sought to achieve a world federation of education associations. Using American-style propaganda, it sent invitations to the educational circles of the whole world to convene the founding conference of the "World Education Conference" in San Francisco. A certain American magnate immediately donated one million gold dollars to bless this new international conference. This charitable patron's favor precisely serves to characterize the San Francisco education federation. In other words, it was merely a product of imperialism. The ruling class, terrified by the brave movement of the Educational Workers' International, sought, under the fine name of peace education, to soften, check, and even shatter the proletarian educators' movement, thereby perpetuating international capitalism.

This association had considerable influence on countries like China, Japan, and India. Because the teachers of the 'colored races' were very submissive to their imperialist domination and easily attracted by Wilsonian sweet talk. However, European educators, having witnessed the horrors of war and personally suffered its bitterness, did not participate. They either viewed this pacifism with the xenophobia born of trauma, or, fervently revolutionary, rejected it as hypocrisy. The second World Education Conference held in Edinburgh, UK in 1925, though it managed to reach the European stage, ultimately failed to achieve any substantial results.

According to its stated rules, the conference was "above politics and religion"; but in reality, this world conference manifested as an educational tool of Anglo-American capitalism. Did not a high-ranking pastor come to bless the Edinburgh conference?

The third conference was originally scheduled for Stockholm, the capital of Sweden, but ultimately failed there and had to cross the Atlantic again, convening in Toronto, southern Canada (1927). It was only with great difficulty that its fourth conference was successfully held in Geneva, the seat of the League of Nations, in 1929.

As mentioned earlier, the European ruling class lacked the power to destroy the Educational Workers' International, but in recent years, it found supporters among European pacifist educators. They competed with the Educational Workers' International, intending to dissolve and suffocate it.

4. The International Federation of Teachers' Associations (The London International Peace Education Movement)

In June 1926, initiated by the French National Education Association, based on mutual pedagogical understanding between France and Germany, and jointly with German educational groups not yet part of syndicalist organizations, the first step was taken to build a pacifist group organization. In September of the same year, a meeting was held at the International Institute of Intellectual Cooperation in Paris with the British National Union of Teachers, which was also not part of syndicalist organizations, thus gaining the support of the League of Nations. In November, Britain joined the Institute of Intellectual Cooperation. Finally, in April 1927, with the participation of France, Britain, Germany, the Netherlands, Sweden, and other Mediterranean countries, the founding conference of the International Federation of Teachers' Associations was held in London. Simultaneously, a congress of the "Peace Through School" movement was held in Prague, the capital of Czechoslovakia, under the semi-official protection of the Geneva-based League of Nations, attended by 400 delegates from 18 countries. The majority were school teachers, and representatives from various pacifist groups also participated.

If the old international peace education movement is called the "San Francisco International Peace Education Movement", then this new one might be called the "London International Peace Education Movement". This new international of pacifist educators is, of course, vastly different from the class-based, proletarian International of Educators. A look at its statutes reveals: "The Association aims solely at cooperation in education, seeking to lead to world peace through the common labor of humanity" (Article 1); "The Association demands no mandatory commitment regarding politics or social forms" (Article 2); "The Association believes that the education of children in various countries for mutual understanding among peoples is a necessary prerequisite for achieving lasting peace" (Article 3).

Eight years after the Great War, as European capitalism restored its pre-war foundation, thoroughly suppressed the revolutionary movement, and world imperialism prepared anew for the Second World War, the new pacifist teachers broadcast their silent cries everywhere, taking the first step towards international organization. These educators, docile as lambs, actually fantasized that they could bring about peace through children's education and pedagogical cooperation among educators, dragging out an ignoble existence on a neutral path outside political and social struggles.

The Educational Workers' International, which stands on the position of struggle and unites the masses of proletarian educators of all tendencies, must combat this temporarily whitewashing pacifism and expose the dangerous illusions of the pacifists, as stated in its open letter regarding the "Peace Through School" movement:

"Neither children nor teachers can give peace to the world. Only the iron fist of armed workers can give peace to the world."

(The above brief history of the international education movement is based on the original work by M. Boubon, council member of the French Teachers' Union, the translation of which was largely supplied by our friend Gongpu.)

From the above account, it is clear that in the modern era where all social life is colored by class antagonisms, even international education movements cannot but bear a class character. Is this not precisely what the facts demonstrate? The difference in nature between the two lies in that the International Peace Education Movement strives to conceal its true colors, while the Educational Workers' International does not shy away from declaring its class character. Let us now proceed to introduce in more detail the latter's development history and its statutes.

1. The Developmental History of the Educational Workers' International (From the Bordeaux Congress to the Leipzig Congress)

As mentioned above, the Educational Workers' International germinated in August 1920 at the congress of the French Teachers' Union in Bordeaux. At this congress, there was only one foreign delegate in attendance: the Italian Ms. Renata. The initial two secretaries, Veldkamp and Brizard, acted courageously. On the basis of the anti-war education common front of the class struggle, they drafted the statutes of the International of Educators and worked to establish national branches.

The formal founding congress was held in Paris (August 1922).

Delegates from branches in five countries and individuals from other countries attended. During these two years, the growth of the International of Educators relied heavily on the efforts of French activists.

At the Brussels congress (August 1924), four new branches were admitted (Belgium, Portugal, Bulgaria, Soviet Union). Due to the number of represented countries, this began to become a grand congress. Influenced by the newly joined branches, especially the Belgian branch, the International of Educators not only adopted the basis of class struggle and the school struggle against war, but also adopted a trade union basis, expanded its scope of activities to include the defense and protection of teachers' rights and interests, created clearer and stronger new regulations, and changed its name from the International of Educators to the Educational Workers' International. The 1924 Brussels congress marked a new stage in the life of the educational international. From then on, it gradually left its infancy, rapidly developed, and matured into an international organization.

The Paris and Brussels congress (August 1925), because the French government denied entry to Soviet delegates, had to conclude in Brussels despite opening in Paris. At this congress, delegates from 7 countries and individual attendees from 15 countries were present. The secretary's report sufficed to prove that this International had already engaged in activities worldwide. Africa and Asia were also represented by native teacher delegates from French colonies (North Africa and Annam), and connections with North America, South America, the Dutch East Indies[113], and China began. In the common atmosphere of this International, a resolution supporting the worldwide united front

---

113 [Special Editor's Note] It is present-day Indonesia

movement of trade unions was passed (among the affiliated countries, British teachers belonged to the Amsterdam International, Soviet teachers to the Red International of Labor Unions). Also, after long debate, the question of the "class education" of capitalist schools was unanimously passed, resolving to unify all educational organs under the banner of class education, i.e., anti-capitalism, marking a new stage in the movement. Simultaneously, under the auspices of this International of Educators, a delegation of British teachers (one from the Teachers' Labour League, one from the National Union of Women Teachers) was sent to the Soviet Union to report on the educational situation there (Note: Their report was published in 1929, titled Schools, Teachers and Scholars in Soviet Russia).

At Vienna (August 1926), the Educational Workers' International, through mass meetings, aroused resonance among Austria's oppressed classes, welcomed the Soviet delegate whom the government had denied entry, and had two delegates belonging to the Amsterdam International – (Kleemann, Luxembourg) and (Peters, Belgium) – criticize the government's conspiracy to split the congress leadership. Peters personally welcomed the Soviet delegate, declaring "This alone is the symbol of the internal unity of the Educational International". Topics such as "School and Morality", "School and Religion", and "The Struggle Against Chauvinism and Imperialism" were hotly debated, and powerful resolutions were made. At this congress, all European countries had representation, and Africa, Asia, and America also had delegates, making it truly a world congress in fact.

After the Vienna congress, the growth of the Educational Workers' International progressed even further. In the spring of 1927, the Scottish Socialist Educators' Association joined, and in May, a portion of the teachers' organizations in a certain East Asian country also participated.

Thus, the Educational Workers' International had established active branches in ten countries, and additionally, groups formed by individual members existed in almost all countries worldwide. The total membership now numbers approximately 800,000.

In Leipzig (April 1928), the Educational Workers' International held an "Education Day", [attended by] the International's executive committee and delegates sent by affiliated groups from all over the world. Through this mass gathering, the purpose of the Educational Workers' International and "Education Day" was announced to the working masses of Leipzig, Germany.

The congress discussed issues of children and educators, peace and schools, under the premise of class struggle. It also invited pacifist or liberal educators, seeking open discussion with them regarding the so-called religious, political, and social "neutralism" of that "moderate" collaboration with imperialism.

"Education Day" began on April 10th and lasted for three days according to the following schedule:

Evening, April 9th: Public Mass Meeting

April 10th: The Situation of the Proletarian Child

Reports –

Material Conditions… Fischer (Berlin)

Psychological Conditions… Döring (Leipzig)

Legal Status… (Giriakos, Greece)

The Situation in the Far East… Dr. (Shimoki, Tokyo)

April 11th: On the Aims of Education

Reports –

School and the State... (Shulgin, Moscow)

School and Religion... (Friedrich Schmid, Berlin)

School and Society... (Pistrak, Moscow)

Others... (Redgrave, England), (Letten, Belgium)

April 12th: Congress Preparation Section Meetings

Morning: Congress participants divided into three groups

A. Organization of the School System

Reports –

Edith Hommes (Hamburg)

Pinkevich[114] (Moscow)

B. Curriculum and Teaching Methods

Reports –

Lupi (Spain)

Rosg (Leipzig)

---

114 [Special Editor's Note] Pinkevich, a prominent Soviet educator of the early 20th century.

Shevts (Moscow)

C. Student Training

Reports –

Dr. Werfel (Berlin)

Freinet (France)

Moore (UK)

Evening: Congress participants gathered together, presenting the outlines approved by the morning section meetings.

April 13th: Congress of the Educational International, where representatives of national branches discussed the general movement policy of the Educational Workers' International.

Note: The 10th to 12th were "Education Day", not the congress. Resolutions defining the attitude and actions of the Educational Workers' International and its branches were not made here. "Education Day" was solely a "day of study". During this period, individuals expressed opinions, discussed and compared them; where opinions remained inconclusive, they were handed over to research committees.

Outside the congress, an international exhibition of textbooks, handicrafts, and school materials was held.

Particularly noteworthy was the participation from Vienna of Dr. Max Adler, who delivered a report on the "Aims of Education". Also, Victor Stern, head of the Vienna Workers' University, attended.

Among educational scholars and the masses of teachers, this Leipzig congress indeed generated great impact and anticipation. The Dutch Education Union (a Syndicate belonging to the Amsterdam International but not part of the Educational Workers' International) sent two people; participants came from Scandinavia, Austria, as well as North and South America. Besides renowned educational scholars and specialist researchers, many educators belonging to educational unions, who were closely related to proletarian children and adults, attended. The discussions were scientific and of a socially practical nature.

In essence, the congress held in Leipzig was an unprecedented event in the history of education. Because the masses of educators struggling alongside the working class, with an international plan and within this international organization, discussed the proletarian significance of educational issues and the direction of the work.

At this congress, it was resolved to issue a manifesto to the educational workers of the world. It was to be signed and issued by the General Secretary after the congress concluded. It is translated as follows:

Dear Comrades

The Fifth Congress of the Educational Workers' International has been held in Leipzig in April 1928.

The congress of the San Francisco International (W.F.E.A., i.e., the World Education Conference) was opened with addresses by representatives of kings, churches, and ministers of education. The congress of the European Pacifist Educational International was declared open with a pre-written speech by the Prussian Minister of Education, Becker, and the travel expenses of the delegates were fully paid by their respective governments. All expenses for the Second International congress held in July were paid by the Romanian government. In contrast, our Fifth Congress, like all our previous congresses, could not avoid encountering many obstacles erected by the bourgeoisie themselves.

The German government refused visa assurance to the Soviet delegates and further prohibited our General Secretary from speaking in public venues. The French authorities also refused visas to two French delegates. Many delegates from other countries could not attend the congress for a simple reason – once they left their home country, they would not go to Leipzig but to the nearest prison.

Yet despite so many obstacles, we managed to hold our congress and education congress. The congress fully approved all activities of the Executive Committee.

We can state with satisfaction: the position on the unification question adopted by the Executive Committee greatly contributed to the development and strengthening of the E.W.I. (i.e., the abbreviation for Educational Workers' International), the expansion of its relations, and the development of the proletarian consciousness of its members.

In the last two years, the E.W.I. has made contact with other proletarian and semi-proletarian organizations such as the International of Ex-Servicemen, the International of Proletarian Freethinkers, and the League against Imperialism.

During this time, previous resolutions concerning activity towards the Orient and Latin America were realized. The congress approved the affiliation of new branches in Uruguay and Scotland.

Within the major part of the reformist union in the French national syndicate, the E.W.I. has gradually increased the number of sympathizers (At the 1927 national syndicate congress in Paris, the E.W.I. received 37 votes out of 101).

For the same unification, the new Executive Committee, realizing a solid position and not neglecting its ultimate aims, strives to engage educational workers in the struggle for daily practical demands. To achieve this aim, it is necessary to continue employing the system of joint committees.

The International's program on various demand items – adopted at the Vienna Congress, based on the struggles of educational workers – shall form the basis for future struggles. The slogans of wage increases and improvement of labor conditions remain, as in the past, an important part of our struggle.

Special attention should be directed towards young teachers and educational workers in countries under imperialist bondage. The E.W.I. in general, and its specific departments in particular, are concerned with the struggle for the equality of status and legal rights of male and female teachers. The special departments active in the groups established by the E.W.I. Executive Committee, and the department active in the Central Executive Committee, must participate in this struggle.

Regarding the profound unemployment among young teachers, it is necessary to struggle for the following: state subsidies for the unemployed, scholarships allocated for their continued study, selection of the unemployed for short-term teaching posts, and salaries to be increased within the public education budget.

As the bourgeoisie offensives against the proletariat, including the ideological offensive in schools, the strengthening of militarism in schools, and the gradual development of war preparations, the E.W.I., which declares itself an organization of anti-imperialists, anti-Fascists, and anti-chauvinists, is bound to suffer increasing persecution from the bourgeoisie. Each branch must gather strength within its own ranks and extend its influence among the masses of educators. The struggle against the crisis of imperialist war and against imperialist ideology in schools must be expanded.

From this viewpoint, it is essential to increasingly develop correct relations with the International Workers' Relief and the League against Imperialism.

We must wage a determined struggle against the persecution of teachers, the exclusion of political opinions, the slander and arrest of those with progressive views, and the destruction of teachers' various organizations. Strengthening the E.W.I. solidarity fund is truly important.

To the extent that it relates to the bourgeoisie, even more cunning methods of struggle are being utilized. Namely, repeated lectures on "achieving peace through schools", and the organization of special pacifist internationals for educational workers (the San Francisco International and the European Pacifist International) are also its supports.

We must confront hypocritical pacifism, resolutely declaring proletarian anti-imperialism, and that only the defeat of capitalism can make war impossible. We demand that educational workers unite with the proletariat and struggle against capitalism. In view of the dangers arising from the incessant increase of armaments and the strengthening of armies and navies, our congress welcomes the proposal for total disarmament made by the Soviet representatives at the Geneva Conference.

The present bourgeoisie utilizes all religious forces to aid its offensive against schools. The hand of clerical reaction reaches deeper into the schools.

We must fight against the influence of the church, defend schools from their control, prevent funding for religious schools, and generally combat clericalism.

In this struggle, we must emphasize maintaining close contact with the organizations of proletarian freethinkers.

At the 1926 Vienna Congress, we unanimously declared a definitive position on the unification question. Consequently, the professional bureau for educational workers established by Amsterdam[^8] actually opposes our position on unification; we must adopt a negative attitude towards it.

The complexity of the situation and the difficulty of the struggle require us to direct our attention decisively towards the masses of educational workers, first and foremost towards primary school teachers.

We can only give the E.W.I. the possibility of developing and deepening its work by gathering the strength of our own class and unifying the masses through proletarian training.

General Secretary

2. Statutes of the Educational Workers' International (Decided at the Brussels Congress, August 1924)

Introduction

In countries dominated by capitalism, science is permitted to be acquired only by a very few and becomes commodified. The laboring masses are naturally excluded from the category of 'people' who should have the possibility of acquiring the knowledge necessary for managing the state and education.

The schools of capitalist society cater only to the interests of the propertied class. On one hand, they aim to cultivate a privileged stratum capable of guiding capitalist society, strengthening the functioning of its institutions, and making its power respected; on the other hand, they aim to keep the vast majority of the populace in a state of intellectual slavery, making them blind tools of capitalism.

In such a society, male and female teachers not only fail to become bearers of excellent education for the youth, but they themselves must also flatter capitalist society, sink into intellectual subservience, and transform into bureaucratic servants and underpaid employees who comply with the capitalists and their state.

For educational workers to liberate themselves from this miserable situation — not only materially but also spiritually — must be combined with liberating the school itself from its capitalist enslaved state and transforming it into a workshop of culture for all humanity. Only social revolution can create free schools and free educators, while also possessing the capacity to liberate the laboring masses. Only the working class holds a genuine and unwavering interest in the transformation of current educational methods.

Therefore, the struggle of educational workers to improve their material and spiritual conditions can never be achieved under a form of struggle that seeks merely some privilege within capitalist society; it is only effective when conducted in the active form of transforming society, in collaboration with the organized working class.

Consequently, the struggle of educators must not be carried out solely for mere economic benefits and narrow professional interests. It should be a struggle against the capitalist ideological system within schools, against imperialist war which glorifies chauvinism, against the religious influence in schools, and a struggle to promote the solidarity of the laboring masses regardless of race or nationality.

The Educational Workers' International (Paris)

To make the struggle for improving the material, legal, and intellectual conditions of educational workers effective, the various national groups composed of actively engaged educational workers should form an international organization.

This international organization, which existed from 1920–1922 as the International of Educators, shall henceforth be called the Educational Workers' International (Paris).

The Tasks of the Educational Workers' International

Its tasks are as follows:

a. To compile and guide the unified struggle actions of affiliated national groups, and to produce directives on strategy and tactics.

b. In countries where educational organizations that have not adopted the above program exist, to strive to awaken class consciousness within the same professional groups and arrange for their affiliation with the International.

c. To collect and publish materials concerning the material, intellectual, and legal conditions of educators in various countries, and data on national school policies and school reform movements, thereby illuminating the fact that capitalism, in all countries it dominates, enslaves schools and educators, exploiting them solely for its own benefit.

d. To study the problems of secular and unified labor schools.

e. To publish a bulletin, hold various conferences, discussions, study tours, etc., to promote mutual contact among educators of different countries, and also to seek the organization of opinion exchange.

f. International solidarity should be strengthened through the organized activity of international educators supporting groups and individuals struggling under particularly difficult circumstances.

g. To unite with all proletarian class organizations, carrying out the struggle against imperialism and all war crises, and against international fascism.

Conditions for Affiliation

National groups that adopt the following tenets, or have statutes and activities consistent with such tenets, may join the Educational Workers' International:

a. The class struggle for the liberation of the working class.

b. The struggle against the crisis of imperialist war and against worldwide fascism.

c. The acknowledgment and adoption of international training.

In countries without a branch, individuals who acknowledge the above tenets may join as members. They must carry out propaganda work in their respective home countries.

Organs of the Educational Workers' International

The Educational Workers' International has three organs:

a. The International Congress

b. The Executive Committee

c. The General Secretariat

The Congress

a. The Congress is the supreme organ of the Educational Workers' International and meets annually.

b. The Congress determines the general policy of the International, decides the location of the General Secretariat, and appoints its personnel and other members of the Executive Committee from lists of candidates selected by the national branches.

c. The Congress elects 3 auditing commissioners whose task is to supervise the organization's expenditures and report to the Congress.

d. Unless otherwise decided by the Congress, the Executive Committee decides the place and time of the next Congress.

e. An extraordinary Congress may be convened by decision of the Executive Committee through the General Secretariat, or upon the proposal of one-third or more of the affiliated branches.

f. Each branch has from one to several votes in the Congress:

Branches with up to 1,000 members: 1 vote

From 1,000 to 10,000 members: 2 votes

Over 10,000 members: 3 votes

g. Individual members may attend the Congress and express

opinions (without voting rights).

The Executive Committee

a. The Executive Committee consists of 11 persons: 3 from the Secretariat, and 8 elected by the Congress upon the recommendation of the scrutineers.

b. The Executive Committee directs the work of the International between Congresses and is responsible to the Congress.

c. The Executive Committee meets at least twice a year.

d. The Congress elects 7 alternate members for the Executive Committee.

The General Secretariat

a. The General Secretariat consists of one General Secretary and two or three Secretaries.

b. The General Secretariat directs all work of the International based on the resolutions of the Congress and the Executive Committee.

It monthly publishes an organ journal in three languages (German, French, and English), representing the International and its Executive Committee.

Membership Dues

Membership dues are collected by the affiliated branches and sent monthly to the General Secretariat.

International Fund for Struggle and Mutual Aid

To effectively continue the struggle for the improvement of the material, intellectual, and legal conditions of educational workers and other struggles against attacks targeting educators, the Executive Committee shall, according to detailed rules, establish an International Fund for mutual aid and struggle, under the management of the General Secretariat.

The Bulletin

The Educational Workers' International monthly publishes a bulletin in three languages (German, French, English).

Each branch shall designate a suitable person from its Executive Committee responsible for liaison with the General Secretariat. A report shall be submitted to the General Secretariat and its own Executive Committee every two months. In urgent cases, special reports shall be made.

Expulsion from the International

A branch that fails to implement Congress resolutions or to follow the instructions of the General Secretariat may be expelled by a resolution of the Executive Committee. Expulsion requires a two-thirds majority vote of the Executive Committee.

When a resolution of the International is not adopted by the organs of a national branch, the International shall appeal to the members of that branch, compelling, if necessary, the convening of a national congress to resolve the immediate problem. Only after a national congress has expressed its own opinion on the issue may the Executive Committee proceed with expulsion.

The Executive Committee may also expel individual members.

For both types of expulsion (of a national branch or an individual member), the next Congress may affirm or deny the resolution of the Executive Committee.

Note: Items a and b of Article 14 were changed at the Paris-Brussels Congress of August 1925. Item d of Article 13 and Article 16 were changed at the Vienna Congress of August 1926. The above statutes have been revised accordingly and are effective from 1926.

The address of the Secretariat is:

Internationale des Travailleurs de l'Enseignement

L. Vernochet, 8 Avenue Mathurin-Moreau, Paris X IX.

From the above statutes of the Educational Workers' International, we can see that it exposes the function of education in capitalist society and seeks the material and spiritual advancement of educators themselves. But it does not seek to pick up the crumbs of material and spiritual benefits under capitalist domination; it aims to cooperate with the general working-class movement to achieve the thorough liberation of the proletariat. Consequently, it strenuously opposes patriotic service to imperialism for the benefit of the capitalist class, and also explains that true peace cannot be placed on the shoulders of children, but can only be guaranteed by the international linkage of the working class and realized only through the worldwide victory of the working class.

Finally, I wish to discuss a powerful branch of the Educational Workers' International, which is the British Teachers' Labour League.

The Teachers' Labour League was established in London in early 1923. It has held an annual congress every December since. Initially just a small local group, it has now grown into a national organization, its importance increasingly significant. In its early days, its activities were limited to the vicinity of the capital. By the end of 1925, it had secured a firm foothold in Lancashire, and now has 22 branches throughout the country. However, due to financial difficulties and other reasons, its rapid organizational development has not fully met expectations, and there are still areas where its influence has not reached.

According to the League's statutes, its aim is to engage the majority in the struggle to transform society. The methods for realization are as follows: a. Engage in political movements locally, nationally, and internationally alongside other male and female workers; b. Endeavor to unify the many existing male and female teachers' groups into an educational workers' union to join the Trade Union Congress (T.U.C.), and further strive to organize male and female teachers internationally; c. Develop the principles and structure of the future education system; d. Arouse public attention to the many conditions that waste educational effort in homes, schools, and other places; e. Secure and defend fully the civil and political rights of educational workers and general workers; f. Strive to exclude imperialist education from various educational facilities in the country, etc.

At its December 1925 congress, the League passed a resolution to become a branch of the Educational Workers' International (Paris). This resolution even led Conservative Party MPs to question the Minister of Education in Parliament about the Educational International. Since then, the League's international work has been carried out on a large scale. Now, the League maintains close contact with educational groups throughout the British Empire and teacher movements in other English-speaking areas like the United States, and continues uninterrupted liaison with the Educational Workers' International. This part of the League's work, having attracted worldwide attention and powerful repercussions, is extremely noteworthy.

In 1926, the League undertook two significant tasks on the international front: firstly, through the introduction of the Educational International, it sent two groups of educational inspection delegations to Soviet Russia (see earlier), with a total of sixteen League members participating. Secondly, it sent eight Executive Committee members as delegates to the Vienna Congress of the Educational International. The delegates, confirmed by a subsequent Executive Committee meeting, made the following decisions: (1) This League holds an important function within the International; (2) The League's affiliation with the International confers significant value upon both organizations.

In April 1928, it sent seven delegates to participate in the Leipzig Congress of the Educational International and its "Education Day".

Since its Sixth Congress in 1927, the League has adopted Esperanto as its official language for communication and has planned for the development of the Esperanto movement and collaboration with workers' and educational groups in various countries using Esperanto. It was also resolved at the congress to expand the previously attempted teacher exchanges on a larger scale, making them truly international exchanges; furthermore, to facilitate travel abroad for members from other countries, it specifically liaised with the Educational International, entrusting the Executive Committee to realize this aim.

During the great British miners' strike of 1926, the various local branches and members of the League were highly active in aiding the strikers, achieving many notable results. Beyond raising strike funds, the League also managed to become the driving force behind larger groups than itself. In November of that year, it began publishing its monthly organ, The Educational Worker. It has been issued regularly since and has now become a powerful weapon politically and educationally.

(Note: The original name of the Educational Workers' International in Esperanto is La Internacio de Eduklaboristoj; translated into English as Education Workers' International, into French as Internationale des Travailleurs de l'Enseignement, and into German as Internationale der Bildungsarbeiter.)

Questions

1. The international movement of educators essentially has two different types of organizations; what are their respective roots?

2. What role does the advocacy of world peace or international friendship in education play?

3. Can advocating for peace through education truly achieve peace? Why or why not?

4. Explain the nature and tasks of the Educational Workers' International.

SECTION 15: EDUCATION IN THE UNITED STATES

Reasons for Specifically Discussing American Education — Sinclair's Two Books Studying American Education: "The Goose-step" and "The Goslings" — Plutocratic Education at Columbia University — Harvard's "Liberalism" — "Armed Education" at the University of California — The General Situation of Ordinary Education — The Great Role of the National Education Association — Questions

In Section 3 earlier, we already discussed the influence of centralized capital on schools and science, using school education and scientific research in Europe and America as examples. Also, in Section 7, we discussed how modern, i.e., capitalist society's education, besides the general transformation of education, also possesses the two major characteristics of monopolization and commodification, and provided a brief explanation.

Now, in this section, we will specifically focus on education in the United States as a specimen for dissecting modern education. There are two reasons for this: first, because American school education is most markedly influenced by capitalism; second, because American school education is precisely the model that China's current educational circles are strenuously imitating and worshipping.

For the sake of convenience, I will base my discussion on Sinclair's works, excerpting and translating them following the order of the original texts. Readers should know that Sinclair's two works are truly worthy of our attention. Because what is currently being researched in education departments of Chinese universities, and what is being taught in education textbooks of normal schools, if not entirely, largely consists of those very "highlights" described by Sinclair. Most of our educators, having learned those "highlight" educational theories in the teachers' college of Columbia University in the United States, are precisely trying to use them to reform Chinese education and instruct Chinese youth (as can be seen in the recently published Student Guides written by American returned students and university graduates who have caught a whiff of the American style). This is by no means a matter that can be overlooked; it is something that deserves our serious attention.

Readers may doubt that I am exaggerating? Absolutely not! Please follow me to see the true face of the American education spectacle, and you will inevitably be greatly shocked.

Let us first look at American higher education, which is described very nakedly in the book The Goose-step (published in 1923).

Sinclair refers to the United States as a Plutocratic empire, where there are monarchs, princes, and aristocrats. The main players there are J.P. Morgan (the wealthiest, a monarch), George F. Baker (President of the First National Bank of New York, the second richest man in the world), William Rockefeller (mentioned alongside Morgan), George M. Reynolds (President of the Continental National Bank of Chicago, the second largest bank in America), etc.

Everything in the United States is manipulated by the "Interlocking Directorates"; New York's three major banks – Morgan Bank, First National Bank, National City Bank – and two trust companies under their control – The Guaranty and The Equitable[115] – control the nation's economy through the hands of

---

115 [Special Editor's Note] The Guaranty and The Equitable were trust companies and securities firms.

the interlocking directorates.

Men die, but such plutocrats are immortal. Therefore, the interlocking directorates require an educational system to perpetuate the survival of the plutocracy, and they have made this system very thorough. In one very large university, Morgan is a lifelong trustee; the university's president is a director of a certain Morgan life insurance company. If the university president writes a book telling Americans to be loyal to the plutocrats, this book can be published by a publishing house where Morgan is a director, and the paper for printing it can be bought from an international paper manufacturing company where a Morgan man is a director. The school superintendent where the paper is made is a graduate of Morgan's university, the textbooks adopted there are issued by a publishing house where Morgan is a director, written by the director of education owned by Morgan, praised by the educational magazine run by Morgan's university president, and further recommended by the editors of Morgan's newspapers and magazines. The school superintendent will promote teachers who attend the university's summer school, and will encourage secondary school students to enter that university. Once a year, he will attend the congress of the National Education Association (see below), electing a president who is a graduate of Morgan's university, a member of Morgan's church, a reader of Morgan's newspapers and magazines... Furthermore, when the Republican Party (Morgan is a shareholder) nominates the president of Morgan's university as a candidate for Vice President of the United States, Morgan's bishop will bless him, Morgan's newspapers will propagandize for him, and Morgan's superintendent will invite school children to a Picnic, let them listen to the candidate Vice President's campaign speech on a gramophone, and provide refreshments supplied by Morgan's election committee, the cost of which is paid by the life insurance company where Morgan's university president is a director, and this company holds the insurance policies of various local superintendents and principals.

This is the system of interlocking directorates, and this is also the part of the plutocratic empire known as the American education system. Sinclair not only describes this skeleton but also proceeds to dissect its nerves, brain, flesh, hair, and claws.

The headquarters of the American plutocratic empire is in New York, and consequently, the headquarters of plutocratic education is also in New York. This headquarters is none other than Columbia University, which has produced a large number of China's educational giants. It is a splendid university of the House of Morgan, a university purely dedicated to the ideal of plutocracy. Its education experts direct the nation's primary, secondary, and university education, and the production of its plutocratic ideals has become an industry as definite, organized, and standardized as the production of automobiles and sausages.

This university's property exceeds 75 million US dollars, with an annual income of over 7 million US dollars. Most of its property is invested in securities and bonds, monitored by interlocking directors. According to a booklet listing the university's investments obtained by Sinclair, it was over 20 pages thick, containing shares in all important American railways and industries. Therefore, he says that within the United States, there is hardly a person whose every waking hour does not pay tribute to Columbia University.

This Morgan university is run by a Board of Trustees. These trustees possess absolute power, are accountable to no one, and no one can remove them. Who are these trustees? Most notably, there is only one educator among them, that is the university president, who is an ex-officio trustee. None are scholars or have any connection with scholarship. There is 1 engineer, 1 doctor, 1 bishop; 10 are corporate legal advisors, 8 are bankers, railroad owners, landowners, merchants, and manufacturers, etc. The chairman of the board, William Barclay Parsons, is a tunnel engineer and a director of many companies. The youngest trustee, Marcellus Hartley Dodge, was elected at age 26; while a student at Columbia, he was already a director of the Equitable Life Insurance Company and is Rockefeller's son-in-law.

In short, those who serve as directors on the coal trust, steel trust, and railroad trust serving the Morgan company are also those serving in American educational administrative organs and schools at all levels. Not only are the trustees of Columbia University indistinguishable from the directors of the New York Central Railroad or the Remington arms company, but the lists of trustees for Harvard University and Lee Higginson company; the University of Pennsylvania and the United Gas Improvement Company; the University of Pittsburgh and the United States Steel Corporation; the University of California and the Hydro-Electric Power trust; the University of Minnesota and the Ore[116] trust; are all identical.

Furthermore, according to Scott Nearing's research, among the over 500 universities and specialized schools in the United States, there are a total of 2,470 trustees. Among them, 208 are merchants, 106 are manufacturers, 112 are financiers/capitalists, 6 are contractors, 32 are landowners, 26 are insurance agents, 115 are corporate officers, 202 are bankers, 15 are managers, 18 are publishers – this plutocratic group totals 903 persons. There are 111 doctors, 514 lawyers, 125 educators, 353 clergy, 8 authors, 43 editors, 70 scientists, 13 social workers, 32 judges – this group of high-level professionals totals 1,269 persons. Additionally, there

---

116 [Special Editor's Note] Ore refers to the mining trust.

are 94 retired merchants, 3 salesmen, 123 farmers, 46 homemakers, 3 artisans, 2 librarians – totaling 271 persons. If lawyers are not counted as professionals but included in their major clients, the commercial and financial class, then that class totals 1,414 persons, or 58% of the total. In state universities, the merchant class constitutes 477 out of 776 trustees, or 61%. And here, retired merchants are not yet included, though their plutocratic nature is certainly no less than active merchants; nor are many doctors, clergy, editors, and educators included, though their plutocratic nature can be just as substantial as bankers.

Currently, many universities in China are actively following the example of American predecessors, organizing boards of trustees and inviting famous business figures to join. Although there is a difference between acting voluntarily and passively, the impact on education is likely to be equally "highlighted".

Having examined the board of trustees of the Morgan university, we must now examine how much of a plutocratic nature the university president selected by this board possesses.

The president of Columbia University is named Nicholas Murray Butler[117]. His father was an artisan, which is not a bad thing in itself; but he considers it a disgrace and seeks to conceal it. The interlocking directors built him an official residence worth over 300,000 US dollars; it was said to be for educational purposes and thus tax-exempt, but according to Professor Cattell's[118] declaration, Butler used it "for social activities and political intrigues". According to general rumor, Butler also receives gifts

---

117 [Special Editor's Note] Butler (1862–1947), American educator. Awarded the Nobel Peace Prize in 1931.

118 [Special Editor's Note] Cattell (James McKeen Cattell, 1860–1944), American psychologist.

from trustees and other wealthy individuals. He is also keen on political honors and engaged in extremely base actions while campaigning for US Vice President. What does such a person exhibit in educational administration?

He rules the university like an absolute monarch, allowing no slight interference. If anyone shows signs of interference, he will not rest until that person is expelled from the university. The so-called faculty council is merely a farce, because it only has advisory power, while he monopolizes authority and can do as he pleases. He uses the trustees to place them above the professors; all actions are executed by the trustees, while what he says to the trustees is unknown to anyone. Professors have no standing whatsoever before the Board of Trustees.

Professors' teaching must strictly follow prescribed methods. Even if one is a genius musician, when the prescribed time arrives, he must abandon the score he is wholeheartedly composing and attend to report. Even if you are a great poet, full of ability to move students, you are forbidden to teach outside prescribed hours and are forbidden to lecture on interesting subjects. If you act arbitrarily, you will be driven out of the university. In the twenty years of his tenure, he has expelled over twenty professors.

The famous economist Beard was also driven out by Butler. He once said: "The position of a Columbia professor is lower than that of a manual artisan."

According to a famous American scientist who told Sinclair, in the past ten years, no distinguished scholar has been invited to Columbia, nor has one been produced from Columbia. He said: The salaries of American university faculty are truly too low; anyone of first-rate talent can always turn to other professions to earn more money. If he remains a teacher, it is because he loves teaching and hopes to receive his reward in other forms – in domestic respect. But if he feels he has no status or power, if he sees himself and his colleagues being threatened and insulted by businessmen, if he knows the whole world does not value his opinion and considers him a puppet for businessmen to play with, then the dignity of academic life is utterly swept away, leaving nothing behind except the small monetary compensation.

The academic status of Columbia University under the rule of the interlocking president can be glimpsed from an article titled "A Statistical Study of American Men of Science" by the university's psychology professor J. McKeen Cattell. Among 1,000 leading American scientists, 38 held doctorates from Columbia University, whereas 102 held degrees from Johns Hopkins University; 78 had studied at Columbia, whereas 237 had studied at Harvard. In 1905, Columbia professors numbered 60 among the 1,000 scientific leaders, whereas Harvard had 66, Yale had 26. By 1910, Columbia had 48, a decrease of 12, whereas Harvard had 79, an increase of 13, Yale had 38, an increase of 12. Regarding universities associated with the 1,000 scientific leaders, Harvard had 22 individuals holding positions among the top 1,000; Chicago had 13, whereas Columbia, despite having more professors, had only 8. Conversely, among those who later lost their leading positions, Harvard accounted for 6, Chicago for 3, but Columbia accounted for 12, more than any other American university! This is the achievement of academic autocracy! That the American Columbia University, long famous in our educational circles, should be so vulgar, must it not disappoint and dishearten our educational leaders?

There is another table showing the ratio between the number of prominent scientists associated with each university and the total number of professors at that university. Accordingly, at Harvard, roughly one out of every seven professors belonged to the top

1,000 scientific leaders; at Chicago, one out of six; at Johns Hopkins, one out of five; at Clark, one out of two – but at Columbia, it took thirteen to have one! Regarding the ratio of prominent scientists to student numbers, at Johns Hopkins, roughly every 21 students had one scientist; whereas at Columbia, it was every 96 students for one scientist. Regarding the relationship to the value of buildings and land, at MIT, there was one prominent scientist for every $35,000 US dollars of value, whereas Columbia required $259,000 US dollars for one. Furthermore, regarding the relationship to income, at Johns Hopkins, there was one prominent scientist for every $10,000 US dollars of income, whereas Columbia required $45,000 US dollars for one. Sinclair says: Although all American universities are plutocratic in nature, there are differences in degree; and the aforementioned figures truly tell us the effect of the plutocratic policy: it destroys intellectual life, turning a great academic institution into soulless bricks and mortar.

Columbia University has a total of about 1,500 professors, but only four or five can be considered creative and possessing character. John Dewey is one of them; he is America's most progressive educator. If even he were to leave, it would certainly cause a detestable uproar. Butler knows that Dewey does not interfere with the university's internal policies; when Dewey found the professors' dismissal oversight committee ineffective, he even politely resigned from his committee duties.

Look at the case of Professor Goodnow to better understand how plutocratic rule eradicates originality and ability. Goodnow taught administrative law at Columbia. When Professor Burgess left his post, Goodnow was elected by the faculty to hold the Ruggles professorship, one of the university's important chairs. Butler had originally allowed faculty departments the right to elect their own, but he was displeased with Goodnow because

Goodnow had published a book suggesting that the current U.S. Constitution might not last forever, which Butler considered dangerous thought. Therefore, the Board of Trustees, without consulting the political science faculty, bypassed Goodnow and appointed another interlocking director to succeed him!

Consider also the case of Professor James McKeen Cattell. He served as a professor at Columbia for 26 years. He was the first professor of psychology in any university worldwide, and the editor of four important scientific journals. But he opposed Butler's policies, such as appointing an unqualified person to a professorship in his field because that person had given him a gift worth $100,000. When Butler failed to force Cattell to resign, he prohibited him from using six classrooms and a psychology laboratory that Cattell himself had raised funds to build. Later, even after Cattell resigned his chairmanship, he could not refrain from voicing opinions against the authorities and was finally expelled by the trustees. Cattell once described Butler thus: "He runs the university like a department store, acting the master towards the faculty, and the obedient cook towards the Board of Trustees."

Butler abuses his position to lavishly award medals to people at home and abroad. For instance, in 1912, he promoted Senator Underwood as a leader of democracy, intending to prevent Wilson from being nominated as the Democratic presidential candidate. In 1922, he bestowed honors upon an Episcopal priest, a Belgian baron, a Portuguese viscount, a Chinese minister, and a follower of the Polish warlord, Paderewski[119].

Butler uses the money of wealthy trustees to build a machine of the alumni association, publishing alumni periodicals to boost his

---

119 [Special Editor's Note] Paderewski (Ignace Jan Paderewski, 1860–1941), Polish pianist and statesman.

image. He also built a faculty machine, composed of those who agree with him and carry out his will wherever Columbia's influence reaches – which extends to all school organizations within the territory of the plutocratic empire.

Butler is also the head of Columbia's Teachers College. He set the direction for this college, aiming to make it a machine for producing "education experts," experts who view life as a battlefield for making money and running schools like operating factories.

This president's influence extends everywhere. The alliance of national school superintendents, the politicians of the National Education Association (see below), colluding with local chambers of commerce and professional patriots, unanimously exclude liberalism in education and reject new ideas in human activity. Here is just one example: When the people of North Dakota sought to reclaim educational rights for their children and liberalize their state's school system, a Columbia University professor of educational administration, George D. Strayer (Note: This gentleman's name is quite well-known in Chinese educational circles as well), spoke to the North Dakota State Board of Education, attacking the newly proposed plan and instead preparing an alternative program for them. As long as it serves the interests of the privileged class, Columbia professors interfering in politics is not considered a violation of academic rules.

Sinclair concludes his discussion of Columbia University as follows:

All this wealth, all this solemnity – within it lies only stupidity and death! You see millions of dollars spent on education and rejoice, thinking it signifies progress. But all these millions can buy is – stupidity and death! Look at Butler managing a ten-million-dollar peace fund, using it to write a history of war! Spending half a million dollars a year to seek peace for mankind, and at this most critical period in history, Butler hires someone to write a history of war!

If you think my words exaggerate, that the Columbia system annihilates new thought and excludes creative tendencies, then listen to this law of the educational discipline laid down by our plutocratic president himself: "The responsibility of one generation is to pass on the institutions inherited from its ancestors, undamaged, to the next generation." That's all! Let humanity remain forever exactly as it has been, world without end, Amen! Is it not everyone's responsibility to discover new truths and conquer nature? Is it not everyone's responsibility to encourage us not to stagnate in the barbarism left by history? Is it not everyone's enterprise to remedy commercial anarchy, to use humanity's collective power to construct life, not destroy it? Doing these tasks is not man's enterprise; we enter university to know our ancestors, to become like them – pitiful sacrifices of blind instinct.

Having discussed Columbia University, let us now turn to Harvard University, also long famous among our countrymen, considered a university of extremely high cultural standing in America.

But, strangely enough, this Harvard also cannot escape the domination of the House of Morgan. The elder Morgan was a lifelong trustee of Columbia, while the younger Morgan became a trustee of Harvard (he graduated from Harvard in 1889). The great Boston bank Lee, Higginson & Company is part of the same entity as New York's J.P. Morgan & Company. Therefore, if New York's Columbia can be called the Morgan university, then Boston's Harvard can be called the Lee-Higginson university.

Harvard's property, valued at 34 million US dollars in 1917, is largely invested in various Morgan-Lee-Higginson enterprises, naturally under the control of the Morgan-Lee-Higginson directorate.

Harvard University has a tradition known as "Liberalism" and respect for scholarship. But these are merely "words." Emerson[120] once said: Harvard University within Harvard University has no opinions; only State Street (Note: where the big corporations are located) has full authority. Freedom of thought is neglected. All youth are molded into aging citizens, not prophets, not poets; they are forbidden to speak, forbidden to breathe, or else they are driven away.

Some say Harvard professors are not expelled for their opinions. This might be true. One reason is that Harvard is very cautious in appointing teachers; when a new teacher enters, he is immersed in an atmosphere of subtle yet powerful politeness. It is not as cold and ruthless as Columbia; it blends scholarly and social qualities, containing elements of friendship. But within this lies potent plutocratic control. One day, an employee of Lee, Higginson & Company telephoned Harvard President Lowell, saying: "We used so-and-so's money to endow this chair, and that young teacher actually lectured to workers, his name appearing in the newspaper. How can this be tolerated?" Immediately, Lowell very politely asked that young teacher to leave.

Others say Harvard's reputation for liberalism comes from President Lowell's willingness to harbor professors expelled from other schools. This is indeed a fact. But one must understand there is also a subtle purpose here, and it is quite calculated.

---

120 [Special Editor's Note] Emerson (Ralph Waldo Emerson, 1803–1882), American essayist and poet. Graduated from and taught at Harvard University.

Generally speaking, the people he harbors have offended plutocrats in some locality but have not harmed "State Street." Or they have violated religious laws, which is irrelevant at Harvard.

As for how carefully Harvard investigates a person's conduct before appointment, Sinclair cites the example of Professor Smith, who underwent such a rigorous test. When Smith was appointed to the local public utilities commission, he discovered that the local gas company was cheating the citizens. This fact was published in the newspaper, and consequently, he was dismissed from his school position by the school trustees, several of whom were connected to the gas company. Later, Smith's friends told President Lowell about this matter; Lowell investigated and, knowing he was a very moderate liberal, invited him for a talk. The content of the conversation, as Smith later told others, was as follows:

"I heard you had some unpleasantness in your city," Lowell said.

"Yes, quite a lot," Smith replied.

"I'm not too clear about it," Lowell said, "was it related to some gas company?"

"Exactly," Smith replied.

"Was it only about gas? Had nothing to do with electricity?"

"Oh, absolutely nothing to do with electricity."

"Are you sure the electric light company wasn't involved?"

"Certainly. They are two different businesses."

"I see," Lowell said, and immediately moved on to other matters.

It turned out Smith didn't understand the purpose of this conversation. He had attacked the city's gas company, not the city's Edison Electric Company; that electric company happened to be part of an electrical trust whose influence extended throughout the United States. Harvard, however, was closely related to this electrical trust. Smith attacked only the gas company without implicating the electric company, meaning people would have to use electricity if they didn't use gas, so President Lowell was quite pleased. Sure enough, within a few days, Harvard's letter of appointment to Smith was issued!

In the summer of 1918, American troops invaded Archangel in Northern Russia and Vladivostok[121] in Eastern Siberia, killing many residents. This event was a great stain on American popular history, condemned by many thinkers. At that time, five Russian children living in New York distributed leaflets pleading with Americans not to kill innocents so recklessly. For this, they were arrested and imprisoned; one died from maltreatment, and the remaining four were sentenced to 15 to 20 years in prison.

Many protested this illegal trial. One was Professor Zechariah Chafee of the Harvard Law School. He wrote a critique and included this essay in his book Freedom of Speech. Other professors jointly signed petitions seeking leniency in the case. This, however, provoked the great anger of the interlocking directorate. A Harvard graduate and New York lawyer, Austin G. Fox, drafted a protest to Harvard's Board of Overseers, co-signed by 20 prominent lawyers, all Harvard alumni. The Board of Overseers referred the matter to a "Committee to Inspect the Law School," resulting in an inquisitorial "meeting" where Fox

---

121 [Special Editor's Note] Vladivostok, a port city in southeastern Asian Russia.

used unreliable propaganda material as a pretext to attack the law school professors. During the "meeting," President Lowell's attitude was that of "a mother hen protecting her chicks from the old Fox." Because this was Harvard's internal "family scandal," it wasn't reported in the outside press, except for one newspaper not within the Boston plutocrats' sphere.

This shows the great power of the Boston plutocrats, but also proves that suppressing news reports only results in rumors spreading everywhere. Or, from the perspective of Harvard's defenders, is suppressing the news precisely to uphold the principle of academic freedom?

In this example, when New York Wall Street[122] lawyers attacked Harvard, even though they were also Harvard alumni, Lowell still had to defend the current Harvard professors to some extent. But once his own plutocrats were under attack – in other words, when it was not Wall Street but State Street seeking his help – his attitude changed completely.

Here we can cite the experience of Morris Llewellyn Cooke. He served as a lecturer at the Harvard Graduate School of Business Administration for five consecutive years. Later, he prepared two lectures on public utility problems in American cities, which he had delivered at many universities. Harvard also invited him and promised free "discussion of actual conditions in public utilities."

But in the second year, his contract was terminated. The reason given was that he violated academic ethics by publishing his lecture outlines in the newspaper. But no such "academic custom" exists in American universities.

---

122 [Special Editor's Note] Wall Street, the concentration of major U.S. monopolies and financial institutions in New York.

So what was the real reason? Sinclair found in the published outlines several passages mentioning the Edison Electric Company's disgraceful practices and the false "Valuation work" of a Harvard professor of electrical engineering. The real reason for the termination lay precisely in these matters. The university president, employed by the interlocking directors, invites their "consulting engineers" and "valuation experts" to teach, thereby enhancing the value of public utilities and expanding company business. If someone exposes these secrets, how can the university president not punish them severely?

Another example. Harvard, inadvertently, actually hired the young writer Harold J. Laski to teach political science. Laski's views on modern capitalism were not orthodox; he believed it needed improvement. He raised this issue with students, causing a great stir on State Street. At that time, Harvard was conducting a fundraising campaign, and many people wrote to the university saying they would not donate if Laski was not dismissed. On the other hand, a Chicago lawyer wrote saying his son, previously inattentive to his studies, had become diligent under Laski's influence; therefore, he would donate $15,000 to cover any loss. The dispute later erupted in the Boston newspapers, and President Lowell actually sided with Laski, stating that no Harvard professor should be expelled for his opinions.

What was this about? It turns out Lowell had written a book explaining the British constitution, which was quite famous in England. He also received an honorary degree from Oxford University and hoped one day to become an ambassador. The English people indeed believe in freedom of speech and, in fact, demonstrate their belief. And Laski happened to be from Manchester, his family connected to the current British ruling class. Moreover, Laski was a capable writer, not easily defeated. If Laski returned to England declaring he had been expelled from

President Lowell's university for his beliefs about the modern state, wouldn't that shatter Lowell's reputation in England? So, if Laski had been German or Russian, the situation would likely have been different.

The true face of Harvard University, reputed for its liberal tradition and reverence for scholarly authority, turns out not to be much different from the model university of plutocracy, Columbia. Isn't this utterly disappointing?

There are many other famous American universities, which we certainly cannot cover here. Below, we will only discuss one famous university in the West: California.

Presiding over this university are figures like Crocker, manager of the New York Equitable Trust Company...; Mortimer Fleishhacker, the largest banker in San Francisco...; and seven others. Besides monopolizing the state government, the university, and their own banks and railroads, they also control many gas and electric companies, as well as newly developed hydroelectric power, etc.

But beyond this, they have an independent vigilante committee called the Better America Federation. Its nature is that of a plutocratic "Black Hand" party, a terrorist organization. This group investigates anyone working in any institution in California; if they are not one hundred percent for the capitalists, they are blacklisted. It intimidates public officials and slanders them in the press. It attacks workers' offices and arrests union organizers; and managing all schools in California, including the state university, is one of its many undertakings.

Its oppression of university professors can be seen in Haldeman's report. He said: "We watch students with radical tendencies. We receive reports from all sides about teachers and students holding radical views."

So this is a detective agency. If a University of California professor is slightly suspect, he is blacklisted, cannot be promoted, or is even expelled immediately. Expelled teachers are prevented from finding jobs elsewhere. University graduates, even with excellent records, cannot obtain teaching positions because the university's placement office is under the Black Hand party's branch.

Professors' sphere of activity is limited to the classroom; they are absolutely forbidden to participate in "extracurricular activities," especially not to approach newspapers.

President Barrows is a militarist adherent who followed the American army to Siberia and was very friendly with the Russian White General Semyonov, vigorously promoting him during Semyonov's stay in the U.S. Students at the university must undergo two years of military training, 55 hours per year. The best location on campus was appropriated by him for a sports field; a professor who resisted his barbaric action resigned in protest. But he openly declared: One benefit of a large-scale university is having abundant material from which to select athletes. So while other universities have their "classics" like Homer, California's "classic" is merely the football game between Stanford and California, intercollegiate track meets, and Pacific coast tennis doubles.

He absolutely forbids students from exposure to new ideas. The most common psychology among students is that of the ruling class. Even students from working-class backgrounds strive to imitate gentlemen. One university student once said: "I think organized workers should be killed." So they are very eager to gain experience in strike-breaking, and their "soldier president" naturally works hard to promote this university tradition. During an electrical workers' strike, the authorities indeed used university students' power to crush the strike. Later, a seamen's strike was also broken by students replacing the seamen.

Meanwhile, the Black Hand party naturally continuously monitors the university. When they find someone with the slightest unorthodox thought, if a student, they are failed; if a teacher, they are immediately dismissed. Consequently, professors with some independent thought go elsewhere to teach, and only the flattering and foolish retain their jobs. The result is naturally a decline in the university's academic standing.

Let us stop here regarding the inside story of American higher education.

In summary: These universities or specialized schools are all controlled by plutocrats; presidents and professors must "obey the law and serve the public" for the benefit of the plutocrats; the education teaches students to be slaves of the capitalists. In cities across the South, the influence of the KKK is particularly great. For example, the Board of Trustees of the University of Oklahoma forbids faculty from opposing the KKK because the board chairman is a Klan member, the vice-president is a Klan member, and two-thirds of the professors are also Klan members, these Klansmen specializing in suppressing poor farmers' movements.

Below, we will discuss American general education), i.e., primary and secondary education, based on Sinclair's The Goslings (published in 1924).

Here, Sinclair reiterates: The forces that dominate politics and industry are also the forces that run the general schools; this invisible government destroys trade unions and also destroys school teachers' associations. These two tasks are one.

He starts with the Black Hand party of Southern California, describing how it controls the board of education, governs all schools, intimidates teachers, and aims to produce students who are loyal servants of the capitalists.

Then he discusses education in Los Angeles, one of America's major cities. Education there is dominated by the Times newspaper. All figures in educational administration are connected to the interests of the Times. Listen to these individuals' views on education: "We don't want you (Note: referring to teachers) bringing opinions here; we only want you to obey orders." A group of teachers went to the board of education to voice a complaint but were loudly rebuked by a board member: "Don't come here stating opinions; all we require you to do is follow our instructions."

At a discussion meeting, a board member explained the definition of education: "In promoting the development of the human mind." Before he could finish, a former military officer serving as a board member became agitated, shouting loudly: "Education? I can tell you what education is! Education is shutting a group of children in a room, teaching them a lesson, hearing them recite it, marking scores, and calculating their results at year's end. That is education, the education we have in Los Angeles, and nothing else."

Another educational administrator, a businessman, stated his educational aims, saying schools are factories, children are raw materials, to be turned into goods of certain sizes and styles, like biscuits and sausages. In his view, teachers are servants or helpers, their duties the same as in any other factory — obey orders, mind their own business, and respect superiors. If a teacher dares to hold their own opinions, or even dares to demand a salary increase, they will face the methods the Southern California Black

Hand party applies to unions – arrest and imprisonment.

The aforementioned Better America Federation published its platform extensively in newspapers:

Teachers must stay away from political and industrial discussions. Teachers are being regarded as guardians of the state. The teacher, like the soldier, owes his first and only loyalty to the state.

Secondary school teachers in Los Angeles once prepared to petition the board of education to organize a "Teachers' Advisory Committee" to consult with the superintendent and assistants on matters concerning child welfare and school affairs. Such organizations exist in other American cities. They thought such a proposal would surely be accepted. Little did they know the Black Hand party's methods could be so severe. One day, the Times suddenly published startling news claiming there was a conspiracy among Los Angeles teachers to organize a "Teachers' Soviet"! Immediately, the Black Hand party sent people to the City Club and the Women's City Club to denounce the evils of the "Teachers' Soviet." The Chamber of Commerce resolved to form an investigation team and summoned teachers for confrontation. They interrogated teachers in a tone used for admonishing stubborn children, fabricated many facts, and allowed no rebuttal from the teachers. Subsequently, the Times continuously "denounced and attacked," and naturally, the committee the teachers had proposed could not be realized.

Under such a school system, teachers' promotions naturally depend entirely on connections. Although there are supposedly evaluation methods, these are merely a facade; with a recommendation from a local plutocrat, direct or indirect, one can safely be promoted without question.

Meanwhile, promoting the capitalists' virtues in schools is a major task for the board of education and school authorities. For instance, the board once issued a notice requiring all schools to hold a "Chamber of Commerce Week." It strictly instructed: "Children below the fifth grade are to write a letter to their father or guardian about a certain undertaking of the local Chamber of Commerce, or mention the benefits of the Chamber's work to the city." Furthermore, teachers at all levels must "use the functions, activities, or achievements of the local Chamber of Commerce as material for compositions and speeches. Pamphlets describing the local Chamber's activities are to be placed in mailboxes. Principals and teachers must actively cooperate in the work."

If a slightly radical teacher is found in a school, a campaign of terror is launched. The principal of a certain middle school was advised by a board member that he could be promoted if he dismissed several teachers accused of liberal thoughts. When the principal said they were good teachers, the board member said: "Can't you find some flaw in their conduct?"

The Black Hand party even uses students as informers, as stated by the Better America Federation's president, Harry Haldeman, himself. At a banquet, he declared in a speech to the audience: "In the schools and universities of this state and the nation, there are already investigators whose duty is to detect what teachers, professors, or students say and report it to the various headquarters of the Association. If the reported speech is unsuitable according to the Association, methods will be devised to have those teachers or professors dismissed. If students, they will also be shown their error. If they persist, then further steps will be taken to prevent them from having a place to earn a living."

In essence, this Black Hand party controls the board of education, controls the superintendents, controls the teachers, controls the students, and even controls the parents. Los Angeles had a Parent-Teacher Association with over twenty years of history, where parents came to schools to discuss their children's welfare with teachers. But this organization has now fallen into the hands of the Black Hand party. The Black Hand party specifically spends money to invite prominent women to the meetings. Other women are employed by the Times; their role is to speak well of the Black Hand party and the Times, boasting and bluffing, making parents believe in them. If you support the Times, you can immediately become a famous lady; your photo will be printed in the paper, your words published, and your reputation will spread far and wide daily.

To prevent parents from having proposals or power, they specifically amended the bylaws to state "shall not interfere with the administration of the Board of Education." So if anyone needs to voice an opinion, they only need to declare, "This is the Board's administration"! And to prevent teachers from having a chance to speak, they always schedule meetings during school hours. One teacher, employed for nearly thirty years, had never once been able to attend such a school meeting. Representing the school at these association meetings are only the principal and a few staff members. Teachers pay one-third of the dues but have no right to speak!

As for those who run this school machinery for the Black Hand party, their prevention of new thought goes without saying. Therefore, they prohibited the purchase of the magazines The Nation and The New Republic for secondary school libraries. Conversely, they spare no effort in promoting books beneficial to capitalists. For instance, the Better America Federation specifically selected Vanishing Landmarks as a textbook for promoting patriotism in all schools. This book was written by former Secretary of the Treasury Leslie Shaw, a character who praised the U.S. Constitution as a defense for the privileged class. "Only socialists, quasi-socialists, and Bolsheviks demand democracy," he declared. He also said capitalists should organize, and the only danger begins when trade unions form. He further denounced the women's suffrage amendment, calling it part of the revolutionary movement. So the Association spent twenty thousand dollars printing this book to distribute to every school teacher. They demanded its adoption as a textbook in all elementary schools — this in a state where women had had the vote for twenty years! According to one teacher, the slogan "Votes for Women" should be changed to "Lies for Children."

The Association also published a textbook called Back to the Republic, vehemently denouncing the initiative and referendum as treason to the ancestors. The publisher called the book a "contemporary masterpiece" and distributed it to every teacher. Here are some excerpts: "Democracy in government is like free love in the family... Democracy in government is like gluttony in the individual... Democracy in government is like drunkenness in the individual... Democracy in government is like cacophony in music... Democracy in government is like insanity in thought," etc. Note, this is used in a textbook! Teachers are required to force children to memorize and recite it!

What kind of people do children become under Black Hand rule? According to many teachers speaking unanimously, they can do anything except study. One secondary school is attended by the children of officials. There, only money is omnipotent; students' ideals revolve around how to spend money; their standard is monetary value. Rows of cars line the school entrance; those young drivers are all social experts; they play around at school and also play around with girls.

Sports competitions and "assemblies" are the school's biggest events. They gather in the auditorium, practice cheers; the cheerleaders tell them: "Yell louder, now let's cheer for the team." They come out of the auditorium emotionally charged, too impatient to read anything. Bookstores sell hydrogen balloon toys, and everyone buys one to fly. Just as they sit down in the classroom holding their hydrogen balloons, they hear the summons for "fire drill." Without these amusements, these young people take powder boxes to powder their noses and paint their lips with rouge; meanwhile, the poor teacher is trying to put something into their foolish heads.

What can teachers do to deal with such a situation? The only method is to make the lessons more interesting, to talk about lighter topics, which might awaken students' originality and guide their thinking. This method isn't bad originally, but the teacher must still be careful not to risk danger. One female student wanted to write a paper titled "The Social Motive in American Literature". This was a good topic, but it was forbidden by the principal.

In 1921, the Black Hand party tried to get the state legislature to pass a provision requiring schools to expel "any teacher who indicates to children in school contempt for any provision of the U.S. Constitution, or verbally expresses to students any opinion, or distributes written or printed opinions to students, favoring any modification of any provision of the U.S. Constitution." The U.S. Constitution itself provides for its own amendment and has been formally and legally amended no less than nineteen times in history! But the Black Hand party wanted to forbid school teachers from having such legitimate opinions, fearing teachers might discuss child labor issues with students!

Another strange incident. In Los Angeles, there was a group

called the Young Workers' League, an educational organ of the Communist Party. They wanted to hold a debate on Communism versus Capitalism. But they couldn't find anyone to defend capitalism and had to assign one of their own speakers, who was naturally reluctant. At this time, three youths – one a secondary school student, two recent graduates – attended the debate. They felt the defense of capitalism was inadequate, stood up, said they could do better, and it was decided to hold another debate. The Young Workers' League rented a venue, and the three students spent most of their summer vacation preparing. Two or three days before the scheduled debate, the Young Workers' League distributed leaflets to all secondary schools, deliberately stating that the three students were "three representatives of a secondary school debating society." Immediately, that secondary school student was notified by the principal that he was absolutely forbidden to participate. The principal explained it wasn't his own decision but an order from the Superintendent of Education. It turned out the Superintendent had learned of the matter.

Who is the Superintendent of Education? He belongs to the Merchants' and Manufacturers' Association!

The above describes the educational situation in Southern California. But Sinclair says, "Southern California is exactly like the rest of industrial America." Whether in San Francisco, Seattle, St. Louis, Chicago, or even New York, Boston, Washington, etc., "we will see the plutocracy dominating commerce and politics, and we will find it is this same group, often the very same individuals, who dominate education. Whether or not they use Black Hand methods depends purely and simply on one question – to what extent the slave class attempts to resist. If the slave class offers no resistance, then the ruling class does not adopt harsh methods. If the slave class attempts resistance, then harsh methods are adopted to suppress it."

Because of this, we will not continue describing general education in other parts of the United States. However, one more item must be briefly explained: the national educational organ.

The remarkable similarity in educational content across the United States is no accident; there must be central control and standardized institutions governing the national school system. The setup is such that the local machinery of townships and municipalities is part of the county machinery; many county machineries are part of the state machinery; and many state machineries are connected, assisted, and standardized by the National Education Association. In addition to this, there is the Bureau of Education under the federal Department of the Interior, along with the assistance of the Rockefeller General Education Board and the Carnegie Foundation for the Advancement of Teaching.

Within the American school system, a county superintendent must be a school politician and almost necessarily a political politician as well. This administrative organ is composed of the superintendent's assistants, clerks, principals, and many other appointees, all of whom must follow his directives. The teachers under his command also lead groups of teachers in implementing his policies. To give teachers a sense of self-respect and make them feel they are contributing to education, they are organized into groups or clubs, all affiliated with the National Education Association but practically controlled by the local educational administration. Therefore, these educational organizations serve the educational world exactly as yellow unions serve the labor world. For the most part, the staff of these teacher organizations are superintendents, principals, and other ruling-class figures. In a small minority, they are teachers who have accepted the directives of the rulers. Only in a few instances have a minority of teachers dared to defy orders and form their own organizations, but their leaders are often subjected to intimidation, persecution, slander, and denial of promotion.

The state superintendent of education must collaborate with local politicians and local financial elites. Whether appointed or elected makes no difference, because even elections require nomination first, and the power of nomination lies with the local political machinery. Those who support nominations do so for their own interests. Among them are land speculators, either looking to sell land or wanting to purchase school sites to make huge profits. There are contractors who profit from constructing school buildings. There are textbook dealers, who are close friends of all superintendents, donating money to elect them, expecting to reap fortyfold profits. These booksellers even act as managers for teachers, capable of influencing their hiring, firing, and promotions—depending on whether the teachers patronize their business.

Naturally, there are also bankers who need to control school funds and teacher salaries; teachers save money and deposit it in banks, which the bankers then use for cashing or political activities. Furthermore, there are capitalists who need child labor and thus hope to abolish or ignore compulsory education laws. Then there are various large commercial propaganda organs—such as the National Association of Manufacturers—which need children to be trained as slaves in factories and shops. There is the American Legion[123] and militarists who want children to serve in the military, filled with patriotic thought; there are newspapers that support all reactionary forces and punish those who do not comply. This is the position occupied by superintendents and boards of education throughout the United

---

123 [Special Editor's Note] American Legion, a United States war veterans' organization.

States—except in a few areas where the people have gained control through the labor and peasant movements.

Next, the situation with state superintendents and state boards of education is no different, only on a larger scale. This state education machine has more money, the state superintendent receives a higher salary, and thus he is also a more agile and meticulous politician. He participates in state political machines, his office is a den for cigar-smoking, idle bureaucrats. He connects with land speculators and bookstores, he belongs to them, and he delivers the education they require to the people. The people are often satisfied with this kind of education—because they cannot see or imagine any other kind of education. Pious American farmers are taught to sing hymns about the "old-time religion," while today's children receive an antiquated education. The average American is taught to believe that public schools are as sacred as churches and that public school educators must be people with noble hearts and impartial attitudes.

Now we come to the pyramid of American schools, that is, the National Education Association. Let me first quote a passage from another text.

Although the educational administrative systems of the various states in the United States differ, and there is no central Ministry of Education, the national educational community has a powerful liaison organization, namely the National Education Association (N.E.A.). Its members include university professors, heads of education departments, other administrative personnel, primary and secondary school teachers, and those enthusiastic about educational affairs, etc., totaling several hundred thousand people. It has many sections, frequently holds meetings, conducts investigations, produces reports, engages in propaganda, and puts forward proposals, exerting considerable influence on the nation's education. Its recommendations are often adopted and implemented by the states. (See Zhuang Zexuan, Comparative Studies on Education in Various Countries, The Commercial Press, p. 25)

Who owns this National Education Association, which possesses such influence, and for whose benefit does it operate?

Earlier we learned that this Education Association was the initiator of the World Conference on Education and the organizer of the "San Francisco International Peace Education Movement." What kind of monster is it really?

It is the professional organization of American educators, wielding immense privilege and power in the educational world. It greatly influences schools everywhere, and its impact is in no way diminished by being indirect. What it does is set standards for the educational community, decided in its open or secret meetings.

The Association currently has (1924) 125,000 members, each regular member paying a fee of $2 (USD). Over 80% of the members are ordinary, average primary and secondary school teachers, whose function is akin to that of daily wage laborers in large factories—producing wealth for consumption by their superiors. The N.E.A. claims to be a "democratic" organization, but this "democratic" nature is quite different from what we might imagine, as will be described below. The N.E.A. welcomes new members; in fact, new members are urgently needed—it conducts "membership drives," and privileges in some schools are established based on having N.E.A. membership. Some schools even compel teachers to join the N.E.A. as members. The September 1922 issue of the N.E.A. magazine proudly quoted the superintendent of Michigan, Onaway: "Future teacher contracts in Michigan, Onaway will stipulate that teachers must be members of the State Education Association and the National Education Association." In St. Joseph, Missouri, the application form for teaching positions includes the following two items: "Is the applicant a member of the N.E.A.? If not, will they join this year?"

What benefits do members get from the N.E.A.? You might not believe it. Members only serve the role of 'carrying the sedan chair' [i.e., doing the legwork for others]. Below we will dissect the true nature of the N.E.A.

The N.E.A. was established before the Civil War. Throughout this not-so-short period, it has consistently been the possession of the ruling class. In the past few decades, not a single primary or secondary school teacher has been elected as an officer. Only recently have a few senior teachers occasionally been elected to embellish the facade. It took many years of struggle before the N.E.A. would consider the living and working conditions of teachers, or acknowledge salaries, pensions, etc., as legitimate topics for discussion. It required a kind of revolution for the N.E.A. to appoint a committee on salaries and pensions in 1903. And it wasn't until 1911 that substantive information on these issues was actually collected. This shows that the N.E.A. does not serve the interests of the average teacher.

By 1917, the Russian Revolution occurred, and then American superintendents recognized the danger of not fully controlling the subordinate classes. They decided to suppress the primary school teachers within the N.E.A. How to suppress them? By using so-called democracy as a threat. You should know that the National Education Association is a public institution and, by law, should be run by its members. Any educator who pays $4 USD can become a special member, attend the annual convention each year, with the right to vote and be elected. But the N.E.A. is not like that.

Originally, at the N.E.A. conventions, two types of special members would attend: one type came from all over the country, 90% of whom were figures from the school administration side. They received public or organizational funding, and attendance was part of their job. The other type were members residing where the convention was held, here 90% were actual classroom teachers. Only they were the teachers who could attend without great expense, and they represented the mass of teachers who could not attend.

Therefore, at the conventions, one could begin to notice the class struggle, a main feature of modern times. On one side were the funded, influential superintendents and principals; on the other were the very ordinary teachers. In any large city, the proletarians often constitute the majority. They might not pay attention to anything or voice any opinions; but perhaps a few radicals from places like New York or Chicago would come to attend, raise issues at the convention, propagandize to the general primary and secondary school teachers, and persuade them to vote for their own class.

Such happenings were deeply hated and feared by the educational employers of the N.E.A. So, at the 1918 winter meeting—the Atlantic City conference of the Department of Superintendence—they devised a plan. It was to change the N.E.A. to a representative system, replacing the method of electing committees by special members at the annual convention. Members from cities, towns, and counties would elect representatives to state bodies, and then local and state representatives would elect representatives to the national convention. Naturally, in these layers of elections, the school administration side had the means to ensure their own politicians were elected. This way, when the convention was held somewhere, local teachers would only be able to send representatives, no longer having the right to vote as special members; and the method of sending representatives was such that one representative was elected for every 100 teachers, and if there were over 500 members, one representative represented 500 members. So, at the convention, it wasn't one vote per teacher, but perhaps one vote per 1% of a teacher, or even 1/500th of a vote! Thus, the N.E.A. was securely placed in the hands of the superintendents!

What kind of democracy is this!

We can see the true nature of the N.E.A. from the convention held in Des Moines in 1921. There are detailed statistics on the composition of attending representatives at this convention. The convention had a total of 553 voting representatives. Among them: 33 state superintendents, 21 county superintendents, 104 city superintendents, 28 university and normal school presidents, 34 high school principals, 54 elementary school principals, 23 supervisors (Note: American supervisors are akin to our inspectors or superintendents. While American superintendents are state/county educational administrators). Thus, on the employer side, there were already 297 people, a majority. If we further note: the statistics list 14 miscellaneous, 46 unclassified, 6 educational magazine editors, and 2 bookstore managers. These numbers can naturally also be added to the 297.

Now look at the representatives from the teacher side: 8 special teachers, 34 university and normal school teachers, 65 high school teachers, 81 elementary school teachers. The total is 188, including university teachers. Compare this number with the 297 above! In reality, the number of school teachers compared to the administration side is about ten or fifteen to one. But in this national representative body, they only constitute 39%, while the administration side constitutes 61%. This is the "democracy" of America's largest educational organization!

This National Education Association is now completely the property of the capitalists. It is a political machine, operated by capitalists, performing its part of the duty for the benefit of the capitalists. Just like in any other large factory, the workers are deprived of power, but on the other hand are flattered as free citizens. At successive conventions, you can hear many speeches praising democracy, while simultaneously taking precautions to prevent teachers from having opportunities to speak. All power is in the hands of a small group; they have people on every committee. They set the plans and force them through when the time comes.

The teachers who attend the annual convention are powerless. Because they are mostly newcomers, inexperienced, they let the so-called ex-officio representatives—past presidents, lifetime trustees, executive committee members, state superintendents, etc.—manipulate everything.

At the 1923 convention, a Miss Flara Menzel was appointed to the credentials committee. She went to the Oakland hotel to find the meeting place, searched for a long time before finding it, but was 15 minutes late, the meeting had already adjourned, and she couldn't find anyone. Later, she learned the committee had met and finished within 15 minutes. At the 1921 convention, they appointed a committee to revise matters concerning elementary education; this committee consisted of university presidents and professors, state superintendents, the head of the federal Bureau of Education—and one elementary school teacher. They were to decide N.E.A. policy on the most important matters in elementary education, yet only placed one person with practical experience with children on the committee!

In essence, the American National Education Association is solely the property of big capitalists and operates for their benefit. Therefore, when it holds its convention in Boston, it is welcomed by the Boston Chamber of Commerce; when in Oakland, it is welcomed by the Oakland Chamber of Commerce. Wherever it goes, it ultimately receives the sincere welcome of big capitalists. This is because their interests are so intertwined. Upton Sinclair said: "It is not an overstatement to say that from the first day of the public school system, its fiercest enemy has been organized commercialism. I know some business individuals, farsighted, who believe in schools and work for them, but business organizations, the class group of exploiters, will do everything in their power to hinder the establishment of public schools, because they know that educating the lower classes is preparing to overthrow the wage slavery system."—We have previously discussed that universal education in capitalist society, while seemingly tending towards integrating education and labor, is actually feared by capitalists. Now, from Sinclair's words, we have factual confirmation.

What capitalists need from children is their labor. Someone proposed in the state legislature to prohibit factories from employing children under 14; but capitalists said that if children study until 14, they are no longer useful; children who study literature, history, and music become unwilling to work. Capitalists demand that manual training in schools only train children's hands; they are also willing to donate generously to let schools train their workers, in order to obtain cheap skilled labor, useful for breaking strikes. Capitalists demand the division of the school system into two types, using different buildings, funds, and teachers; and they see no need for collaboration between the two types of schools. Their purpose is that when this plan is realized, they can vigorously nurture vocational schools while starving ordinary cultural schools. Furthermore, some capitalists propose to parliament that vocational training be funded publicly but must be under employer control, without interference from school authorities. The education they need is only that which is related to their interests—learning the techniques of commodity production, cultivating talent to break strikes; anything beyond this is superfluous and should be abolished!

Well, regarding the signs of "commercialization" in American education, one could originally write tens or even hundreds of thousands more words, but it's sufficient without writing more, enough to let us understand the true nature of this education. Do you think this is education for humanity? Is this worthy of imitation by China? Educational philosophy guides educational practice and is also its reflection. Given this state of American education, can American educational theory still be available for our use? I ask readers to pay attention to the current propositions in Chinese education and the statements of educational leaders; we must guard against this kind of "imperialist aggression"!

Questions

1. Investigate how many individuals holding positions in national educational administrative organs, university education departments, or senior normal schools are returned students from America.

2. Criticize the educational discourse published by these returned students from America.

3. Do you still believe American education has aspects worthy of

our imitation? Please list them.

4. From this section, what characteristics of American education can you identify?

5. Investigate the educational institutions established by the United States in China and their influence.

SECTION 16: EDUCATION IN THE SOVIET UNION

Education under the Dictatorship of the Proletariat—The Theoretical Basis of Education—An Overview of Educational Organization—Cultural Development Expenditure—"Cultural Development over a Decade"—Resolutions on Education by the Soviet Central Government—Questions

Regarding the theory and facilities of Soviet education, the section of Education in Socialist Society has already provided a general introduction. Now, immediately after exploring American education, proceeding to explore Soviet education will, I believe, certainly give readers a fresh perspective.

The teacher organizations and student organizations in the Soviet Union are already known to us. This section will naturally only supplement points not mentioned before. Furthermore, as there are already several Chinese translations of specialized works on Soviet education, those seeking details can refer to those books. Therefore, the narration in this section will also only outline key points.

First, we must clearly recognize that the Soviet Union is a state ruled by the working class, and its education is accordingly the education of the working class. This stands in direct contrast to the United States, ruled by the bourgeoisie, whose education is that of the bourgeoisie. Both are class-based education, except that the Soviet Union does not shy away from declaring it as such, while capitalist countries like the United States try hard to conceal this class function.

The ultimate ideal of the Soviet Union is to build a socialist organization of life, from which a communist society will emerge.

In this process towards the ideal, the current goal of Soviet education can be said to be the cultivation of Soviet citizens—people with the psychology and ideas of the working class, capable of independent activity, self-reliance, and actively struggling for these ideals. Relying on these people to build and defend socialism in Russia, and to support workers in other parts of the world in overcoming capitalism and imperialism.

The methods adopted to achieve these goals follow several principles:

First, education is based on labor or physical work. The method of learning is through practical work. "Labor becomes the pivot around which all education revolves," as Professor Pinkevich said. Life and livelihood depend on labor. Therefore, schools and other educational institutions are closely linked with the lives of the surrounding people and industrial production. Between schools and factories, mining areas and farms, cities and villages, Russia and the rest of the world, there is mutual aid and interrelation. Teachers and students first study the labor and life of workers and peasants in their local area and county, then extend to a province, a republic, and further to the entire Soviet Union and the world.

Second, from pre-school education on, the curriculum is built on a threefold foundation. (1) The natural phenomena surrounding each individual; (2) The labor by which people cooperate with or resist nature to control and utilize it; (3) The social characteristics arising from labor, and the relationships or connections between these three categories (this relationship is commonly referred to in Russia as the "principle of integration"). Knowledge obtained in this way is unified, not a miscellaneous mixture of many subjects.

Third, in various collective activities, children and teachers must participate like laborers. Co-education is universal at all levels of schooling. This ability to labor collectively needs to form from the start a socialist attitude towards life in children and immerse them in communist ideals. This means that children must have a clear understanding of the political situation in their own and other countries. This is a scientific (realistic) world outlook, not a nationalistic one. Finally, they must, from the earliest school age, be able to apply this knowledge to labor alongside their companions and to resist anti-labor class or anti-social behavior.

Soviet teachers must be able to use various methods to encourage the highest degree of initiative, originality, and self-discipline, and to develop each child's innate energies. Such a teacher is akin to a guide, an advisor, seeking to lead children into freedom in both studies and school administration, thereby fostering the qualities necessary for Soviet citizens. Shatsky[124] said, "Any valuable idea grasped by children should be advanced to a state accessible to them." Clearly, a school atmosphere and methods based on compulsion, obedience, and testing are naturally unsuitable for the fighters and builders on the path of socialism. The world outlook, fundamental to all truly socialist ideas, requires teachers to critique religion, nationalism, patriotic exclusivism, and sentimental idealism from a scientific materialist perspective, thereby sweeping away various prejudices and obsessions related to religion, nation, and sentiment. Russian educators give students a clear concept of fundamental economic needs, these economic needs determining the development of modern class society, and the forces that, upon its abolition, will establish a truly human and just society. Therefore, Soviet education aims to

---

124 [Special Editor's Note] Shatsky (Станислав Теофилович Шацкий, 1878–1934), i.e., Stanislav Teofilovich Shatsky, a famous Soviet educator.

instill a consciousness of solidarity with all laborers worldwide, regardless of their religious beliefs, cultural level, or racial differences; it also prepares them to struggle for the ideas of the working class as a whole and focuses on the capacity for rationally and systematically building a worldwide federation of socialist republics.

In fact, this concept is the great enemy of all capitalist countries and those hostile to communism; but in this transitional period, Russia's class education has indeed done its utmost to approach all humanity. American education serves the interests of a minority of capitalists, while Soviet education serves the interests of 95% of the worker and peasant masses. That is truly democratic, preparing for the enlightenment of all. The poorer the child, the better the opportunities they receive. The abnormality where the right to education follows ownership is completely eliminated here. Naturally, Soviet education is not yet 100% sufficient or widespread, but its authorities are urgently striving to achieve this. By the year the Five-Year Plan is completed (1933), the radiance of Soviet culture will surely shine even brighter upon the earth.

The above is the theoretical basis of Soviet education. Now, let's discuss some general aspects of its organizational structure.

Educational Administration

Within the sphere of education, each constituent republic of the Soviet Union has complete autonomy. According to the Soviet Constitution, the central authorities only have the authority to "establish general principles for educational administration."

Therefore, the Central Education Committee's authority is limited to determining the proportions of budgets for the constituent republics, and collaborating with the Central

Executive Committee of trade unions, the Communist Party, the Communist Youth League, and the central executive organs of various cooperatives. All these bodies liaise with the People's Commissariat of Education to promote educational activities. Simultaneously, through the Soviet State Scientific Council—a committee of experts appointed from among teachers, approved by the Educational Workers' Trade Union—it drafts curriculum outlines and sets general educational policies.

The People's Commissar of Education for each republic is elected by the Soviet Congress of that republic and is responsible to its Executive Committee. Education departments are appointed by the People's Council of each republic. The Soviets of large cities, counties, and provinces have their own educational organs. The purpose of this organization is to involve the broad masses of working people in educational administration, and due to the close relationship between the Soviets and trade unions, cooperatives, and political organizations, this goal has been effectively achieved.

Outline of the School System

Pre-school Education. Accommodates children from 3 to 7 or 8 years old in kindergartens and nursery schools. Younger children are placed in crèches when their mothers are working, and are breastfed by their mothers at scheduled times.

Unified Labour School. The meaning and importance of this school have already been discussed in the section on education in socialist society. It forms the foundation of the entire school system, rooted in social education, and is provided for children from 8 to 15 or 17 years old. It is divided into two levels: the first level for children aged 8 to 11 or 12, and the second level for children over eleven. By age 14 or 15, many bright children begin specialized training; the majority enter factory schools, industrial schools, agricultural schools, or vocational schools. The purpose of these schools is to train skilled workers, specialists, and managerial personnel to meet the needs of developing industry and agriculture.

Higher Education Institutions and Universities. Around age 17, capable young workers pursue university courses.

Education for Orphans and Homeless Children. Due to the disasters of war, civil strife, and famine, the Soviet Union was once filled with orphans and homeless children. The Soviet authorities took active responsibility for educating these children, and their numbers have greatly decreased in recent years.

Adult Education. The illiteracy legacy of Tsarist Russia became a most important part of Soviet educational work. The weapons used by workers in the struggle against illiteracy are: (a) Literacy schools; (b) Schools for political education, a distinctive feature of Soviet education; (c) Workers' Faculties (Rabfac), offering secondary-level courses to meet the needs of workers and peasants who, due to environmental constraints, could not formally enter higher education institutions or universities.

National Minorities. Russia has many internal national minorities, each with its own language. But in Tsarist times, the use of non-Russian languages was prohibited. After the revolution, over a hundred nationalities gained complete autonomy in educational affairs. Consequently, books were published in various languages, and their cultures naturally grew accordingly.

Museums and Art Education Galleries. Committees manage academies of sciences, museums, and art galleries. The use of these facilities is an important part of public education, marking the beginning of human culture serving humanity.

State Publishing Houses. Perhaps the world's largest and unique publishing organ. Individual teachers and teacher organizations directly participate in producing textbooks used at all educational levels. This is entirely different from commercial textbook publishers.

Army Education. The Soviet Red Army is a huge educational institution; illiteracy among soldiers was quickly eliminated. The education soldiers receive aims not to create militarist and nationalist ideas, but to train good defenders of the revolution. Soviet soldiers have political rights and are free to participate in social life.

Cinemas and Theaters. Educational authorities have management rights over films, radio, and theaters, all of which are state-operated. Soviet films are reviewed by educational authorities, unlike in capitalist countries where police censorship is used. Many schools have set up radio clubs and children's theaters, with equipment mostly made by the children themselves. There are also special children's theaters established specifically for children.

Teacher Training. There are two types of teacher training institutions: one is specialized schools training primary teachers; the other is pedagogical institutes within universities, training advanced teachers. Students typically engage in social activities within their own regions. The programs are generally four years.

Inspectors. Inspectors are appointed by educational authorities jointly with the Educational Workers' Union from among teachers. They cannot oppress teachers but are regarded by teachers as skilled experts and friendly guides. Unlike American inspectors who belong to the employer side, they belong to the same Educational Workers' Union as the teachers.

Judging from the aforementioned educational organization of the Soviet Union, it encompasses schooling, theaters, cinema, arts, publishing, and all other cultural undertakings. Earlier, when discussing education in capitalist society, we noted that its ideological dominance extends not only through schooling but also permeates all cultural institutions such as news, magazines, lectures, libraries, drama, films, and sports. Fundamentally, this is not surprising. The Soviet Union remains a class-based state, still rigorously practicing class struggle; consequently, its educational enterprise cannot be separated from its role in this class struggle. As long as we can distinguish the different natures of the two ruling classes, we can naturally perceive the differences between the two types of class education.

From the two brief summaries above, the essential principles of Soviet education should now be clear. We know that since the success of its revolution in 1917, the Soviet Union has firmly stood for a full 12 years. Its socialist construction is steadily advancing, achieving successful financial outcomes year after year. Starting from the 1928 fiscal year, it further established a Five-Year Plan for economic development, accompanied by very detailed and concrete planning for cultural facilities. I will now present, using figures, the state budget for cultural undertakings within the Five-Year Plan for the National Economy of the Russian Republic as follows:

Russian Socialist Federative Soviet Republic Cultural Development Expenditure (Unit: Million Rubles)

Cultural Development Sector	Year	Fiscal Year Expenditure (Million Rubles)		
		Investment Amount	Other	Total

Cultural Development Sector	Year	Fiscal Year Expenditure (Million Rubles)		
		Investment Amount	Other	Total
Public Education	1928~1929	165.4	751.8	917.2
	1932~1933	432.2	1782.5	2214.7
	5-Year Period	1597.4	6311.8	7909.2
Public Health Services	1928~1929	74.0	411.9	485.9
	1932~1933	181.0	702.8	883.8
	5-Year Period	628.0	2766.0	3394.0
Social Policy Facilities	1928~1929	0.6	63.2	63.8
	1932~1933	3.2	127.7	130.7
	5-Year Period	10.9	478.7	489.9
Total	1928~1929	240.0	1226.9	1466.9
	1932~1933	616.4	2612.8	3229.2
	5-Year Period	2236.3	9556.5	11792.8

Furthermore, according to the statement made by the Soviet Financial Commissar Bryukhanov on December 1st, 1929, the Soviet Union's military budget was significantly reduced, with the army and navy budget accounting for less than 9% of the total; however, the army and navy budgets of imperialist countries often reach 40%. Revenue totaled 11.4 billion rubles (compared to 8 billion rubles last fiscal year), of which 7 billion rubles were allocated to the economy and 2.4 billion rubles to cultural and social undertakings.

This Soviet planning differs greatly from the deceptive social policies of bourgeois states, which are akin to dishonored checks. This stems from the fundamental difference in the nature of the

Soviet political structure compared to that of bourgeois states.

Let us leave the future for later discussion. To conclude this article, a summary account of cultural undertakings prior to the 1928 fiscal year—that is, during the first decade of the Soviet Union's existence—is presented here. This allows us to glimpse how, despite such a decade of suffering and hardship, the development of cultural endeavors progressed at an astonishing speed and yielded astonishing results. This summary is based on the report "Cultural Development Over the Decade" delivered by Anatoly Lunacharsky[125], People's Commissar of Education of the RSFSR, at the celebration meeting of the 10th anniversary of the Central Executive Committee of the USSR. A resolution from the Central Committee regarding this report is also appended below.

"Cultural Development Over the Decade"

The topic of this report, "Cultural Development Over the Past Ten Years," is an extremely broad subject that cannot be detailed exhaustively under the heading of "People's Education" alone.

Politics, Economics, and Education are Inseparable

Lenin said that political achievements can only be attained by raising the cultural level of the masses; this statement is correct. In his article on cooperatives, he wrote: "Once Soviet power is established, all we need is culture among the masses in order to build socialism."

This approach to problem-solving necessitates considerable

---

125 [Special Editor's Note] Anatoly Lunacharsky had already resigned as People's Commissar of Education in September 1929, succeeded by Bubnov. Lunacharsky was subsequently appointed Chairman of the Council of Scientific Institutes under the Central Executive Committee of the USSR.

emphasis on a nation's cultural development.

Our efforts in economics and culture [as Comrade Rykov's report mentioned] are visible everywhere. However, these efforts are not unique to our current stage of economic and cultural development. These efforts existed from the very beginning of the October Revolution. Our school system expanded significantly in 1917, 1918, and 1919, and we witnessed the initial growth in the number of universities. This increase in the number of ordinary schools and specialized schools in the early years of the October Revolution sufficiently demonstrates our aspirations and efforts for education, although these were far from commensurate with our material possibilities. This situation continued until 1921. At that time, we felt there was no way to realize our aspirations, and many schools had to close down again.

In 1923, the foundation for people's education within the Russian Soviet Federative Socialist Republic was established. In other republics within the Soviet Union, because their Commissars of Education were appointed later, the establishment of this foundation was also slightly delayed. By 1923, the position in the field of education had been strongly restored. The public's enthusiasm for education grew year by year, and the material basis for realizing these efforts became increasingly solid.

In short, the people of the Federation are yearning for universal primary education. Therefore, as proclaimed in the declaration (Translator's Note: The Central Executive Committee of the USSR issued a declaration on October 15, 1927, addressed to all workers, poor peasants, the Red Army of the USSR, and the proletariat and oppressed peoples of the world. One section stated: "7. In the 1927-1928 state budget, an additional 15 million rubles, over and above the total allocated for the same purpose, are earmarked for the construction of schools in village factories and working districts"), the allocation of 15 million rubles by the federal government for school use, on the occasion of the tenth anniversary of the October Revolution, was certain to receive special welcome from the people. But the people are also demanding the establishment of more secondary schools with the same urgency; the popular slogan is: "Give us schools!"

We observe the urgent demand of the people for education; this urgent demand is driving millions of workers and peasants.

Literacy Campaign: Education

Recent data published by the Central Statistical Administration prove the irresistible progress of the literacy eradication movement within our country. In 1920, in the European part of Soviet Russia, out of 1,000 men and women, 355 were able to read and write. Today, this number has increased to 445. Over the past five years, we have achieved a general progress of approximately 28% to 29%.

Women lag behind men in literacy knowledge, but over the past five years, while the number of men learning to read and write increased by 25%, the number of women increased by 32%. These figures refer to Soviet Russia; other republics are exceptions.

Upon this foundation of fundamental knowledge, a multifaceted structure is being built. This includes various higher Soviet schools, industrial schools, and specialized institutes.

Efforts on another front involve establishing reading huts, libraries, and clubs, using political enlightenment to extend various forms of people's education. We further utilize science to formulate new scientific problems, disseminate acquired knowledge, and apply it to practical undertakings. Additionally, there are the arts, for which methods are being devised to bring them closer to the people, thereby facilitating the realization of socialism.

Financial Basis of Education

In 1913, the total amount allocated to people's education from the state and local budgets was 276.1 million pre-war rubles. In the 1925-1926 fiscal year, the total expenditure for education from the state and local budgets, plus funds under the Commissariat of Transport (for educational purposes within the transport sector), reached 302.6 million pre-war rubles. In the just past year, 1926-1927, the expenditure for people's education from the same types of budgets mentioned above reached 396.2 million pre-war rubles.

In 1913, education expenditure accounted for 7.76% of the total state budget; in 1925-1926, it accounted for 10.88%; in 1926-1927, it accounted for 10.63%.

Although the current year's budget is not yet fully finalized, the expenditure on people's education in the USSR is bound to increase, both in absolute and relative terms.

The education expenditure per capita was as follows: 1913: 2 rubles, 8 kopecks; 1925-1926: 3 rubles, 86 kopecks; 1926-1927: 4 rubles, 79 kopecks.

Primary Education, First Level

Before the war, in 1914, the total number of schools was approximately over 104,000. Immediately after the October Revolution, during the period of active increase in educational institutions, the total number of primary schools rose to 114,000. In 1923, the number of schools dropped to 87,500; by 1926-1927, it increased to 108,000, which is 3.6% more than in 1914. In 1914, the student population was 7.2 million; during the period of rapid school expansion, it reached 9.2 million. Finally, last year, there were 9.9 million students within first-level primary schools.

Currently, 65% to 70% of children are enrolled in school. The Soviet government has already decided upon the great task of expanding the school system so that by 1933, all school-age children can be enrolled.

In terms of quality, our schools still have many areas requiring improvement; funding is insufficient, facilities are incomplete, and teacher training is often unsatisfactory.

However, the four-year curriculum schools have recently made rapid progress. New plans are being proposed everywhere; in this regard, much achievement is certain.

Our school education system has received high praise from foreign education experts and scholars visiting the Soviet Union. This praise, expressed by foreigners far from Communism, proves that the Soviet school is a major educational laboratory for the world.

School Reorganization Based on Teaching in National Languages

The most important element in people's education has been the emphasis on national languages (Translator's Note: The Soviet Union comprised many different nationalities, each using their own distinct language). All schools were uniformly reorganized, with the first level of primary education compulsorily implementing this reorganization plan, even for nationalities with extremely low cultural levels. This school reorganization using native languages was a very difficult task because, before the war, such schools either absolutely did not exist or were extremely pitiful. But regardless of the difficulties, progress was ultimately achieved.

For example, in Ukraine, the number of schools teaching in the native language increases annually. On January 1, 1924, such schools accounted for 66% of all schools; on January 1, 1925, 77%; on January 1, 1926, over 79%. Similarly, increases in the number of schools teaching in native languages can be observed in other republics of the Federation.

Education for Pre-School Age Children

Since the October Revolution, education for pre-school age children in the USSR has made remarkable progress.

A great expansion of pre-school educational institutions became apparent after the revolution. In the 1920-1921 school year, there were 4,723 kindergartens and nurseries, accommodating over 245,000 children. When these institutions ceased receiving state subsidies and relied solely on local finances, their numbers temporarily decreased; but in recent years, they have increased again. In 1924-1925, there were 1,139 kindergartens and nurseries; the following year this increased to 1,364, and in 1926-1927, there were 1,629. The number of children accommodated also increased correspondingly.

The establishment of children's playgrounds in recent years has been particularly notable. There were 1,500 in 1924-1925, rising to 4,000 by 1926-1927. Currently, 200,000 children spend their leisure time in these playgrounds.

The Struggle Against Destitution

The struggle against destitution among children is being carried out using various methods. This unfortunate situation is gradually being eliminated. The number of homeless and uncared-for children is decreasing, as is the number of children living in state-supported children's homes. Children now enjoy a better life and are engaged in the production process, similar to young workers.

The countryside has done considerable work in reducing the number of homeless children; many such children have been fostered within their own families.

Secondary Schools

The major shortcoming of secondary schools lies in their insufficient organizational expansion. They accommodate only about one-tenth of the children who have completed the first-level schools. However, it is also a fact that the Soviet Union has transcended the unfortunate legacy left by the bourgeois social order. Consequently, as early as 1923, the number of students enrolled in secondary schools already exceeded that of 1914; today, the number of children in such schools is over 4% more than pre-war levels.

Regarding secondary education, one thing must be pointed out: the systems adopted by these schools. The system in the Russian S.F.S.R. is fundamentally different from that in the Ukrainian Socialist Soviet Republic. In the Russian S.F.S.R., there are two types of schools: five-year secondary schools and seven-year secondary schools, whereas in Ukraine, there is only one type of secondary school with a uniform seven-year curriculum. Attached to these are three-year schools called Professional Schools, and above the Professional Schools are Colleges.

The existence of two systems of secondary schools is naturally not very ideal. However, whichever system remains must be maintained for some time, in order to use experience to prove which system best promotes the interests of national development.

Schools for Young Peasants

Within the Soviet Union, there is a special form of secondary school: the schools for "Young Peasants". The education provided by these schools aims to turn young peasants into educated individuals knowledgeable about Cooperatives.

The following data illustrates the development of Young Peasant schools. In the 1924-1925 school year, there were 229 such schools with over 20,000 students; in 1925-1926, the number of schools increased to 491, with over 36,000 students; in 1926-1927, there were 686 schools with nearly 50,000 students.

Factory Schools

Factory Schools can be classified as secondary schools.

We often hear people say that, since the result of national industrialization can reduce the work of qualified laborers merely to operating machines, Factory Schools are already excessive. This view is wrong; Factory Schools have various possibilities for continued development. But this must be achieved by expanding the organization of such schools and striving to increase student numbers. In the 1923-1924 school year, there were only 789 Factory Schools within the Soviet Union; in 1926-1927, there could be 1,678. During this period, the number of students increased from 60,000 to 110,000.

Vocational Education

The industrialization of the nation has made vocational education one of the most important sectors of our culture. Here, close cooperation is essential, on one hand between the economic authorities and the People's Commissariats representing the economy, and on the other hand with the People's Commissariat of Education.

However, this cooperation has not yet been realized in practice. For this reason, the work done in organizing Professional education is not yet fully satisfactory. Especially the lower-level Professional Schools are in an unfavorable state. There are only a few such schools, and they are not very suited to practical needs. This is evidently still a legacy of Tsarist Russia. But lower-level Professional Schools are necessary for training qualified laborers for the nation, and such laborers are in very short supply. Some provinces have voiced many complaints due to a lack of blacksmiths, saddlers, cabinetmakers, etc.

Technical Schools

The organization of Technical schools, like that of Professional schools, has been taken over from old Russia and expanded. But the number of schools and their content have not adapted to the nature of the various localities within our Federation and their organizational requirements. Plans are currently underway to open many new industrial schools in the near future; this should be very useful for improving matters in this area.

The expansion of the Technical School network and the increase in student numbers have been enormous. From the 1920-1921 school year to 1926-1927, the number of Technical schools increased from 585 to 1,017, nearly doubling; the student body also increased from 70,000 to 180,000, more than two and a half times.

Specialized Schools and Workers' Faculties

Tsarist Russia left us a legacy here that requires major renovation. The professorial syllabi and the system of Specialized Schools must be changed, especially as the state now faces the extremely important task of proletarianizing higher education.

Currently, Specialized Schools have clearly become schools for workers and peasants, largely due to the Workers' Faculties; the Workers' Faculties are preparatory institutions intended to send outstanding young workers and peasants to Specialized Schools.

Various methods are now being considered to improve the teaching in the Workers' Faculties, so that the students' production work does not hinder their studies. Therefore, the People's Commissariat of Education is planning evening instruction.

Our task is not to increase the number of Specialized Schools, but to improve the knowledge they impart. The period when there was an urgent need to establish new Specialized Schools in our country has ended; hereafter, what is needed is a period of selecting the best Specialized Schools and improving instruction. The current Specialized School system accommodates 160,000 more students than the pre-war Specialized Schools.

The following figures show the social origins of the enrolled students. Compared to 1924, the proportion of workers entering Specialized Schools increased from 10% to over 25%, and the proportion of peasants increased from 22% to 26%. Although the requirements set by the Syllabus have been raised, the percentage of Party Members and young workers applying to Specialized Schools has greatly increased. The difference between (current) students and those of previous years lies in their deep interest in the subjects they study. The teaching staff is gradually adapting to modern teaching conditions and the activities of the youth. Young teachers trained in scientific pedagogy are being prepared to replace the old-style professors.

Political Enlightenment

The organs of the People's Commissariat of Education, both central and local, are zealously applying themselves to the area of Political Enlightenment.

The first step in this area is the eradication of Illiteracy among adults. A large organization of Literacy Centres has been formed. The number of these centres was 41,000 in 1921, and is now nearly 47,000; the number of students has also increased from 1 million to 1.5 million. Over the past 7 years, approximately 7 million people have received instruction in reading and writing.

The general population actively participates in the struggle to abolish illiteracy. The society "Away With Illiteracy" now includes about 27,000 Nuclei, comprising one to two million men and women, of which about 65% are in the countryside and 35% in cities.

General educational institutions (schools, nurseries, etc.) must also be included within Political Enlightenment. In 1921, there were 780 such institutions, while now there are 866, with about 100,000 students. Parallel to this is the expansion of the Workers' Universities network. Currently, we have 31 Workers' Universities, with 7,868 students who are simultaneously working.

Apart from the aforementioned general educational institutions, there is also remarkable work being done by male and female workers who teach in rural reading huts; this corps of young workers teaches at 22,000 reading huts.

The activities of Workers' Clubs can guide the working masses to the clubs to spend their leisure time. Sometimes it is felt that the clubs' functions are overemphasized on instructional and organizational activities, setting excessive lessons. Consequently, many workers shy away from the clubs, precisely because after work, they are already tired and cannot concentrate anymore. Therefore, these clubs must become places truly for workers' rest and sensory entertainment. Women must occupy a primary role in this work; they have already proven to be the best organizers and leaders in this area.

On the front of Political Enlightenment, a powerful ally has recently emerged: Radios. Just four years ago, only a few people understood the significance of radio; most people regarded reports from America as fairy tales – such as that radio could broadcast at any time, and music performances and lectures could be heard anytime. But today, almost every household in the cities has installed a radio set. There are now 47 broadcasting stations that can supply nearly a quarter of the entire Federation's population.

Cinema has developed at an equally rapid rate.

Before the revolution, 75% of films were foreign, and the remaining 25% were very worthless productions. Now our output and quality have reached a high level, and foreign films are gradually being excluded.

Publishing

The progress of our culture, as indicated by our publishing industry, is also very significant. We publish 556 newspapers, with a total circulation reaching 8 million copies. This greatly exceeds the pre-war standard of newspaper circulation. Compared to pre-war times, the impact on the public has increased infinitely.

Publishing in scientific fields has shown equal progress. The number of scientific publications also sufficiently indicates the increase in people's interest in scientific books. In 1910, considered the most prosperous year for this publishing sector, there were 464 new book titles published; but this year, the number of classified new publications totals 945.

Science

Science is very important for socialist construction. According to S.F. Oldenburg, Secretary of the Academy of Science of the Soviet Union, the progress of scientific work in the USSR coincided with the establishment of the "Central Commission for the Improvement of the Material Status of Scientists" in 1920. From that time on, science was able to develop systematically. Scientists' work occurs not only in Specialized Schools and scientific research institutions; a significant part is also within state organs, starting from the organization of the Commission for Planned Economies of the Union. Through this, they can make definite and significant contributions to the progress of socialist construction.

Developing Marxism in our science is a task of utmost importance. Here we must focus on publishing more works by Marxists, developing general Marxist literature and journalism. On the other hand, it is also necessary to ensure that important scientists across various fields and all scientific research institutions grasp the principles of the Marxist viewpoint.

The Marxist institutes established by the revolution hold the first position, such as the Marx-Engels Institute. Headed by Comrade Ryazanov, in its organization and scientific work, it can truly be called the world's primary institution for scientific Marxism.

Others, like the Communist Academy, the Lenin Institute, and many other scientific research institutions, have also done much work, tirelessly instilling Marxist principles into various departments of scientific research.

The activities of the Academy of Sciences of the Soviet Union have seen enormous development in the present period.

Art

The masses, the Party, and government authorities are beginning to pay attention to art. We can observe, on one hand, a general increase in creative artistic activity, and on the other hand, a trend towards expressing our ideology in art. A purely proletarian literature has emerged, and here there are already some striking, beautiful examples worthy of a permanent place in our literary history.

Our theaters, which were well-protected even in the most difficult periods after the revolution, have received infusions of new strength. Therefore, today, whether in management or performance, they are undoubtedly among the best in the world. There is a strong tendency to portray real life in our theaters, an impulse to participate in the tide of cultural development.

Immediately after the revolution, our painters and sculptors, having broken free from the influence of previous patrons, were somewhat disconcerted. In the initial period, mostly Futurist painters came over to our side, but they could not produce the works hoped for by the revolutionary proletariat at that time. Only recently have painters and sculptors determined the correct path of serving the people. Artists can also achieve success by meeting the practical needs of the people; whether using a brush or a chisel, they feel their work has been gratefully accepted by the people.

The art of music has also achieved great progress.

National Culture

Under Tsarist rule, all nationalities were forced to use the Russian language. The October Revolution proclaimed the absolute equality of the languages and dialects of all small nationalities. Now, children in the backward regions of various nationalities are entering schools; much work is being done to disseminate national literature and train women for public Soviet work.

Human society can only be established on the basis of harmonious transformation; we must first and foremost guarantee the cultural development of minority nationalities, the development of national cultures based on the equality of rights of all nations.

The Next Generation

One of the most important centers of our cultural development is the Young Communist League, whose development simultaneously indicates the enormous cultural development of the entire Federation.

This generation is, of course, largely possessed by our most active Collaborators. But the next generation will belong to the youth of our Pioneer Organizations, whose era is continuing this one. Here a powerful ally is developing; they are the successful ones, and we can without fear entrust to them the great task of building a new human society.

The entire cultural development of Western European countries is suited to the satisfaction of individual interests; however, our culture is directed towards the goal of the progress of all human culture and the improvement of living standards.

We would do well to know this distinction if we visit foreign countries. When we return from a wealthy foreign country to our poor Soviet Union, we feel a deep, pleasant sensation – the joy of work, the joy of our own cause in our own country (enthusiastic applause).

Resolution on the Report of Lunacharsky

Ten years have passed since the Great October Revolution freed the working class and the peasantry from the oppression of Tsarism and capitalism and laid the foundations for the socialist organization of the economy. This great revolution has had an even broader impact: it has brought about a fundamental transformation of culture and education for the vast majority of the people.

Formerly, education for the people lay entirely in the hands of the propertied classes, and the Tsarist Empire was a vast prison of peoples. Brutal Russification was one of the main methods of Tsarist rule. Peoples oppressed by this overpowering force were deprived of every possibility of cultural development. Many nationalities were even forbidden to establish elementary schools teaching in their native languages. The culturally backward regions were in the most unfortunate position: they grew up in the darkest spiritual conditions, lacking culture, and were therefore subjected to extremely barbaric methods of exploitation and division. The October Revolution put an end to all this and made the promotion of mass culture one of its foremost objectives.

The working class of our country, having seized state power, has further proved true its responsibility to carry forward the progress of humanity. While the proletariat has sought methods to raise culture and knowledge, it has simultaneously labored with zeal to advance and enlighten all working people and all nationalities of the Soviet Union.

The great cultural revolution born of the October Revolution will achieve successful results, because it rests upon the activity and creative power of many millions of workers in the cities and countryside. It is solely thanks to the October Revolution that our country has been able to free itself from the dead weight of a barbarous past, to take charge of cultural progress, and to open the road to building socialism.

Nowhere else in the world has any state proclaimed complete equality of men and women as the Soviet Union has done, nor pursued this principle so earnestly and consistently.

The Soviet Union holds first place in Europe in the protection of motherhood and childhood.

During the period of revolutionary struggle against feudalism, the bourgeoisie were drawn into combat with religion—one of the fundamental pillars of the feudal order—and often placed the question of freeing culture from religion in the forefront. But in the period that followed, as the proletarian revolutionary movement began, the bourgeoisie turned to rely upon religion and allied themselves with the clergy. Only in the Soviet Union, which proclaims freedom of conscience for all, is there sustained effort to clarify the minds of adults—and especially of the new generation—so that they may cast off religious prejudices. Here, in the struggle against religion, the Soviet Union employs no method other than thoroughgoing enlightenment. The cultural development of our vast country has been freed from the prison of religion; the culture of humankind here is, for the first time, wholly founded upon real science.

Only in the Soviet Union do we find consistent and complete adherence to the principle of equality among peoples. The peoples belonging to the Soviet Union are equal; the development of their national cultures proceeds with the support of the proletarian dictatorship. They are organized in a free union of peoples.

The Central Executive Committee of the Soviet Union notes with great satisfaction that, thanks to the efforts of the majority of workers and peasants, the ten years since the October Revolution have yielded victorious results in raising the culture and education of the laboring masses and of all nationalities. General elementary education for the people has made great strides; the campaign to eradicate adult illiteracy is pressing forward with vigor. The school system has been greatly expanded, and the plans drafted for 1933–1934 will enable us to achieve universal general schooling. Various forms of secondary schools continue to supply the state with semi-skilled labor, and they send well-prepared, socially useful youth on to specialized institutions. Political education advances with the close support of clubs, libraries, reading rooms, people's houses, theaters, cinema, radio, and workers' universities and evening schools, and now reaches the great majority of the working class and the peasantry.

The October Revolution itself set the task of eliminating the cultural gap between urban and rural populations, and the Soviet Union is now pursuing this task with unremitting effort.

Great efforts are likewise being made to create healthy conditions of work and life for laborers, as seen in the reduction of infectious diseases, the fall in mortality rates, and especially the marked decline in infant mortality.

The cultural development of the backward nationalities is advancing rapidly, proportionally raising the collective cultural level of our Union.

All cultural work is carried out on the basis of the doctrine of the emancipation of labor and the fundamental concept of training the people of the new era in the spirit of communism.

Soviet publications are entirely different from those of the bourgeoisie—the latter being powerful instruments for the exploitation and deception of the people, whereas the former serve the workers and convey to them genuine truth.

Soviet newspapers penetrate to the most remote parts of the country, are printed in the languages of the various nationalities, and enjoy circulations far surpassing those before the war. Tens of thousands of worker and peasant correspondents submit articles to these papers, ensuring the closest, most practical contact with the broad masses.

The demands of socialist construction have imposed upon Soviet power an exceedingly complex task: to create a stratum of worker- and peasant-intellectuals. In qualifications they are in no way inferior to the intellectuals of the old Russia or to the specialists of the bourgeois states, while at the same time remaining in the closest contact with the working class and possessing the most penetrating revolutionary consciousness. Here, too, we have achieved great success: for the first time in human history, hundreds of thousands of workers and peasants—and their children—are able to partake of the highest intellectual culture, thanks to our workers' preparatory universities and specialized schools.

The revolution has proved capable of bringing the nation's scientific forces to their fullest effectiveness—resulting not only in scientific achievements far surpassing pre-revolutionary standards, but also in a science most perfectly adapted to the concrete needs of life and to the work of building socialism within the Soviet Union. The greatest achievements have been in the domain of the social sciences. In that sphere, the bourgeoisie deny the very cornerstone—the scientific method of Marx; yet in the Soviet Union, guided by Lenin's teachings, the fundamental principles of Marxism have been applied to the most varied aspects of public life. The first true home of Marxist thought is the state of the proletarian dictatorship.

The Soviet Union has employed every means to protect the artistic treasures of the past and to render them fully accessible to the working masses.

Another area of work is the development of new literature and of the stage, the promotion of painting and sculpture, music and cinema—so that they can reproduce the substance of the revolution and meet the demands of our great creative era. Here, art is no longer the exclusive property of the rich; it is increasingly becoming the common possession of the working class. The use of art to advance national culture and to awaken the creative powers of all the peoples of the Soviet Union is something that has come about only since the October Revolution.

The great successes achieved in cultural progress over the past ten years in the Soviet Union have, for the most part, been due to the efforts of mass organizations such as the trade unions, the Communist Youth League, the cooperatives, and various voluntary societies.

Such are the achievements of the Soviet system over ten years—even though the first five years of this decade were a difficult time of civil war, famine, epidemics, and every kind of loss.

In reviewing the cultural development of the Soviet people over the past decade, the Central Executive Committee of the Soviet Union considers it its duty—on behalf of the country's working class—to extend thanks to those engaged in educational and cultural work, who, in the most arduous years, remained faithful to their mission and found a way of cooperation friendly to the proletariat, thereby clearing away the last remnants of the past.

While the Central Executive Committee of the Soviet Union may take satisfaction in the country's general cultural progress, it also recognizes, in light of the revolution's lofty aims and the people's demands for education, that what has so far been achieved is by no means sufficient. The Central Executive Committee therefore deems it necessary to focus on the continued, unremitting task of raising the nation's culture, and it instructs the Soviet Government to deploy every possible means to realize this goal—making it one of the primary joint tasks of the Union republics and the autonomous republics. Now, as we stand on the threshold of the second decade of the Soviet revolution, the Central Executive Committee holds that the entire program of cultural advancement must be seen as an inseparable element of the unified socialist plan for national reconstruction, and as an inseparable part of the work of the country's industrialization. (End of section.)

The Central Executive Committee of the Soviet Union attaches great importance to the right—proclaimed by the October Revolution and enshrined in the Constitution of the Soviet Union—of each nationality to develop an independent national culture, and it declares that the development of the national culture of all peoples shall continue to receive the support of the Soviet power in the future.

In accordance with the foregoing, the Central Executive Committee resolves:

1. To consolidate firmly and systematically the material foundations of social and cultural work within the Soviet Union, so that the pace of development in these areas does not lag

behind the general pace of economic development.

2. To place among the most important immediate tasks of the Government of the Soviet Union and of the governments of the Union republics and autonomous republics the following: the establishment of universal elementary education; the eradication of adult illiteracy; the elimination of child poverty and destitution; improvement of public health and of living and working conditions; training in healthy habits and hygiene; large-scale vocational and technical education; support for workers' universities and evening courses; the admission of broad masses of workers and peasants to specialized schools; and the improvement of institutions of higher education so that they may undertake work of value to the Soviet state.

3. To persevere in elevating the cultural level of the culturally backward countries.[126]

4. To continue, with even greater seriousness, the work of raising the cultural level of working women in both city and countryside.

5. To continue the systematic improvement of the material conditions of all those engaged in cultural and scientific work.

6. To continue to promote artistic culture and to make it more accessible to the working masses (theater, cinema, music, painting).

7. To ensure that all cultural development proceeds in the direction of socialism, we must:

---

126 [Special Editor's Note] "culturally backward countries" refers to certain Union republics located in the more remote regions of the Soviet Union.

(a) Conduct cultural, educational, and training work in the spirit of collectivism and international solidarity of workers;

(b) Continue our efforts to draw the broad masses of workers and peasants—and their public organizations—into the work of construction;

(c) Expand the ranks of qualified workers (cadres) required for the development of socialist industry, and provide guidance for the countryside along the path toward socialism;

(d) Continue forming a new cohort of worker- and peasant-intellectuals among the peoples of the Soviet Union, and from among them draw the highly qualified personnel needed for scientific work and research.

If the working class of the Soviet Union follows this course, and applies to the program of socialist cultural development the same capacities it displayed in civil war and in times of economic ruin—and if it has the support of the Russian workers and peasants—then it will succeed in winning the final and complete victory of socialism in our country.

Questions

1. What are the fundamental aims and current tasks of Soviet education?

2. What are the theoretical foundations of Soviet education?

3. With what other institutions is Soviet educational administration linked, and why must it be so?

4. Compare the differences between American education and

Soviet education.

5. In what ways do children and youth in Soviet Russia differ from those in other countries?

BIBLIOGRAPHY

Li Haowu, ABC of the History of Education (World Book Company).

Shima [author's name as printed], Class Culture and the Revolution in Education (in Japanese).

Morito Tatsuo, Schooling as a Weapon of Struggle (in Japanese).

Nakasone Genwa, A Reader in Education (in Japanese).

Nakasone Genwa, A Study of the New Education of Laboring Russia (in Japanese).

Shigaki Hiroshi, A Journey through the New Education of Soviet Russia (in Japanese).

Korehito Kurahara, A Study of New Russian Culture (in Japanese).

Korehito Kurahara, Education in the Soviet Union (in Japanese).

Ognyov, Diary of a Communist Schoolboy, 1928. (Chinese translation: New Russian Schoolboy's Diary, tr. Lin Yutang and Zhang Yousong, Spring Tide Press.)

Ognyov, Diary of a Communist Undergraduate, 1929. (Chinese translation: New Russian Undergraduate's Diary, tr. Jiang Shaoyuan, Spring Tide Press.)

Upton Sinclair, The Goose-Step, 1923.

Upton Sinclair, The Goslings, 1924.

E. & C. Paul, Creative Revolution: A Study of Communist Ergatocracy.

E. & C. Paul, Proletcult (Proletarian Culture).

Lucy L. W. Wilson, New Schools in New Russia, 1928.

Scott Nearing, Education in Soviet Russia, 1926. (Three Chinese translations:
— Commercial Press edition, tr. Xu Chongqing, Education in Soviet Russia [price considered high];
— Minzhi Press edition, tr. Du Zuozhou, Education in the Soviet Union;
— Beixin Press edition, tr. Pan Zinian, Education in the Soviet Union.)

W. T. Goode, Schools, Teachers and Scholars in Soviet Russia, 1929. (Chinese translation: Living Education in the Soviet Union, tr. Wang Xizheng, Huatong Press.

Earl August Wittfogel, Die Wissenschaft der bürgerlichen Gesellschaft, 1922.

L. Trotsky, Problems of Life.

Stalin–Bukharin Collected Works, The Struggle for Socialist Construction (in Japanese).

Stalin–Bukharin Collected Works, Proletarian Revolution and Culture.

K. Kautsky, Ethics and the Materialist Conception of History. (Chinese translations include: Guo Mengliang, Philosophy of Life and Historical Materialism, Commercial Press; Dong Yixiang, Ethics and the Materialist View of History, New Culture Book House.)

Bogdanov, Die Entwicklungsformen der Gesellschaft und die Wissenschaft. (Chinese translations: Shi Cuntong & Chen Wangdao, Outline of Social Psychology, Da Jiang Bookshop; Sa Mengwu, Sociology of Socialism, New Life Press.)

Bogdanov, A Short Course of Economic Science. (Chinese

translation: Shi Cuntong, Outline of Economic Science, Da Jiang Bookshop.)

Ruo Jun (translator), On Ideology (Nangqiang Book Company).

Liu Daosheng[127] (translator), Outline of World History.

Cai Hesen (translator), A History of Social Evolution (Minzhi Press).

Karl Marx & Frederick Engels, The Communist Manifesto.

Karl Marx, A Contribution to the Critique of Political Economy.

Bukharin and Preobrazhensky, The A.B.C. of Communism.

Bukharin, Historical Materialism. (Chinese translation: Xu Chusheng, Historical Materialism and Philosophy, Beixin Press.)

I. Stalin, The Theory and Practice of Leninism.

N. Lenin, State and Revolution. (Chinese translation commonly titled State and Revolution.)

F. Engels, The Origin of the Family, Private Property and the State. (Chinese translation: Li Yingyang[128], The Origin of the Family, Private Property, and the State.)

F. Engels, Socialism: Utopian and Scientific. (Chinese translation included in Lin Chaozhen's Philosophy of Religion and Socialism, Hubin Bookstore.)

---

127 [Special Editor's Note] "Liu Daosheng" was the pen name of Yang Xianjiang. The first edition of this book was published by the Creation Society in Shanghai in August 1928.

128 [Special Editor's Note] "Li Yingyang" was the pen name of Yang Xianjiang. The book was published in 1929 by the New Life Book Company in Shanghai, as the first complete Chinese translation. Its title is rendered here as The Origin of the Family, Private Property and the State.

Plekhanov, Les questions fondamentales du marxisme (Chinese translation: The Fundamental Problems of Marxism).

A. Bernard, Rôle et méthode de l'enseignement léniniste.

Karl Marx, Selected Essays. (Chinese translation: Li Yimang, Selected Essays of Marx, Hubin Bookstore.)

Nathan Miller, The Child in Primitive Society.

Educational Worker (organ of the British Teachers' Labour League).

Teachers' International (journal published in Paris, in English and French).

"Proletarian Science" (Japanese monthly; title as printed).

The following were added in the reprint:

Yamashita Tokuji, Education in the New Russia (in Japanese; translated by Li Haowu[129]).

Albert P. Pinkevitch (Pinkevich), The New Education in the Soviet Republic (translated by Li Haowu; Chinese title: The New Education of the Soviet Republic[130]).

---

129 [Special Editor's Note] "Li Haowu" is also a pen name of Yang Xianjiang. The book was published in 1931 by the Commercial Press in Shanghai under the title Education in the New Russia, signed "Zhu Kang" (another pen name of Yang Xianjiang).

130 [Special Editor's Note] Judging from Yang Xianjiang's frequent introductions and citations of Pinkevich's educational writings, the statement that this book "had been translated by Li Haowu" is highly credible. However, for decades many scholars have "searched everywhere to no avail," leaving a not-insignificant "mystery" in the field. We welcome anyone who can shed light on this.

According to the February 1930 edition of The Outline of New Education (Shanghai: Nangqiang Book Company).

www.ingramcontent.com/pod-product-compliance
Lightning Source LLC
Chambersburg PA
CBHW052054300426
44117CB00013B/2122